PROVINCETOWN MASSACHUSETTS

CEMETERY INSCRIPTIONS

Compiled by
Lurana Higgins Cook
Hugh Francis Cook
Anne Gleason MacIntyre
John Stuart MacIntyre

HERITAGE BOOKS
2011

HERITAGE BOOKS
AN IMPRINT OF HERITAGE BOOKS, INC.

Books, CDs, and more—Worldwide

For our listing of thousands of titles see our website at
www.HeritageBooks.com

Published 2011 by
HERITAGE BOOKS, INC.
Publishing Division
100 Railroad Ave. #104
Westminster, Maryland 21157

Copyright © 1980 Lurana Higgins Cook,
Hugh Francis Cook, Anne Gleason MacIntyre
and John Stuart MacIntyre

All rights reserved. No part of this book may be reproduced or transmitted in any form or by any means, electronic or mechanical, including photocopying, recording or by any information storage and retrieval system without written permission from the author, except for the inclusion of brief quotations in a review.

International Standard Book Numbers
Paperbound: 978-0-7884-5293-2
Clothbound: 978-0-917890-18-5

CONTENTS

PREFACE

PART ONE

CEMETERY NUMBER TWO - OLD SECTION   3
    INDEX   111
        LOT MAP   after 122

PART TWO

GIFFORD CEMETERY   127
    INDEX   197
        LOT MAP   after 255

PART THREE

HAMILTON CEMETERY   209
    INDEX   243
        LOT MAP   after 255

PART FOUR

SMALLPOX BURIALS   251

PREFACE

Nowhere is one struck more tangibly by a sense of one's own mortality than when standing alone in a quiet cemetery. This is especially true at Cape Cod in Provincetown, Massachusetts, where countless storms have caused the stones in the cemeteries to weather and crumble, so that some are now almost illegible, and where intermittent vandalism has resulted in stones being damaged or stolen.

We began our project with the thought that the coming years would certainly worsen the condition of these cemeteries and that, if at all possible, the information remaining on the stones and recorded here should be preserved. As we worked, we became increasingly aware that these old stones could also help us to recapture a time when Provincetown was very different from the tourist attraction it is today, a time when busy wharves lined its harbor, masts of ships were silhouetted on the horizon, and Provincetown's seamen touched all corners of the earth.

Since the inscriptions from Provincetown's oldest cemetery, known as Cemetery Number One, were published between 1906 and 1908 in the *Mayflower Descendants, An Illustrated Quarterly Magazine of Pilgrim Genealogy, History and Biography* by the Massachusetts Society of Mayflower Descendants, Volumes 8, 9 and 10, we began our recording with the next three oldest cemeteries, Number Two - Old Section, Gifford and Hamilton and have also included the smallpox cemetery.

From its beginning in 1800, Cemetery Number Two - Old Section has been town owned, while Gifford and Hamilton cemeteries were privately owned until the 1960's. All are now maintained by the town of Provincetown. Originally, it was our intent to record only Cemetery Number Two - Old Section; however, during the same period of time many persons were buried in the two private cemeteries, so it seemed appropriate to record all three.

Wherever stones were difficult to read we have attempted to check the vital records of the town and where there were lots without stones we have consulted old cemetery records to ascertain the owners of these lots. Variations between the dates and spelling of the names on the stones and in the vital records can be attributed, in many cases, to errors made by town clerks, stone cutters, and even the families of the dead.

These three cemeteries have a total of over 900 lots and over 4000 burials and often span three generations of families. Each cemetery's contents are recorded by lot numbers in a separate part of this volume and each part is indexed by names of persons, places and ships; all citations are to lot numbers. Lot maps of the three large cemeteries are also included for reference.

While working on this project we have heard many interesting reminiscences of Provincetown...intricate mixtures of fact and legend that make up the local history. One of the most fascinating of these concerns the smallpox deaths and isolated burials; therefore we have included the results of our research, identifying for the first time we believe, fourteen numbered but unnamed graves.

As individuals we have ties of blood and/or affinity with these past generations of Provincetown. When they were laid to rest in these cemeteries it was certainly with a hope of a lasting remembrance, a hope that today seems to be threatened by the passage of time. By preserving these cemetery inscriptions we are trying to extend that remembrance into the future.

The authors acknowledge with thanks the assistance given to them in compiling these records by the staff of the Provincetown Town Offices, the Cemetery Superintendent, as well as our many friends who helped with various phases of this book. A special thanks to Kay Touchette for her assistance in recording Gifford Cemetery inscriptions.

July 1979

PART ONE

CEMETERY NUMBER TWO - OLD SECTION

CEMETERY NUMBER TWO - OLD SECTION

LOT #1 -- 1 Stone

    1. Charles R. Wright 1831-1909

LOT #2 -- 1 Monument - 1 Footstone

    1. Klaas D. Wessels, Coxwain USN, born February 3, 1869, died June 4, 1898. Erected by his shipmates of the U.S.S. San Francisco.

    2. Footstone - Our shipmate

LOT #3 -- 2 Stones

    1. Obadiah S. Browne 1879-1936
       his wife Wilhelmina R. 1882-1943

    2. Front: John F. Joseph 1861-1959
            his wife Eloise G. 1862-1927

       Rear: Frank Joseph 1826-1872
               Frances 1814-1888
               Ellen F. 1859-1874
               Amelia F. 1862-1891

LOT #4 -- 2 Stones

    1. Charles A. Colburn died Oct. 19, 1908

    2. Georgie E. Williams 1872-1910

LOT #5 -- 2 Stones

    1. Heman S. Smith 1836-1916
       Mercie Knowles Smith 1836-1884
       Jane Wood Smith 1847-1936

    2. Mother - Elizabeth Smith Dec. 3, 1797 - Oct. 19, 1887
       Father - Jesse Smith Oct. 9, 1793 - Nov. 5, 1871

LOT #6 -- 1 Stone

    1. Eliza A. Ricker died Jan. 28, 1869 age 28 yrs.

CEMETERY NUMBER TWO - OLD SECTION

LOT #6 (continued)
    wife of William R. Ricker
    Also there (sic) child Jessie May died Jan. 28, 1867
    age 7 months

LOT #7 -- 3 Stones

1. Reuben Nickerson born May 13, 1810, died Jan. 14, 1860

2. Lucia S., wife of Reuben Nickerson, died Sept. 24, 1839 ae 27

3. Nellie F., daughter of Hiram B. and Lucinda A. Nickerson died June 19, 1862 aged 2 years 4 months 7 days
"I heard an Angel's voice saying, 'Mother the fold is not full in Eden,' and then we gave our darling Nellie back to the Great Shepherd's care."

LOT #8 -- 4 Stones - 1 Footstone

1. Father - Robert Savage died Oct. 24, 1877 ae 77 yrs. 4 mos. 7 days
Mother - Betsey Savage died Apl. 5, 1881 ae 77 yrs. 4 mos. 5 dys.

2. Father - William H. Hammond born Feb. 4, 1821, died Aug. 31, 1890
Hattie M. Hammond born Aug. 9, 1861, died Sept. 15, 1876
Robert H. son of Charles R. and Ella C. Farrin Jan. 12, 1902-Aug. 31, 1902
Lizzie F. Hammond born July 4, 1865, died July 23, 1870
John W. Hammond born May 25, 1854, died Dec. 10, 1872

3. Adelia H. wife of Charles D. Thompson died Sept. 19, 1863 ae 26 yrs. 3 ms. 2 days

4. Elnora daughter of Charles and Adelia Thompson born Feb. 14, 1857, died July 22, 1857

5. Footstone - Baby

LOT #9 -- No Stone

LOT #10 - 1 Stone - 4 Footstones

1. Front: Capt. Duncan McDonald 1830-1873 Lost at sea
       Isabella 1861-1862
       Walter S. 1867-1869
       Joseph W. 1870-1870
       Charles D. 1873-1879

   Side: Capt. Archibald McDonald 1844-1869 Lost at sea
       Jane Ferguson 1841-1869

   Rear: Capt. John McIntyre 1848-1932
       Betsey Gruchie 1840-1935
       Jennie Lee 1877-1879
       Katherine I. 1878-1943

CEMETERY NUMBER TWO - OLD SECTION

LOT #10 (continued)

    2. Footstone in front of Stone #1 - Children

    3. Footstone - Father

    4. Footstone - Isabella daughter of Duncan and Elizabeth McDonald died Nov. 4, 1862 aged 1 year 6 days

    5. Footstone - Kate

LOT #11 -- 2 Stones

    1. Father - Ephraim S. Ghen died May 2, 1875 aged 70 years 14 days
       Mother - Mary Ghen died May 7, 1885 aged 75 yrs. 4 mos. 27 dys.

    2. Addie - Adelaide L. Ghen died July 12, 1874 aged 23 yrs. 6 ms. 12 ds.

LOT #12 -- 1 Stone

    1. Francis W. Cook 1815-1889
       Elizabeth B. 1821-1885
       Frank A. 1845-1899

LOT #13 -- 1 Stone

    1. Lemuel F. Nickerson 1842-1925
       Cinderella K. Nickerson 1842-1933
       Ernest W. Saunders 1878-1953
       Amy N. Saunders 1881-1955

LOT #14 -- 3 Stones

    1. Front: Father - Mother
       Rear: Mary S. Smith died June 23, 1867 ae 57 yrs. 6 mos. 2 days
            Seth Smith died Nov. 8, 1873 ae 71 years 1 mo. 26 days

    2. Front: Philip R. Smith died Jan. 18, 1860 ae 33 yrs. 3 mos. 20 days
            Mary A. wife of Philip R. Smith died Jan. 23, 1867 ae 36 years 7 months 18 days
       Rear: Charles A. son of Philip R. and Mary A. Smith died Sept. 12, 1853 ae 2 yrs. 1 day

    3. My husband - Truman Smith died May 18, 1874 ae 33 yrs. 9 mos.

LOT #15 -- 1 Stone

    1. Capt. James M. Turner died Nov. 16, 1881 ae 66 yrs. 7 mos.

CEMETERY NUMBER TWO - OLD SECTION

LOT #16 -- 1 Stone

    1. Front: Seth Smith 1837-1912
               Fannie C. Smith 1835-1920

       Rear: Solomon R. Higgins 1833-1864
              Freddie S. 1862-1871
              Aqilla (sic) Higgins 1806-1875
              Abigail Higgins 1803-1875
              Abbie 1843-1903
              Sarah N. 1839-1916
              Philena 1844-1927

LOT #17 -- No Stone

LOT #18 -- No Stone

LOT #19 -- 3 Markers

    1. Elisha S. Newcomb 1858-1933

    2. Hattie W. Newcomb 1859-1932

    3. Elmer W. O'Donnell 1916-1924

LOT #20 -- 3 Stones

    1. Father - Jesse Wiley Sept. 11, 1827 - Feb. 4, 1906
       Mother - Azubah S. Wiley Aug. 10, 1829 - Feb. 16, 1906

    2. Jesse W. son of Jesse and Azubah S. Wiley died April 2, 1860 ae 2 months 29 days

    3. Austin A. son of Jesse and Azubah S. Wiley died April 16, 1864 ae 5 years 6 months

LOT #21 -- 2 Stones

    1. George H. Lewis 1837-1905
       Mary H. his wife 1843-1920

    2. Mattie E. Lewis 1876-1896
       Freddie E. Lewis 1861-1862

LOT #22 -- 1 Stone

    1. Charles H. Hodgdon 1856-1931
       Bessie G. Hodgdon 1856-1926

LOT #23 -- 2 Stones

    1. Joseph Weeks Aug. 18, 1814 - April 11, 1894
       Betsy S. Weeks April 8, 1814 - Dec. 17, 1893

    2. Celestia A. daughter of Joseph and Betsey Weeks died Sept. 11, 1862 ae 7 yrs. 13 days

LOT #24 -- 1 Stone - 5 Footstones

    1. Capt. Thomas Lewis Jan. 15, 1834 - June 7, 1909

CEMETERY NUMBER TWO - OLD SECTION

LOT #24 (continued)

    Flora A. Sept. 8, 1835 - May 8, 1904
    Thomas J. Nov. 1, 1858 - Aug. 23, 1862
    Carrie A. Nov. 19, 1865 - April 29, 1867
    Nettie H. June 27, 1874 - Aug. 3, 1874

  2. Footstone - Thomas J.

  3. Footstone - Carrie A.

  4. Footstone - Nettie H.

  5. Footstone - Father

  6. Footstone - Mother

LOT #25 -- 2 Stones

  1. Lewis L. Chapman Nov. 23, 1818 - May 19, 1898
     Anastasia his wife Aug. 5, 1830 - Jan. 6, 1905

  2. Ellen M. dau. of Lewis L. and Anistia (sic) Chapman died March 9, 1864 ae 7 yrs. 7 mos. 4 days

LOT #26 -- 1 Stone

  1. Frederick E. Williams 1860-1928
     Emma L. Williams 1858-1923

LOT #27 -- No Stone

LOT #28 -- 1 Monument - 2 Stones - 2 Footstones

  1. Monument Front: Reuben S. Snow 1831-1903
                   his wife Hannah D. Payne 1835-1897

     Monument Rear: Nathaniel son of Sally and Nathaniel Payne drowned April 26, 1847 ae 14 years 7 months 9 days

  2. Footstone - Reuben S. Snow 1831-1903

  3. Footstone - Hannah D. wife of Reuben S. Snow 1835-1897

  4. Stone - Mother - Sally Payne died Sept. 18, 1890
                   ae 87 years 5 months 25 days
         Father - Nathaniel Payne, lost at sea, Sept. 1837
                 ae 33 yrs. 5 mos.

  5. Stone - Louisa F. wife of Alfred Hall Aug. 23, 1837 - Nov. 22, 1906

LOT #29 -- 1 Stone - 1 Burial, no stone

  1. John Rautio 1877-1955

  2. No Stone - Cemetery records: Frank A. Souza died May 15, 1974 ae 67 years 3 months 6 days

CEMETERY NUMBER TWO - OLD SECTION

LOT #30 -- 2 Monuments - 1 Stone - 10 Footstones

   1. Monument Front: Capt. David Smith died April 19, 1888
                      ae 74 yrs. 1 mo. 15 days
                  Lucy wife of Capt. David Smith died
                      Sept. 21, 1861 ae 42 yrs. 2 mos. 23 days

      Monument Right: Joseph Lewis died Oct. 23, 1857 ae 32 yrs.
                  1 mo. 11 days
                  Joseph H. son of Joseph and Jerusha A.
                  Lewis died Dec. 15, 1891 ae 33 yrs.
                  10 mos. 1 day
                  Jerusha A. widow of Joseph Lewis and widow
                  of Capt. David Smith died Feb. 13, 1894
                  ae 59 yrs. 5 mos. 4 days

      Monument Left: An infant daughter of David and Jerusha A.
                 Smith died Nov. 10, 1862
                 Eddie Elmer son of David and Jerusha A.
                 Smith born July 8, 1865 died Aug. 8,
                 1865

   2. Monument Front: Lurana C. daughter of Richard C. and Alsey
                  P. Smith died Aug. 26, 1840 ae 1 yr.
                  3 months 6 days
                  Isaiah H. son of Richard C. and Alsey P.
                  Smith died March 15, 1864 ae 17 years
                  8 months 1 day

      Monument Left: Richard C. Smith born Feb. 25, 1809 died
                 April 17, 1851
                 Alsey P. wife of Nathaniel Freeman died
                 Jan. 26, 1879 ae 64 yrs. 3 mos. 14 days

   3. Stone - Joseph Lewis died Oct. 23, 1857 ae 32 yrs. 1 mo.
      11 days (see Monument #1)

   4. Footstone - An infant

   5. Footstone - Eddie Elmer

   6. Footstone - Mother

   7. Footstone - Joseph H. Lewis died Dec. 15, 1891 ae 33 yrs.
      10 mos. 1 day

   8. Footstone - David Smith

   9. Footstone - Lucy Smith

   10. Footstone - Richard

   11. Footstone - Mother

   12. Footstone - Lurana

   13. Footstone - Isaiah

LOT #31 -- 5 Stones

   1. George V. Williams died Jan. 29, 1873 ae 27 yrs. 2 mos.

CEMETERY NUMBER TWO - OLD SECTION

LOT #31 (continued)

    2. Marietta F. Cross Nov. 27, 1828 - Oct. 9, 1902

    3. Francis Nickerson 1827-1913

    4. Mary F. Nickerson died March 24, 1895 ae 59 yrs. 2 mos. 21 days

    5. Bessie Wyman only daughter of Frank and Mary F. Nickerson died April 13, 1869 ae 14 yrs. 3 mos. 7 days
"Gone to the land where the flowers never die."

    Charlie Vernon only son of Frank and Mary F. Nickerson died Oct. 6, 1859 ae 16 months
"Transplanted from earth to heaven."

LOT #32 -- 2 Stones - 2 Footstones

    1. Father - Henry Rich died Nov. 28, 1866 ae 40 yrs. 6 mos. 16 days
Mother - Hannah Rich died Feb. 25, 1864 ae 34 yrs. 1 mo.

    2. Leonard B. Rich July 11, 1851 - April 30, 1904
Sarah L. his wife Sept. 15, 1854 - March 20, 1938
Fred L. their son Sept. 16, 1876 - Feb. 13, 1899
Lottie B. 1879-1914

    3. Footstone - Fred

    4. Footstone - Lottie

LOT #33 -- 3 Stones - 1 Footstone

    1. Mary W. Pierce Oct. 13, 1825 - Oct. 23, 1898

    2. Footstone - Father (VR: John Pierce, husband of Mary W. Pierce, died May 24, 1902 ae 76 yrs. 9 mos. 23 days)

    3. James W. Pierce 1870-1948

    4. Eva M. Pierce 1881-1968

LOT #34 -- 8 Stones

    1. Daniel S. Small died July 17, 1883 aged 80 years 10 mos. 17 days

    2. Mary H. wife of D. S. Small died April 25, 1877 ae 76 ys. 5 ms. 7 ds.

    3. Susan J. daughter of Daniel S. and Mary H. Small died May 15, 1861 aged 34 yrs. 7 mos.

    4. Ruth S. died June 5, 1838 aged 1 yr. 1 mo.
Ruth S. died Dec'r. 3, 1839 aged 5 mos.
Ann C. Small died Dec'r. 27, 1842 aged 1 yr. 10 mos.
Daniel S. died Oct. 3, 1844 aged 2 years 10 months
Children of Daniel S. and Mary H. Small

    5. Ruth C. wife of John T. Small died Feb. 20 1868 aged 34 years 11 mos.

CEMETERY NUMBER TWO - OLD SECTION

LOT #34 (continued)

    6. Wife Mary L. Brundage 1871-1929

    7. John G. Cooey 1823-1879
       Elizabeth T. his wife 1828-1909

    8. Tommie son of J. G. and L. T. Cooey died Sept. 6, 1865 aged 11 months 17 days

LOT #35 -- 1 Stone

    1. Horace G. Berry died January 28, 1881 ae 49 years 6 months
       Patty S. Berry died Dec. 25, 1901 ae 69 yrs. 11 mos. 25 days

LOT #36 -- 4 Stones

    1. Our Mother - Ruth W. Bailey died Dec. 1, 1863 aged 71 years

    2. Oliver E. Bailey Jan. 26, 1825 - Feb. 19, 1894
       Marilla S. his wife 1830-1918

    3. Daniel F. Bailey died March 28, 1838 ae 18

    4. Sister - Mary Bailey died Feb. 24 1886 aged 72 years 1 mo. 12 ds.

LOT #37 -- 1 Stone

    1. Front: Theodore Nickerson 1834-1920
           Emorie F. his wife 1846-1914
           Nellie H. Shepard 1867-1935
           Edward Shepard 1871-1950

       Rear: Isaac Nickerson 1807-1870
            Mary B. his wife 1816-1882
            Isaac H. 1842-1867
            Ellen S. Cook 1838-1863

LOT #38 -- No Stone

LOT #39 -- No Stone

LOT #40 -- 5 Stones

    1. Father - Prince Freeman Nov. 7, 1822 - Sept. 20, 1909

    2. Mother - Eliza A. wife of Prince Freeman Aug. 15, 1825 - Feb. 15, 1895

    3. Willie L. son of Prince and Eliza A. Freeman died April 1, 1864 ae 3 yrs. 5 mos. 3 dys.

    4. Willie L. son of Prince and Eliza A. Freeman died June 3, 1889 ae 24 yrs. 3 mos. 3 das.

    5. Frank Chase Aug. 18, 1853 - Dec. 5, 1924
       Laura P. his wife Nov. 11, 1857 - Jan. 16, 1944

CEMETERY NUMBER TWO - OLD SECTION

LOT #41 -- 5 Stones

1. Father - Francis Chase died April 16, 1884 aged 65 years 7 months 16 days

2. Mother - Cathrine (sic) wife of Francis Chase died March 24, 1888 aged 58 years

3. M. Elizabeth Chase wife of Henry F. Burt 1855-1887

4. Clarence F. son of H. F. and M. E. Burt 1884-1886

5. Cora Burt wife of Edward B. Gross 1874-1965

LOT #42 -- 1 Marker

1. Chas. F. A. Farnsworth 1859-1907

LOT #43 -- 1 Stone - 1 Footstone

1. James Cashman 1825-1896
   Nancy E. 1830-1911

2. Footstone - Jas. Cashman Co. I. 3rd Mass. Cav.

LOT #44 -- 4 Stones - All buried

1. Father - Freeman Smith 1790-1869
   Mother - Zilla Smith 1801-1860

2. Mother - Sarah E. Smith 1848-1920
   Father - Capt. S. (Samuel) Jones Rich 1839-1922

3. Jennie daughter of Capt. S. Jones and Sarah E. Rich 1873-1874

4. Lillian N. Rich wife of Arthur O. Messer 1876-1932

LOT #45 -- 1 Stone - Buried

1. Edmun (sic) T. Smith Aug. 15, 1836 - Jan. 25, 1898

LOT #46 -- 3 Stones

1. Father - James Sullivan died at sea July 31, 1852 aged 41 years
   Mother - Polly wife of James Sullivan died March 15, 1886 aged 72 years

2. George Crosby 1841-1899
   Eliza A. Crosby 1843-1908
   Edith C. Young 1881-(not cut) (VR: died Nov. 26, 1946 ae 65 years 2 months 27 days)

3. George W. son of George and Eliza A. W. Crosby died Oct. 17, 1867 ae 3 mos. 25 ds.

LOT #47 -- 1 Stone

1. George L. son of Geo. W. and Kate E. Vesty died Dec. 10, 1866 aged 15 yrs. 1 mo. 28 ds.

CEMETERY NUMBER TWO - OLD SECTION

LOT #48 -- No Stone

LOT #49 -- No Stone - Cemetery records list lot in name of
Otis R. Lovering

> (Editor's note: Vital Records indicate Otis R. Lovering died Nov. 1, 1870 ae 57 years 9 months 4 days, and Charles O. son of Otis R. and Cordelia Lovering died Sept. 29, 1849 ae 1 year 11 mos. 1 day)

LOT #50 -- 2 Stones - 1 Footstone

1. Enos S. Burch 1844-1924
   Sarah A. Burch 1846-1923

2. Footstone - Baby

3. Eva H. Burch 1874-1895

LOT #51 -- 1 Stone

1. Father - Capt. Chas. H. Walker April 16, 1830 - Dec. 13, 1903
   Mother - Nancy S. Walker Dec. 8, 1837 - Nov. 6, 1892

LOT #52 -- 2 Stones

1. Josiah Ghen June 6, 1812 - Nov. 30, 1883

2. Rebecca wife of Josiah Ghen died Sept. 23, 1866
   ae 49 yrs. 2 mos. 11 dys.

LOT #53 -- 5 Stones - 1 Base with no stone

1. Richard G. Tarrant 1828-1914

2. Ruth A. wife of Richard G. Tarrant died Jan. 10, 1858
   aged 22 years

3. Phoebe S. wife of Richard G. Tarrant died Nov. 30, 1869
   ae 25 years

4. Eva Agnes dau. of R. G. & P. S. Tarrant died Oct. 7, 1869
   ae 3 mos. 16 dys.

5. Susan A. Tarrant 1839-1903

6. Base (VR: Possibly Ann M. daughter of Richard G. and Ann R. Tarrant died Feb. 8, 1858 ae 2 years 11 mos. 28 days)

LOT #54 -- 2 Stones

1. Ann Butler died Jan. 9, 1884 ae 69 yrs.

2. William H. son of J. (Joseph) and A. Butler born in Boston Sept. 30, 1850 died of the Small Pox in Provincetown Jan. 7, 1873 ae 23 yrs. 3 mos. 8 dys.

LOT #55 -- 1 Stone

1. Elijah Rodgers 1834-1925

CEMETERY NUMBER TWO - OLD SECTION

LOT #55 (continued)
    Zipporah 1838-1920
    Charles 1873-1893
    Adelaide Williams 1875-1918

LOT #56 -- 1 Stone - 1 Footstone

1. Nathan S. Hudson 1835-1908
   George W. 1873-1927
   Elizabeth A. Hudson 1841-1902
   Isabelle Blanchard 1872-1941

2. Footstone - George

LOT #57 -- No Stone

LOT #58 -- 2 Stones - 2 Markers

1. Front: James G. Hunt born in Boston, Mass. Oct. 10, 1810 died in Boston Sept. 15, 1874
        Clarissa J. Hunt born in Billerica, Mass. Dec. 5, 1811 died in Boston Sept. 3, 1881

   Side: James G. Hunt Jr. born in Boston, Mass. Nov. 1, 1835 died in Provincetown Nov. 3, 1865

2. Front: Caleb D. Smith April 24, 1834 - May 30, 1905
        his wife Charlotte M. Hunt June 8, 1837 - July 3, 1895

   Rear: Their children Clara H. April 11, 1857 - Nov. 22, 1873
        Robert C. Aug. 4, 1862 - April 7, 1864
        Pearl & Daisy Sept. 26, 1865

3. Marker - Mother - Charlotte M. wife of Caleb D. Smith June 8, 1837 - July 3, 1895

4. Marker - Bertie - Robert C. Smith Aug. 4, 1862 - April 7, 1864

LOT #59 -- 3 Stones

1. Father - Charles A. Young Dec. 7, 1826 - May 16, 1898
   Priscilla B. Young Nov. 11, 1832 - March 20, 1904

2. Front: Our little Fannie

   Rear: Daughter of Charles A. and P. B. Young died June 6, 1864 ae 3 yrs. 8 mos. 22 dys.

3. Charles L. Young 1853-1910

LOT #60 -- 4 Stones

1. George B. Burch Nov. 25, 1827 - Apl. 6, 1890

2. Elizabeth Burch March 4, 1833 - Dec. 15, 1912

CEMETERY NUMBER TWO - OLD SECTION

LOT #60 (continued)

    3. Lizzie Brewer daughter of George B. and Elizabeth Burch died Dec. 2, 1863 aged 3 y. 4 mo. 24 d.

    4. Alexander T. Burch Aug. 12, 1865 - July 12, 1866
       Lizzie B. Burch Sept. 3, 1866 - Aug. 24, 1867

LOT #61 -- 2 Stones - 1 Footstone

    1. Charles P. Rogers 1855-1898
       Mary 1854-1932
       Loretta E. Sanford 1885-1908

    2. George E. Sanford 1906-1964

    3. Footstone - George

LOT #62 -- 1 Stone - 2 Footstones

    1. Manuel Joseph Barnes lost at sea (No date)
       Frank 1873-1894
       Rose 1869-1953
       Antone 1871-1953
       his wife Lillian 1879-1942

    2. Footstone - Frank

    3. Footstone - Rose

LOT #63 -- 1 Monument

    1. Front: John C. Lurten 1834-1864
           Emma A. Howland 1858-1883
           William J. Lurten 1863-1893
           Joan Woods (No date)

       Right: John A. Woods 1866-1867

       Left: Phares L. Woods 1871-1915

LOT #64 -- 2 Stones

    1. George A. Settes Sept. 15, 1878 - Feb. 10, 1903
       "Faithful son and loving brother."

    2. Mary Elizabeth wife of John E. Morrill died Jan. 16, 1890 aged 22 yrs. 9 mos. 19 dys.
       Bessie their daughter died July 26, 1889 aged 8 mos. 22 dys.

LOT #65 -- No Stone

LOT #66 -- 1 Stone

    1. Front: Camelu Pallam lost at sea April 4, 1883 ae 42 yrs. 16 days
           Nancy T. wife of Camelu Pallam died Nov. 2, 1876 ae 36 years

       Rear: Bertha G. Pallam died Sept. 20, 1870 ae 2 yrs. 3 mos.

CEMETERY NUMBER TWO - OLD SECTION

LOT #66 (continued)
    An infant died Aug. 8, 1866

LOT #67 -- No Stone

LOT #68 -- No Stone

LOT #69 -- No Stone

LOT $70 -- 1 Stone

1. Nathaniel T. Burch 1857-1911
   Catherine his wife 1860-1932
   Enos S. Burch 1818-1864
   Mary A. Burch 1822-1883

LOT #71 -- No Stone

LOT #72 -- No Stone

LOT #73 -- 3 Stones

1. Husband - Frank N. Days 1861-1908

2. Wife - Annie Days 1872-1941

3. Charles E. Days 1894-1963
   his wife Olive C. 1896-(Not cut)
   "Together Forever"

LOT #74 -- 2 Stones

1. Nathaniel Atkins died Sept. 16, 1865 ae 76 years

2. Betsey wife of Nathaniel Atkins died Sept. 7, 1862
   ae 72 years

LOT #75 -- 1 Stone

1. Matilda Nickerson 1846-1872
   Cecelia G. 1871-1872
   Sparrow 1779-1881

LOT #76 -- No Stone

LOT #77 -- 2 Stones

1. Henry Atwood Nov. 19, 1821 - Feb. 13, 1899
   Urania T. Atwood Jan. 18, 1830 - Dec. 10, 1905

2. Arthur C. died Jan. 12, 1863 ae 1 year 6 mos. 5 days
   Eugene F. died July 2, 1868 ae 3 years 11 mos. 15 days
   Wallace H. lost at sea Nov. 13, 1870 ae 16 years 10 mos.
      14 days
   Children of Henry and Urania T. Atwood

CEMETERY NUMBER TWO - OLD SECTION

LOT #78 -- 2 Stones

    1. Capt. William Wareham 1836-1905
       Alice Wareham 1837-1903
       William W. Wareham 1858-1862
       William Wareham 1805-1861
       Jedidah Wareham 1800-1877

    2. Disintegrated stone - probably Wareham family

LOT #79 -- No Stone

LOT #80 -- 1 Stone

    1. An infant son of G. (George) W. and Sarah Adams died Aug. 16, 1861

LOT #81 -- No Stone

LOT #82 -- 1 Stone

    1. Daniel L. Small died April 30, 1880 aged 50 years

LOT #83 -- No Stone

LOT #84 -- 4 Stones

    1. John Williams 1854-1918
       Georgie E. Williams 1860-1932

    2. Our darling Lillian Dec. 27, 1901 - June 26, 1902 daughter of Mr. & Mrs. John Williams

    3. Charles F. Williams - Massachusetts Surfman U. S. Coast Guard June 25, 1890 - July 16, 1961

    4. Elizabeth C. Pond June 15, 1893 - Feb. 18, 1971

LOT #85 -- 1 Stone

    1. Our Babes - Children of E. (Eben) & H. (Hannah) West (VR: infant male died July 30, 1853 ae 4 days Walter H. died Sept. 20, 1853 ae 1 mo. 19 days)

LOT #86 -- 3 Stones

    1. Manuel F. Caton 1870-1943
       Bertha M. 1880-1957

    2. Winthrop C. Caton 1897-1915

    3. Mother - Stella Caton May 26, 1876 - Sept. 13, 1894

LOT #87 -- 2 Stones

    1. Mary E. wife of G. B. Spencer died Aug. 7, 1870 ae 39 yrs. 4 mos.

    2. Alfred J. son of G. (Gilbert) B. and M. E. Spencer died Oct. 20, 1866 ae 4 yrs. 3 mos. 10 days

CEMETERY NUMBER TWO - OLD SECTION

LOT #88 -- 5 Stones

1. George N. Whelden 1859-1939
   Mary F. 1864-1940
2. Ann S. Whelden died Dec. 24, 1899 ae 70 yrs. 1 mo. 23 dys.
3. Johnnie T. died Oct. 1862 ae 6 yrs. 8 mos.
4. Freddie H. died Oct. 1872 ae 2 yrs.
5. Mamie A. died Aug. 1864 ae 11 months
   Children of E. (Eliphalet) H. and Anne S. Whelden

LOT #89 -- 1 Stone

1. Henry Holway born in Sandwich July 18, 1812 died Sept. 18, 1862

LOT #90 -- 1 Stone

1. Henry K. Porter died Jan. 6, 1856 aged 3 mos. 10 days

LOT #91 -- 3 Stones

1. Capt. Henry K. Pierce died May 25, 1854 aged 34 years
2. Gamaliel T. son of Henry K. and Eliza P. Pierce died April 26, 1841 ae 5 mos. 13 days
3. Eliza P. wife of Wm. S. Kendall born Dec. 28, 1821 died June 17, 1894

LOT #92 -- 1 Stone

1. Jesse son of John W. and Rachal S. Small died Sept. 9, 1836 ae 10 mos. 16 dys.

LOT #93 -- 3 Stones

1. Louisa W. wife of Mark G. Smith died March 5, 1858 aged 32 years
2. Addie Louise daughter of Mark G. and L. W. Smith died Aug. 24, 1855 ae 18 ms. and 24 dys.
3. Addie Louise daughter of Mark G. and Louise W. Smith born Feb. 20 died July 17, 1858

LOT #94 -- 5 Stones

1. John Atkins died July 1, 1860 ae 62 years 10 months
2. Bethia wife of John Atkins died March 27, 1840 ae 34 years 5 months
   Isaiah, John, Silas and Maria S. Children of John and Bethiah Atkins
3. Capt. John Atkins 1834-1913
   Jane M. his wife 1845-1932

CEMETERY NUMBER TWO - OLD SECTION

LOT #94 (continued)

    4. Sarah F. wife of John Atkins died August 22, 1872 ae 33 years 11 months

    5. George A. son of John and Sarah F. Atkins died March 18, 1883 ae 17 years 5 months 11 days

LOT #95 -- 4 Stones

    1. Mr. Amaziah Crowell died March 23, 1856 ae 50 years

    2. Avis J. wife of Amaziah Crowell died Sept. 9, 1881 ae 67 years 11 months 9 days

    3. Albert F. son of Amaziah and Avis L. Crowell died Oct. 15, 1850 ae 3 years

    4. Mrs. Addie S. wife of Edwin Crowell died May 20, 1875 ae 28 years 8 months 21 days
"She died when the world seemed the brightest.
She died in the flower of her youth:
At that age when the heart bounds the lightest,
full of virtues and honor and truth.
Worn out with pain her body sleeps.
No more it mourns. No more it weeps.
In Christ the Lord she puts her trust.
And He will raise her sleeping dust."

LOT #96 -- 2 Stones

    1. Mr. Jonathan Hopkins born Jan. 19, 1790 died Sept. 14, 1862

    2. Betsey wife of Jonathan Hopkins died July 30, 1857 ae 62 yrs. 8 ms.

LOT #97 -- 4 Stones

    1. Joshua Mayo Jr. died Feb. 21, 1861 ae 41 years

    2. Mary T. wife of Joshua A. Mayo Jr. died June 18, 1864 ae 32 years

    3. Mary Lizzie (VR: died Jan. 4, 1857 ae 4 yrs.)
Joshua (VR: died Sept. 23, 1858 ae 4 mos.)
Anna (VR: died March 16, 1850 ae 4 mos. 16 days)
Children of Joshua A. and Mary T. Mayo

    4. Anna Spilmun died Sept. 19, 1859 ae 18 years

LOT #98 -- 2 Stones

    1. Mother - Ann wife of Lewis Johnson 1835-1880

    2. Frank L. son of A. & L. Johnson died July 12, 1860 ae 6 mos.

LOT #99 -- No Stone

LOT #100 -- No Stone

CEMETERY NUMBER TWO - OLD SECTION

LOT #101 -- 1 Stone

   1. William Turner Dec. 26, 1857 ae 77 years
      Rhoda his widow died Jan. 21, 1861 ae 72 yrs. 6 ms.

LOT #102 -- 2 Markers

   1. Margaret Hill 1882-1975

   2. Cyrus C. Burch 1877-1915

LOT #103 -- 5 Stones

   1. Capt. Isaiah Atkins died Sept. 21, 1870 ae 40 years 9 mos.

   2. Experience E. wife of Isaiah Atkins died March 15, 1858 ae 23 years 5 months

   3. Isaiah M. son of Isaiah and Jane M. Atkins died July 24, 1889 ae 23 years 1 month 4 days

   4. Emily C. daughter of Isaiah and Experience Atkins died May 30, 1857 ae 1 year 4 mos. 8 days

   5. Emily C. daughter of Isaiah and Jane M. Atkins died Nov. 9, 1883 ae 14 years 11 mos. 29 days

LOT #104 -- 2 Stones

   1. Capt. Peter Avery lost at sea Apl. 9, 1873 aged 44 yrs. 4 mos. 10 ds.

   2. Austine ae 1 yr. 14 ds. (VR: died Sept. 17, 1856)
      Emmie ae 4 ms. 3 ds. (VR: died Jan. 10, 1858)
      An infant ae 2 days (VR: died Oct. 3, 1863)
      Children of Peter and Hannah K. Avery

LOT #105 -- No Stone

LOT #106 -- 1 Stone

   1. Mr. Heman Harvender died Aug. 6, 1875 aged 52 years
      Saphronia (sic) G. died Feb. 8, 1859 ae 33 yrs.
      Henrietta S. died Feb. 15, 1868 ae 33 yrs. wife of Heman Harvender

LOT #107 -- No Stone

LOT #108 -- 1 Stone

   1. Edmund B. Lord died May 8, 1865 ae 59 yrs. 6 ms.
      Sarah A. C. his wife died May 24, 1858 ae 57 ys. 3 ms.

LOT #109 -- 1 Stone

   1. Charles E. Hopkins Aug. 2, 1849 - Apl. 11, 1909
      his wife Maria L. Nov. 22, 1855 - Apl. 13, 1894

CEMETERY NUMBER TWO - OLD SECTION

LOT #110 -- 1 Stone

    1. Rebecca L. died Oct. 7, 1857 ae 21 years 7 mos.
Sophronia D. died Sept. 18, 1859 ae 17 years 12 days
Children of John L. and Maria Smith

LOT #111 -- No Stone

LOT #112 -- 3 Stones

    1. George Lewis 1829-1915
John W. 1856-1935
Albert F. 1870-1952

    2. Mother - Mrs. Arozana Lewis died Mar. 8, 1892
aged 61 yrs. 4 mos. 20 dys.

    3. Hopey R. died Aug. 3, 1862 aged 3 years
Hopey R. died Dec. 7, 1863 aged 1 yr. 2 mos.
Infant died Nov. 25, 1861 ae 6 weeks
Children of George and Arozana Lewis

LOT #113 -- 7 Stones

    1. Capt. George Lewis died March 23, 1845 ae 56 yrs. 8 mos.

    2. Mrs. Mary widow of George Lewis died Nov. 23, 1858
ae 66 years

    3. Mary eldest dau. of Capt. Geo. and Mary Lewis died
Oct. 19, 1819 ae 1 year

    4. Mary 2nd dau. of Capt. George and Mary Lewis died
Sept. 23, 1823 ae 1 yr. 20 ds.

    5. George son of Capt. Geo. and Mary Lewis died
Nov. 4, 1825 ae 1 yr. 1 mo. 2 ds.

    6. Sophronia B. dau. of Capt. Geo. and Mary Lewis died
June 7, 1832 ae 1 yr. 15 dys.

    7. Olin M. born Aug. 14 and died Sept. 21, 1848
Joshua M. born Aug. 14 and died Sept. 27, 1848
Children of Joshua and Mary A. Lewis

LOT #114 -- 2 Stones

    1. Jonathan D. Smith 1835-1904
Marinda Stubbs Smith 1837-1898
Minnie Smith Plaisted 1865-1929

    2. Benjamin J. Smith 1837-1909
Mary F. Smith 1841-1909
Martha O. Nichols 1875-1931

LOT #115 -- No Stone

LOT #116 -- No Stone

CEMETERY NUMBER TWO - OLD SECTION

LOT #117 -- 4 Stones

   1. Father - Nathaniel H. Small 1802-1879
      Mother - Peggy Small 1808-1885

   2. Nathaniel H. son of Nathaniel H. and Peggy Small died March 15, 1842 ae 5 mos. 15 ds.

   3. Uriah son of Nathaniel H. and Peggy Small died Nov. 7, 1832 ae 5 ys. 6 ms.

   4. Annie W. Small 1850-1920
      Nath. H. Small 1847-1920

LOT #118 -- 3 Stones - 1 Footstone

   1. Front: Ruben (sic) W. 1832-1904

      Rear: George R. 1868-1888
               Ansel L. 1874-1876
               Alvin F. 1858-1917

   2. Footstone - R. W. Rich - Co. H 56 Mass. Inf.

   3. Mary S. N. Rich 1837-1910

   4. Ida L. daughter of Reuben W. and Mary Rich died Aug. 26, 1857 ae 8 mos. 13 dys.

LOT #119 -- 3 Stones

   1. Xenophen Rich died July 28, 1856 ae 48 yrs.

   2. Olive wife of Joseph Atkins and widow of Xenophen Rich died Dec. 14, 1879 ae 67 yrs. 2 ms. 8 ds.

   3. Joseph Atkins 1819-1900

LOT #120 -- No Stone

LOT #121 -- No Stone

LOT #122 -- 4 Stones

   1. John Ghen died June 14, 1884 aged 78 yrs. 7 mos.

   2. Our Mother - Delia wife of John Ghen died Oct. 18, 1871 aged 62 yrs. 8 ms. 9 dys.

   3. Front: Gordon

      Rear: John G. son of John and Delia Ghen died Dec. 5, 1873 ae 27 yrs. 4 days

   4. Mother - Suvina L. wife of John Ghen died May 24, 1880 ae 58 yrs. 11 ms. 10 ds.

LOT #123 -- 1 Stone

   1. Charles W. Burch 1851-1926
      Elizabeth S. 1854-1919
      Nellie T. 1882-1883

CEMETERY NUMBER TWO - OLD SECTION

LOT #123 (continued)
    Alice M. 1884-1913

LOT #124 -- 5 Stones

1. Isaiah A. Small died May 28, 1887 ae 62 yrs. 3 mos. 2 ds.

2. Lucy A. wife of Isaiah A. Small died Apr. 29, 1880 ae 52 ys. 1 m. 16 ds.

3. Freddie son of Isaiah and Lucy A. Small died April 11, 1861 ae 4 ms. 23 dys.

4. Ida Bernette daughter of Isaiah and Lucy A. Small died April 15, 1863 ae 4 months

5. Lucy Idella daughter of Isaiah and Lucy A. Small died July 24, 1856 ae 5 ms. 19 ds.

LOT #125 -- 2 Stones

1. Henry W. Marston 1839-1924
Adelia his wife 1843-1876
Lydia his wife 1840-1919
Infant son (VR: Charles S.) died 1865

2. Edward Marston 1806-1882
Julia D. his wife 1806-1903
Edward S. 1835-1855

LOT #126 -- 1 Stone

1. James E. son of Joseph M. and Mehitable Farwell died Sept. 23, 1858 aged 7 yrs. and 10 mos.

LOT #127 -- 2 Stones

1. Eldredge F. Smith died March 11, 1862 ae 42 ys. 5 ms.

2. Rachel A. Smith died April 20, 1889 ae 70 yrs.

LOT #128 -- No Stone

LOT #129 -- 1 Stone

1. Capt. John Nicholson (no date)
his wife Jane N. 1840-1907
Mary (no date) (VR: born Dec. 15, 1860)

LOT #130 -- 1 Stone - 3 Footstones

1. Front: Thomas V. Mullins Aug. 11, 1835 - March 21, 1907
      his wife Mary J. Jan. 15, 1837 - Jan. 1, 1921

   Right: Freeman V. July 11, 1871 - Aug. 5, 1873

2. Footstone - Wife

3. Footstone - Husband

CEMETERY NUMBER TWO - OLD SECTION

LOT #130 (continued)

    4. Footstone - Baby

LOT #131 -- 1 Stone - 1 Footstone

    1. Rodolphus Atwood 1829-1890
       Mary E. Nye 1836-1925
       Mary N. (Luce) 1869-1893
       Laura E. 1859-1861
       Clara F. 1864-1867

    2. Footstone - Our Mother

LOT #132 -- 1 Stone

    1. John R. Morrison 1902-1953
       Helen J. 1902-19 (not cut)

LOT #133 -- 4 Stones - 1 Base with no stone

    1. Anna wife of Edwin M. Williams died March 27, 1856 ae 19 yrs. 4 ms.

    2. Clara Anna daughter of Edwin M. and Anna Williams died Aug. 28, 1856 ae 9 ms. 28 ds.

    3. Base with no stone (unknown)

    4. Mrs. Betsey W. wife of John Williams died Sept. 21, 1845 ae 40 yrs. 4 mos.

    5. Ann T. wife of John Williams died Sept. 8, 1861 aged 52 yrs. 9 mos.
       Bethiah H. died Nov. 11, 1857 aged 24 yrs. 8 dys.
       John T. died in Hankow, China April 9, 1863 aged 22 yrs. 8 mos.
       Children of John and Betsey Williams

LOT #134 -- 1 Stone - 6 Footstones

    1. Front: Nathaniel Paine 1791-1863
             Fanny Paine 1800-1883

       Rear: Nathan Chapman 1821-1879
              Fannie R. Chapman 1829-1906
              Nathaniel P. 1853-1854
              Austin F. 1859-1864

    2. Footstone - N. P.

    3. Footstone - F. P.

    4. Footstone - N. C.

    5. Footstone - F. R. C.

    6. Footstone - N. P. C.

    7. Footstone - A. F. C.

LOT #135 -- No Stone

CEMETERY NUMBER TWO - OLD SECTION

LOT #135 (continued)

(Cemetery records indicate owner of lot was Reuben Goodspeed. VR: Reuben Goodspeed died Jan. 25, 1857 ae 77 yrs. 7 mos. 22 ds.)

LOT #136 -- 4 Stones

1. Albertina L. Nickerson died July 11, 1877
    ae 11 yrs. 3 ms. 20 ds.
   Henry Nickerson - Co. D 22nd Mass. Vols. died at Hiogo, Japan Dec. 20, 1878 ae 37 yrs. 6 ms. 5 ds.

2. Mother - Surmentha wife of Henry Nickerson died Dec. 10, 1892 ae 51 years

3. Laura A. Young April 4, 1854 - Sept. 7, 1906

4. Sarah L. Young March 30, 1815 - Dec. 23, 1893

LOT #137 -- 1 Stone

1. John F. Caton 1865-1927
   Justine S. 1875-1934

LOT #138 -- No Stone

LOT #139 -- 3 Stones

1. Elijah Doane died May 7, 1883 ae 70 ys. 3 ms. 13 ds.

2. Lydia A. wife of Elijah Doane died June 25, 1861
    ae 47 ys. 6 ms.
   Philip S. Doane died at sea July 16, 1862 ae 22 ys. 4 ms.

3. Betsey A. Wilson 1832-1916

LOT #140 -- 1 Stone

1. Wm. Otis Manuel 1859-1924
   Catherine K. Manuel 1865-1958
   Wm. K. Nickerson 1863-(not cut)
   Annie A. Nickerson 1866-1920
   Lucia & Annie (no dates) (surname Nickerson)

LOT #141 -- 1 Buried Stone

1. Charles B. (no date)
   Asaph S. (no date)
   Wally C. (no date)
   Georgie W. died April 15, 1867 ae 5 yrs. 4 mos. 7 dys.
   Children of Thomas and Eliza Ryder

LOT #142 -- 1 Stone

1. Front: Civil War Veteran Paron C. Young Aug. 12, 1838 - Apr. 26, 1912
   Susan E. Young Feb. 10, 1845 - June 7, 1903

CEMETERY NUMBER TWO - OLD SECTION

LOT #142 (continued)

    Rear: Arthur C. Aug. 25, 1866 - Nov. 3, 1874
           Bessie C. March 22, 1872 - July 19, 1872

LOT #143 -- 3 Stones

1. Groce Ghen born Oct. 17, 1799 died June 27, 1853
2. Capt. John Dunlap died Oct. 9, 1876 aged 77 ys. 3 ms. 10 ds.
3. Almira widow of John Dunlap died Oct. 16, 1890 aged 82 yrs. 4 ds.

LOT #144 -- No Stone

(Cemetery records indicate the lot owner was George F. Twombley. VR: Hannah A. Twombley died Dec. 21, 1857 ae 4 yrs. 9 mos. 10 days daughter of George F. and Thankful Twombley)

LOT #145 -- 4 Stones

1. Father - Joshua F. Atkins died Jan. 18, 1882
      ae 28 ys. 7 ms. 10 ds.
   Mother - Genie G. Atkins died Sept. 27, 1884
      ae 31 ys. 6 ms. 14 ds.
2. Father - Samuel Knowles Co. I 41st Reg. Mass. Vols. died Nov. 26, 1893 ae 62 ys. 9 mos.
3. Mother - Hannah E. wife of Samuel Knowles died Aug. 29, 1893 aged 58 ys. 8 ms. 21 ds.
4. Carrie E. Knowles born Sept. 17, 1860 died Aug. 17, 1901

LOT #146 -- 1 Stone

1. Charles Holway died June 22, 1883 ae 79 yrs. 9 mos. 10 dys. Angeline wife of Charles Holway born Sept. 2, 1807 died Sept. 12, 1840

LOT #147 -- 2 Stones

1. Mr. Nathan Young died Aug. 10, 1856 ae 62 ys. 6 ms.
2. Mrs. Sally Young died Mch. 16, 1890 ae 86 ys. 9 ms. 16 ds.

LOT #148 -- No Stone

LOT #149 -- 1 Stone

1. Mr. David Ryder died Feb. 26, 1846 ae 55 yrs. 4 mos.

LOT #150 -- No Stone

LOT #151 -- 1 Stone

1. Michael Freeman 1839-1907
   Abbie L. Freeman 1843-1911

CEMETERY NUMBER TWO - OLD SECTION

LOT #151 (continued)

    William E. 1885-(not cut) (VR: died March 9, 1953 ae 67 years 7 mos. 18 days)

LOT #152 -- 1 Stone

  1. Front: Francis C. Miller 1829-1891
          Lucinda A. Miller 1836-1919
          Francis S. Miller 1858-1933

     Rear: Robert S. Miller 1797-1837
          Patty Miller 1798-1822
          Polly S. Miller 1799-1879
          Hicks S. Miller 1826-1848

LOT #153 -- 1 Buried Stone

  1. Charles H. died April 4, 1851 ae 5 mos. 27 dys.
     Isabel F. died July 27, 1856 ae 10 mos. 22 dys.
     Children of Robert M. and Mercy F. Miller

LOT #154 -- No Stone

LOT #155 -- 1 Monument

  1. Front: Mrs. Bethiah P. Grozier died April 9, 1857 aged 43 years

     Left: Richard Elliot died Feb. 16, 1826 ae 37 years 10 months
         Anna wife of Richard Elliot died Jan. 21, 1835 ae 42 years

LOT #156 -- 1 Stone - 2 Footstones

  1. Capt. Thomas Gross Atkins 1819-1854
     Rachel C. Brown his wife 1823-1900

  2. Footstone - Mother

  3. Footstone - Father

LOT #157 -- 5 Stones

  1. Father - Capt. Lemuel Cook born Sept. 21, 1804 died May 7, 1869

  2. Mother - Belinda Cook died May 31, 1889 age 83 yrs. 2 mos. 29 dys.

  3. Aphia L. dtr. of Lemuel & Belinda Cook died June 21, 1833 ae 1 yr. 4 mos.

  4. Lemuel son of Lemuel & Belinda Cook died Jan. 22, 1836 ae 1 yr. 10 months. Also Lemuel F. died Aug. 22, 1830 ae 18 days

  5. Eliza A. Cook March 9, 1839 - Oct. 23, 1927

CEMETERY NUMBER TWO - OLD SECTION

LOT #158 -- 4 Stones - 7 Footstones

    1. Reuben Dyer was lost at sea Nov. 7, 1831 aged 31 years
       Milly T. wife of Reuben Dyer died Nov. 20, 1857
          aged 52 years
       Reuben died Sept. 24, 1828 aged 1 year 21 days
       Reuben died July 7, 1831 aged 1 year 6 months 5 days
       Children of Reuben and Milly T. Dyer

    2. Elisha M. Dyer Sept. 6, 1825 - Jan. 2, 1885
       his wife Rebecca A. July 7, 1832 - Nov. 18, 1895

    3. Front: Joshua Dyer June 13, 1818 - March 10, 1900
              his wife Laura A. Sept. 24, 1822 - Sept. 25, 1843
              his wife Elizabeth D. May 18, 1829 - Dec. 12, 1915

       Rear: Children of Joshua and Laura A. Dyer
               Joshua Thomas 1843-1843

               (Children of) Joshua and Elizabeth D. Dyer
               Joshua Walter 1851-1855
               Millie Frances 1863-1931
               Laura Elizabeth 1858-1939
               Mary Hersey 1865-1939

    4. Joshua son of Joshua and Laura A. Dyer died
       Aug. 2, 1843 ae 4 months 16 days

    5. Footstone - Walter "He is not lost, but gone before"

    6. Footstone - J. D.

    7. Footstone - L. A. D.

    8. Footstone - E. D. D.

    9. Footstone - L. E. D.

    10. Footstone - M. H. D.

    11. Footstone - N. Y. (This footstone probably belongs on
        LOT #366)

LOT #159 -- 3 Stones

    1. Silas C. Mott Jan. 28, 1839 - May 2. 1919
       Jane B. Mott June 24, 1844 - Sept. 9, 1917

    2. (Buried stone) Edward P. Mott May 11, 1872 - March 15, 1901

    3. Wallace C. son of Silas C. and Jane B. Mott died
       April 10, 1873 ae 9 months 20 days

LOT #160 -- 1 Buried Stone

    1. Reuben A. Adams died Sept. 11, 1879
       ae 52 years 5 mos. 15 days

LOT #161 -- 5 Stones

    1. Mr. Elijah Dyer died May 25, 1848
       ae 58 years 6 months 12 days

CEMETERY NUMBER TWO - OLD SECTION

LOT #161 (continued)

2. Mrs. Rebeckah wife of Elijah Dyer died Oct. 26, 1846 ae 51 years 27 days

3. Sibyl H. wife of Phineas Freeman died May 11, 1884 ae 57 years 3 months 2 days

4. Elijah son of Phineas and Sybill (sic) Freeman died July 15, 1849 ae 1 year 8 months 17 days

5. Aphia daughter of Phineas and Sybil (sic) H. Freeman died July 17, 1858 ae 10 months 9 days

LOT #162 -- 5 Stones - All buried

1. P. Tillinghast son of Pardon T. and Bridget D. Kenney died Sept. 27, 1850 ae 16 months 22 days

2. Sophia Clark infant daughter of Rev. E. and S. Blake (no date)

3. Wm. McKendree son of Rev. J. M. and Nancy Bidwell died July 25, 1837 ae 3 years 9 months 21 days

4. Newton Church son of Rev. J. M. and Nancy Bidwell died March 10, 1838 aged 2 months 17 days

5. Flora F. daughter of Rev. R. K. and Candace Bosworth died July 5, 1857 ae 7 months

LOT #163 -- 1 Stone

1. Front: Willis Higgins 1844-1930
   Icena A. Higgins 1844-1881
   Zetta F. Higgins 1850-1932

   Right: Willis 1881 (VR: died Sept. 9, 1881 ae 2 mos. 2 dys)

LOT #164 -- 7 Stones

1. Father - Joshua Cook died Jan. 25, 1881 ae 86 years 11 months

2. Our Mother - Rebecca wife of Joshua Cook died April 29, 1861 aged 63 years 7 months

3. Mercy P. wife of Joshua Cook born in Eastham March 18, 1814 died in Provincetown Oct. 6, 1891

4. Capt. Moses Young 2nd born Oct. 27, 1821 died Feb. 15, 1872

5. Hannah daughter of Moses and Marilla N. Young died Oct. 31, 1849 ae 3 years 10 months 13 days

6. Melvina F. daughter of Francis and Melvina Nickerson died August 27, 1849 ae 9 years 11 months 15 days

7. Nellie Sears wife of George B. Young 1859-1914

CEMETERY NUMBER TWO - OLD SECTION

LOT #165 -- 1 Monument - 2 Stones - 4 Footstones

   1. Monument Front: J. Young (no record)

      Monument Right: Hannah daughter of Reuben and Priscilla P. Young died July 9, 1842 ae 5 months 6 days
                    Mary Young died Nov. 1, 1888 ae 68 years

      Monument Rear: Reuben Young died Sept. 28, 1883 aged 70 years
                    Priscilla P. wife of Reuben Young died Oct. 15, 1863 ae 45 years 4 months

   2. Footstone - Mother

   3. Footstone - Hannah

   4. Footstone - Priscilla

   5. Footstone - Reuben

   6. H. B. Nickerson, Ensign USN Feb. 7, 1831 - May 25, 1897
      Martha M. his wife Sept. 21, 1834 - March 28, 1910

   7. George H. Nickerson, Lieut. 43rd MVM 1837-1890
      Mary G. his wife 1843-1908

LOT #166 -- 1 Monument - 2 Stones - 4 Footstones

   1. Monument Front: Hon. Stephen Hilliard died August 2, 1852 ae 44 years

      Monument Right: Sarah G. Hilliard died Dec. 16, 1864 aged 26 years

      Monument Rear: Mrs. Stephen Hilliard died Oct. 11, 1892 age 80 years (VR: Sarah)

      Monument Left: Stephen A. Hilliard died May 20, 1869 age 33 years

   2. Footstone - Mother

   3. Footstone - Father

   4. Footstone - Sarah

   5. Footstone - Stephen

   6. Edward Cook son of Stephen and Sally Hillyard died Aug. 7, 1834 age 9 mos.

   7. Cordelia Holmes dtr. of Stephen and Sally Hillyard died Aug. 31, 1832 age 8 mos.

LOT #167 -- 1 Monument - 1 Stone - 5 Footstones - 1 Base with no stone

   1. Monument Front: Nathan Freeman died Jan. 29, 1876 age 78 yrs. 4 months 16 days
                     Mary wife of Nathan Freeman died Jan. 23, 1854 age 50 yrs. 5 months

CEMETERY NUMBER TWO - OLD SECTION

LOT #167 (continued)

    Monument Right: Benjamin F. Freeman died Cienfuegos, Cuba Aug. 3, 1858 age 41 yrs. 2 days
    Louise Russell wife of Benj. F. Freeman died Jan. 12, 1859 age 27 years 5 months 3 days
    Louise Russell dtr. of Benj. F. and Louise R. Freeman died Feb. 24, 1859 age 6 months

    Monument Rear: Helen died June 11, 1830 aged 11 months
    Sylvester died May 23, 1837 age 10 months

    Monument Left: Nathan D. Freeman died at Boston Sept. 12, 1888 age 57 yrs. 4 mo. 3 days
    Aphia C. wife of N. D. Freeman died July 20, 1884 age 48 yrs. 6 mo. 27 days
    Mary H. died Aug. 13, 1859 aged 2 yrs. 23 days
    Mary H. died Aug. 29, 1864 age 3 yrs. 1 mo. 11 days
    Children of Nathan D. and Aphia C. Freeman

2. Footstone - Nathan
3. Footstone - Aphia
4. Footstone - Little Mamy
5. Footstone - Benjamin
6. Footstone - Louise
7. Base to footstone
8. Sarah B. Freeman 1855-1905

LOT #168 -- 7 Stones - 1 Marker

1. Capt. Gideon Bowly died July 3, 1843 in the 57 year of his age
2. Mrs. Mary Y. wife of Gideon Bowly died Sept. 7, 1842 in 58th year
3. Eliza wife of the late Warren Howard dtr. of Capt. Gideon and Mary Bowly died Sept. 11, 1840 at 31 years
   Warren Howard died at Turk's Island Jan. 22, 1840 at 35 years
4. Mary Ann dtr. of Capt. Gideon and Mary Bowly died April 6, 1839 at 15
5. Gideon Bowly Aug. 25, 1816 - July 20, 1893
6. Mary W. wife of Gideon Bowly died Oct. 1, 1856 age 36 yrs. 8 mos.
7. Gideon Bowly 1849-1922
   Mary W. his wife 1852-1900

CEMETERY NUMBER TWO - OLD SECTION

LOT #168 (continued)
    8. Edith M. Conwell 1874-1936

LOT #169 -- 9 Stones
1. Capt. Joshua Paine died Feb. 19, 1850 aged 62 years 7 months
2. Nancy wife of Joshua Paine died Aug. 29, 1871 aged 78 years 2 months 26 days
3. Solomon Dyer Paine son of Joshua and Nancy Paine died Jan. 14, 1836 aged 18 years 5 months
4. Joshua Paine born Sept. 1, 1819 died July 20, 1891
5. Mrs. Nancy W. wife of Joshua Paine Jr. died June 3, 1849 aged 27 years 26 days
6. Martha F. Paine wife of Joshua Paine Oct. 16, 1830 - Jan. 11, 1913
7. Francis A. Paine 1829-1910
8. Ann S. Paine 1832-1896
9. Addie A. daughter of Francis A. and Ann S. S. Paine died April 30, 1857 ae 3 years 9 months 10 days

LOT #170 -- 1 Stone
1. Front: Joseph P. Johnson 1813-1891
        Polly Cook 1815-1842
        Susan Fitch 1821-1846
        Mary Whorf 1813-1869

   Right: Jerusha Parker (Johnson) aged 8 months
        (VR: died 1847)
        Joseph Hall (Johnson) aged 6 weeks (VR: died 1849)
        Arthur Clarence (Johnson) aged 20 months
        (VR: died 1861)

   Rear: Josephine P. Johnson 1850-1932

   Left: Timothy Parker (Johnson) aged 4 days (VR: died 1836)
        Isaac Thomas (Johnson) aged 1 month (VR: died 1837)
        Lemuel Cook (Johnson) aged 13 months (VR: died 1841)
        Polly Cook (Johnson) aged 11 weeks (VR: died 1843)

LOT #171 -- 5 Stones
1. Capt. John R. Lavender died June 9, 1878 aged 55 years buried at Miragoane, W.I. (West Indies)
Sally Mayo Lavender died April 28, 1915 aged 89 years
John Adams Lavender 1854-1922

2. Joseph Henry son of John and Sarah N. Lavender died March 9, 1851 ae 1 year 1 month 22 days

3. Simeon L. Lavender born Jan. 31, 1808 died Aug. 25, 1854

CEMETERY NUMBER TWO - OLD SECTION

LOT #171 (continued)

    4. Mr. Robert Lavender Jr. died April 8, 1849 ae 31 years 4 months
Susan E. daughter of Robert and Mary Ann Lavender died Dec. 3, 1846 ae 5 months 14 days

    5. William R. Lavender born 1806 died 1880
Mary Lavender born 1806 died 1896

LOT #172 -- 11 Stones

    1. Robert Knowles died April 25, 1880 aged 75 years 11 months 3 days

    2. Mary J. wife of Robert Knowles died Feb. 26, 1861 ae 49 years 1 month 26 days

    3. Willard Knowles (no date) (VR: born Jan. 25, 1854)

    4. Elizabeth D. Knowles 1818-1892

    5. Harbeck son of Robert and Mary Jane Knowles died April 20, 1851 ae 2 months 5 days

    6. Mary William daughter of Robert and Mary Jane Knowles died Sept. 6, 1844 ae 1 year 3 months

    7. Mercy Ann daughter of Robert and Mary Jane Knowles died Feb. 29, 1844 ae 3 years 5 months

    8. Mr. Robert Lavender died Oct. 6, 1848 ae 67 years

    9. Mrs. Ann B. widow of Robert Lavender died Dec. 23, 1850 ae 68 years

    10. Lewis C. son of Robert and Ann Lavender died Oct. 4, 1838 ae 9 years 6 months

    11. Mrs. Jane widow of Lewis Alline died April 2, 1847 ae 84 years 4 months

LOT #173 -- 2 Stones

    1. Father - Caleb Cook Oct. 20, 1808 - Nov. 10, 1894
Mother - Eliza G. Cook Dec. 16, 1818 - Feb. 16, 1889

    2. Daughter and son of Caleb and Eliza G. Cook (no names - no dates) (VR: infant female died Dec. 24, 1850 ae 17 days and infant male died in 1841)

LOT #174 -- 2 Stones

    1. Mr. Reuben Ryder died June 10, 1855 ae 75 years
Reuben Ryder Jr. drowned off Long Point April 17, 1839 ae 33 years

    2. Susannah Swift wife of Reuben Ryder born Nov. 16, 1785 died Feb. 20, 1860 aged 74 years 3 mos. 4 days

CEMETERY NUMBER TWO - OLD SECTION

LOT #175 -- 2 Stones

    1. Husband - Father - Benjamin Allstrum died July 9, 1871 ae 49

    2. Charles an infant died Sept. 30, 1846
       Tamsin died Sept. 8, 1849 aged 22 months
       Lizzie B. died March 29, 1851 ae 7 months
       Children of Benjamin and Susan S. Allstrum

LOT #176 -- 1 Stone

    1. Mrs. Jane S. wife of Charles S. Belcher died Feb. 13, 1850 ae 27 years 8 months

LOT #177 -- 7 Stones

    1. Israel Russell died April 15, 1850 age 52 years
       Elizabeth his widow died Oct. 14, 1851 age 56 years 5 mos.

    2. Capt. Edward G. Burt Nov. 2, 1822 - June 27, 1905
       Ruth L. Burt May 25, 1823 - April 17, 1875

    3. Our Babe (VR: Edward C. Burt died Oct. 10, 1847 ae 1 mo. 26 ds.)

    4. Sarah L. Burt Sept. 4, 1850 to June 27, 1902

    5. George W. White died June 17, 1887 at 22 years 11 mos. 24 days
       Capt. Richard S. White lost at sea 1867 ae 36 years

    6. Babes: Lizzie S. died Aug. 7, 1863 at 1 month 27 days
            Lizzie S. died Aug. 24, 1867 at 10 months 24 days
            Children of Capt. Richard S. and Rosetta White

    7. Alexander G. Small 1833-1906
       Rosetta S. Small 1841-1917

LOT #178 -- 1 Monument - 3 Stones - 3 Footstones

    1. Monument Front: J. Snow (date monument erected) 1859

       Monument Right: Josiah Snow died September 8, 1896
                    ae 69 years 11 days
                    Elizabeth wife of Josiah Snow died
                      June 22, 1858 ae 29 years 7 months 19 days

       Monument Left: Sarah E. wife of Josiah Snow died
                    July 21, 1885 ae 56 years 19 days

    2. Capt. Josiah Snow born March 21, 1791 died April 21, 1852

    3. Ruth widow of Josiah Snow died Jan. 14, 1868 aged 68 years 4 months 9 days

    4. Joseph Willis son of Josiah and Ruth Snow died Jan. 15, 1830 ae 7 months 17 days

    5. Footstone - Josiah

CEMETERY NUMBER TWO - OLD SECTION

LOT #178 (continued)

    6. Footstone - Sarah

    7. Footstone - Lizzie

LOT #179 -- 1 Stone

    1. Front: Dr. Isaiah Whitney Jan. 25, 1799 - Dec. 10, 1866
           Henrietta A. June 21, 1815 - Aug. 21, 1848
           Sarah P. Nov. 3, 1827 - Feb. 10, 1851
           Hannah E. May 15, 1816 - Nov. 5, 1904

       Left: Lauretta 1835-1836
            Felicia 1841-1842

       Rear: Electa July 12, 1833 - Aug. 1, 1861
            Charles H. December 11, 1854 - March 24, 1905
            Isaiah Whitney Aug. 30, 1843 - Aug. 31, 1917
            Henrietta Whitney Oct. 3, 1838 - Aug. 18, 1921

LOT #180 -- 1 Stone

    1. Front: Lemuel Cook Nov. 21, 1811 - Jan. 15, 1888
           Mary J. Cook August 29, 1821 - Aug. 20, 1859

       Right: Martha S. 1846-1848
            Albert M. 1852-1853
            Infant 1856 (VR: died 1856)

       Rear: Capt. Emerson D. Cook 1850-1904
            Kathleen O. Cook 1857-1909
            B. Lombard Cook 1888-1905

       Left: Lemuel 1878- (VR: died 1878 ae 4 months)

LOT #181 -- 3 Stones

    1. Clara J. daughter of Nathan and Clarinda B. Adams died Aug. 27, 1848 ae 2 years 16 days

    2. Clara J. daughter of Nathan and Clarinda B. Adams died June 17, 1850 ae 1 year 6 months

    3. Nathan son of Nathan and Clarinda B. Adams died August 7, 1853 ae 2 years 9 months

LOT #182 -- No Stone

LOT #183 -- 1 Monument - 5 Stones - 1 Marker - 2 Footstones

    1. Monument Front: David Conwell 1818-1898
                     Almira Taylor wife of David Conwell died Aug. 29, 1881 ae 60 years 8 months 19 days

       Monument Left: Capt. George Stull Jr. lost at sea on passage from Boston to St. Thomas, W.I., Dec. 1851 ae 42 years (also see LOT #212 for Capt. George Stull Jr.)

CEMETERY NUMBER TWO - OLD SECTION

LOT #183 (continued)

    2. Footstone - Mother

    3. Footstone - Father

    4. Eliza P. wife of George Stull Jr. born Sept. 17, 1816 died Feb. 21, 1851

    5. Three children of George Jr. and Eliza P. Stull (no dates)

    6. A. Frank Conwell Dec. 12, 1856 - July 6, 1895

    7. Hattie B. wife of A. Frank Conwell died July 26, 1880 aged 23 years 6 months 18 days daughter of Charles Rice

    8. Mrs. Eleanor widow of David S. Conwell died Oct. 10, 1846 ae 51 years 9 mos.

    9. Mr. David S. Conwell was lost at sea in the year 1818 ae 25 years
       "Here in the ray of morn and eve
       Gleams the white stone that bears his name
       While far away beneath the sea
       Is sepulchred (sic) his frame"

LOT #184 -- 3 Stones

    1. Mother - Nancy L. Small died June 3, 1874 aged 63 years
       Father - Samuel Small died Jan. 27, 1854 aged 45 years

    2. Charles Edwin son of Samuel and Nancy Small died Jan. 15, 1853 ae 6 months

    3. Samuel D. son of Samuel and Nancy Small died July 10, 1850 ae 8 years 11 months

LOT #185 -- 1 Stone - 6 Footstones

    1. Capt. John Burt 1814-1892
       his wife Rosetta Small 1817-1892
       Capt. John S. Burt lost at sea 1844-1867
       Capt. Mathias W. Burt 1851-1926
       his wife Alma P. Nickerson 1857-1938
       John S. Burt 1877-1955
       his wife Esther A. Hull 1878-1960

    2. Footstone - J. B.

    3. Footstone - R. S.

    4. Footstone - J. S. B.

    5. Footstone - M. W. B.

    6. Footstone - A. P. N.

    7. Footstone - E. A. H.

LOT #186 -- 3 Stones

    1. Josiah Cutter died Feb. 2, 1871 aged 67 years

CEMETERY NUMBER TWO - OLD SECTION

LOT #186 (continued)

    2. Rebecca G. Cutter 1815-1906

    3. Ardelle J. daughter of Josiah and Rebecca G. Cutter died July 1, 1873 ae 22 years 5 months

LOT #187 -- 2 Stones

    1. Freeman Atkins born Oct. 8, 1790 died Aug. 15, 1854

    2. Miriam wife of Freeman Atkins and daughter of Deacon Thomas Gross (stone broken here) born August 27, 1794 died March 28, 1877

LOT #188 -- 5 Stones

    1. Father - Joshua Nickerson April 20, 1802 - Dec. 31, 1892
       Mother - Amanda Nickerson March 29, 1808 - July 1, 1892

    2. Albert H. son of Joshua and Amanda H. Nickerson born Nov. 3, 1839 died April 11, 1852

    3. Capt. Joshua S. Nickerson 1842-1927
       Angelia B. his wife 1853-1942
       Albert S. 1879-1975
       Byron H. 1881-1883
       Blanche L. 1888-1892
       Helen Page 1887-(not cut)

    4. Byron son of Joshua S. and Angelia Nickerson died Aug. 4, 1883 ae 1 year 11 months 24 days

    5. Blanche L. daughter of Joshua S. and Angelia B. Nickerson 1888-1892

LOT #189 -- 5 Stones

    1. Capt. John M. Smith died on the Spanish Main May 3, 1840 ae 32
       Mary O. daughter of John M. and Rebecca G. Smith died Feb. 12, 1837 ae 2 years 3 months

    2. Mary J. daughter of John M. and Rebecca G. Smith born Sept. 24, 1836 died June 29, 1851

    3. George O. Smith 1838-1914

    4. Freeman A. Smith - Co. H 56th Mass. Vol. INFT. Oct. 20, 1832 - Nov. 24, 1910
       Maria L. Smith Jan. 11, 1834 - April 17, 1905

    5. Mary Osborne daughter of Freeman A. and Maria L. Smith died Sept. 8, 1863 ae 8 year 8 months 8 days

LOT #190 -- 5 Stones

    1. George DeWolf died Feb. 9, 1869 ae 52 years

    2. Abby L. DeWolf died March 12, 1890 ae 72 years 1 month 3 days

CEMETERY NUMBER TWO - OLD SECTION

LOT #190 (continued)

    3. Mary L. DeWolf died Sept. 4, 1914 ae 60 years 5 months 18 days

    4. George son of George and Abby L. DeWolf died Sept. 20, 1849 ae 3 years 1 month

    5. Wm. Sanborn son of George and Abby L. DeWolf died July 19, 1851 ae 2 years 4½ months

LOT #191 -- 1 Stone - 1 Base with no stone

    1. Herman A. Jennings 1833-1897
       Hannah M. 1843-1895
       Charles A. 1863-1889
       Nathaniel (twin) 1865-1865
       Heman (twin) 1865-1865
         "FINIS"

    2. Base with no stone (unknown)

LOT #192 -- No Stone

LOT #193 -- 3 Stones - 1 Marker

    1. George B. Bennett - U. S. Navy (no date)

    2. Eliza A. Bennett 1848-1934

    3. Marker - Little Lonnie (no date)

    4. Walter Russell son of George and Eliza A. Bennett died Jan. 12, 1874 ae 3 years 4 months 7 days

LOT #194 -- 1 Stone

    1. Eugene Burden 1860-1902
       Christie A. 1860-1892
       Nellie M. 1884-1891
       Mary L. 1886-1891

LOT #195 -- 2 Stones

    1. Abbott L. Cobb 1854-1927
       Etta S. 1860-1948

    2. Harold W. son of Abbott L. and Etta S. Cobb died March 22, 1892 ae 4 years 3 months
       Lawrence W. son of Abbott L. and Etta S. Cobb died July 9, 1891 ae 2 months 13 days

LOT #196 -- 1 Stone

    1. Samuel Atwood died Sept. 24, 1866 age 90 years 3 months 13 days
       Anna wife of Samuel Atwood died March 22, 1868 age 89 years 8 months 20 days

CEMETERY NUMBER TWO - OLD SECTION

LOT #197 -- 2 Stones

    1. Rufus H. Hopkins 1841-1920
       Ruth L. his wife 1843-1915

    2. Vashti L. wife of William Quinn died June 26, 1864
       ae 39 years 7 months 10 days

LOT #198 -- 9 Stones - 2 Footstones

    1. Joseph B. Dyer 1832-1910
       Mary A. Dyer 1835-1914

    2. Jottie L. son of Joseph B. and Mary A. Dyer died
       June 8, 1867 ae 8 years 3 months

    3. Joseph B. Dyer Jr. 1857-1939
       Ella M. 1859-1909
       Mary A. 1851-1934

    4. Jottie L. son of Joseph B. Jr. and Ella M. Dyer died
       Nov. 4, 1886 ae 2 months 22 days

    5. Vashti wife of Jonathan Dyer died June 7, 1881 ae 85 years
         6 months 18 days
       Jonathan Dyer 1791-1858

    6. Joseph H. Butler 1869-1941

    7. Anna E. Butler 1863-1944

    8. Joseph M. Whitney 1866-1929

    9. Vashti O. Whitney 1865-19(not cut)

    10. Footstone - Mary A.

    11. Footstone - Grandma Smith

LOT #199 -- 3 Stones

    1. Joseph H. Smith 1797-1880
       Lucinda Smith 1806-1888
       John S. Smith 1832-1912
       Cushing H. Emery 1841-1918
       Lurana A. Emery 1842-1923

    2. James T. Kenney March 7, 1827 - Nov. 7, 1855
       Tamzain Kenney May 19, 1827 - Sept. 25, 1891

    3. Eliza C. wife of James N. Hopkins died Oct. 12, 1869
       ae 40 years 2 months

LOT #200 -- 1 Stone

    1. Capt. John McLeod 1850-1895
       his wife Mary A. 1853-1918
       Wallace E. 1875-1897

LOT #201 -- 4 Stones

    1. Nathaniel W. Ayers 1827-1907

CEMETERY NUMBER TWO - OLD SECTION

LOT #201 (continued)

    Clara P. Ayers 1827-1914

  2. Willie - William H. Ayers Oct. 12, 1857 - Aug. 22, 1891

  3. N. W. (Nathaniel W.) Ayers 1862-1948

  4. Benj. B. Ayers 1864-1930

LOT #202 -- 12 Stones

  1. Francis Abbot died Dec. 6, 1879 aged 70 years 3 days

  2. Mother - Melinda Abbot died Oct. 7, 1894 aged 79 years 5 months 10 days

  3. Melinda daughter of Francis and Melinda Abbot born March 1, 1841 died Oct. 6, 1858
    Capt. Walter R. lost at sea Sept. 1867 aged 29 years 6 mos.
    George R. lost at sea Sept. 1867 ae 20 years 7 months

  4. George R. son of Francis and Melinda Abbott born Feb. 28, 1845 died Oct. 13, 1847

  5. Lawrence E. eldest son of Francis O. and Clara Abbot died May 17, 1868 aged 3 years

  6. Francis O. Abbot died April 2, 1873 aged 36 years 5 months

  7. Frances M. R. Abbot, "Fannie", died May 3, 1880 aged 30 years 16 days

  8. Mother - Achsah S. Abbot Sept. 14, 1836 - Feb. 7, 1898

  9. John W. Abbott 1852-1936

  10. Etta R. Abbott 1863-1951

  11. Mrs. Rosetta wife of Andrew Davis born Oct. 4, 1833 died Jan. 19, 1852

  12. Mrs. Martha W. widow of Walter Russell died Oct. 17, 1855 ae 52 years

LOT #203 -- 6 Stones

  1. Caleb Fisher died Spet. 11, 1857 ae 66 years
    Mary K. his widow died Feb. 8, 1866 ae 70 years 1 month

  2. Rufus Hopkins died August 16, 1881 ae 66 years 9 mos. 22 days
    Julia A. Hopkins died July 5, 1879 ae 59 yrs. 8 mos. 12 dys.

  3. Julia A. C. daughter of Rufus and Julia A. Hopkins died June 19, 1849 ae 8 months 6 days

  4. John W. Young Jan. 20, 1836 - Aug. 2, 1894

  5. Mary F. Young Oct. 1, 1838 - January 22, 1912

  6. Frank J. Anthony died Oct. 6, 1870 ae 25 years 8 mos.

CEMETERY NUMBER TWO - OLD SECTION

LOT #204 -- 5 Stones - 1 Marker

1. Abram Pierce died June 4, 1877 ae 61 years 3 months

2. Elizabeth wife of Abram Pierce died Dec. 12, 1843
    ae 24 years 17 days
   John W. White died in Old Canso (Nova Scotia) Aug. 3, 1837
    aged 14 years 6 months

3. Mother - Betsey N. wife of Abram Pierce died Nov. 10, 1884
   ae 58 years 11 months 2 days

4. George Warren son of Abram and Betsey Pierce died
    March 29, 1863 ae 6 years 7 months 4 days
   Ira H. Pierce died June 29, 1868 ae 7 years 10 months
    20 days

5. Grandmother - Hephzibah White Oct. 9, 1799 - Nov. 17, 1873
   Grandfather - Nicholas White July 7, 1799 - May 15, 1867

6. Large granite marker - PIERCE-WHITE

LOT #205 -- 1 Stone

1. Mary Elsa daughter of Christopher and Mary Edwards died
   Aug. 26, 1849 ae 19½ months

LOT #206 -- 1 Stone

1. Reuben Pierce - U. S. Navy (VR: died April 27, 1868
   ae 33 years 3 months 8 days

LOT #207 -- 1 Stone

1. Clarissa died Jan. 10, 1841 ae 3 months 3 days
   John B. Dods died March 23, 1842 ae 2 ys. 9 ms.
   Children of Benjamin F. and Abigail Johnson

LOT #208 -- No Stone

Cemetery records indicate this lot in the name of Ansel Crowell (VR: Ansel H. Crowell died March 28, 1855 ae 1 year 1 month 15 days son of Ansel and Rebecca Crowell. Also, infant male died Sept. 29, 1850 ae 21 days son of Ansel and Rebecca Crowell. Also, Lewis H. died Aug. 6, 1850 ae 1 year 5 mos. 3 days son of Ansel and Rebecca Crowell)

LOT #209 -- 1 Stone

1. Elkanah Paine died May 7, 1875 aged 67 years 2 months

LOT #210 -- 1 Stone

1. Jabez W. Atwood died June 18, 1890 aged 81 years 7 months
    6 days
   Eleanor D. Atwood died Jan. 14, 1892 aged 71 years 9 months

CEMETERY NUMBER TWO - OLD SECTION

LOT #211 -- 7 Stones - 3 Footstones

1. Nancy P. wife of Alonzo Smith died in Cohasset July 19, 1872 ae 35 years 4 months 12 days

2. Alonzo Jr. died Oct. 6, 1861 ae 13 days
   George W. died Oct. 11, 1861 ae 1 year 9 months 21 days
   Children of Alonzo and Nancy P. Smith

3. Joshua son of Joshua and Lydia Smith died April 29, 1845 ae 2 years 4 months 18 days

4. Clara Smith 1855-1874

5. George H. Miller 1834-1909
   Eliza Y. Miller 1840-1903

6. Avis M. wife of Alex. Joseph 1885-1911
   Alex. Joseph 1878-1938

7. Footstone - Joe.

8. Footstone - C. A. J. and J. B. D. J.

9. Footstone - Aunt and Uncle

10. Bessie M. daughter of John P. and Eva L. Silva died Feb. 8, 1895 ae 5 months 26 days

LOT #212 -- 2 Stones

1. Mr. George Stull died Nov. 20, 1854 ae 76 years

2. Mrs. Lydia wife of George Stull died April 20, 1850 ae 72 years
   Capt. George Stull Jr. lost at sea Dec. 1852 ae 42 years
   (see LOT #183 also for Capt. George Stull Jr.)

LOT #213 -- 2 Stones - 2 Markers

1. Mrs. Sabra Sawtele died May 12, 1839 ae 55 yrs.
   Capt. Joseph Sawtele lost at sea Oct. 17, 1832 ae 55 yrs.
   Joseph Sawtele Jr. lost at sea 1831 age 27 years

2. Herbert F. Mayo 1907-1966
   Margaret A. 1908-(living 1979)

3. David Atkins Mayo (died) 1934

4. Herbert F. Mayo 1932-1934

LOT #214 -- 2 Stones

1. In memory of Capt. Daniel Small who died March 31, 1828 at 60

2. To the memory of Mrs. Joanna widow of Capt. Daniel Small died Oct. 5, 1849 aged 75 years

LOT #215 -- 3 Stones

1. Edward T. Starr Aug. 1, 1827 - July 1, 1893

CEMETERY NUMBER TWO - OLD SECTION

LOT #215 (continued)

    2. Mother - Sarah H. wife of Edward T. Starr died June 26, 1874 ae 41 years 10 months 13 days

    3. Sarah Lizzie daughter of Edward T. and Sarah H. Starr died Oct. 12, 1880 ae 23 years 10 months 23 days

LOT #216 -- 2 Stones

    1. To the memory of Asa S. Bowly who died Nov. 20, 1865 ae 72 years 2 days

    2. Mrs. Cynthia consort of Mr. Asa S. Bowly died Dec. 21, 1826 ae 28 years 8 months 15 days

LOT #217 -- No Stone

LOT #218 - 3 Stones

    1. Capt. Phillip Cook born Oct. 15, 1781 died April 9, 1849

    2. Anna H. widow of Capt. Phillip Cook died Feb. 2, 1869 aged 89 years 4 months 15 days

    3. Capt. Anthony Brown sailed from Boston for Port au Prince on the 24th of January 1839 and was never after heard of. He was born April 14, 1805
    Almira his widow born Dec. 10, 1808 died March 24, 1851

LOT #219 -- 3 Stones

    1. Sacred to the memory of Mrs. Mary widow of Capt. Jonathan Cook who died Dec. 6, 1835 age 66

    2. Elizabeth P. wife of Charles Derby died June 1, 1863 ae 63 yrs. 11 mos. 16 days

    3. Henry Willard son of Mr. Charles and Mrs. Elizabeth Derby died May 8, 1832 ae 6 years 4 months 14 days

LOT #220 -- 4 Stones

    1. Deacon John Dyer died May 15, 1885 ae 82 years 6 months 2 days

    2. Mrs. Clarissa wife of Mr. John Dyer, formerly wife of Mr. Jesse Kendall died May 31, 1833 ae 30 years 1 month 13 days

    3. Hannah B. wife of Deacon John Dyer died April 4, 1883 ae 73 years 9 months 10 days

    4. Mr. Jesse Kendall died March 20, 1826 aged 30 years 11 mos. 6 days

LOT #221 -- 4 Stones

    1. Capt. Thomas Smalley died June 17, 1831 ae 70

    2. Hannah widow of Thomas Smalley died Jan. 4, 1861 ae 85 yrs.

CEMETERY NUMBER TWO - OLD SECTION

LOT #221 (continued)

    3. Thomas son of Thomas and Hannah Smalley died Dec. 18, 1838 aged 34 years on his passage from Auxcayes to Boston
Isaac Smalley died in Port au Prince Nov. 20, 1843 aged 27 years

    4. Sally Smalley died Aug. 12, 1872 ae 70 years 1 month

LOT #222 -- No Stone

LOT #223 -- 1 Stone

    1. Mrs. Judith E. wife of Edward Q. Weeks born July 4, 1789 died Sept. 3, 1863
Edward son of Edward Q. and Judith E. Weeks born Oct. 1, 1825 lost at sea from Brig Rienza Sept. 16, 1846

    (Ed. Note: Brig Rienza wrecked Sept. 16, 1846, of twenty-one men, only five survived)

LOT #224 -- 2 Stones - 1 Marker - 1 Footstone

    1. Mr. Andrew N. Williams died Oct. 9, 1831 ae 60
Mrs. Anna his widow died Dec. 27, 1858 ae 86 years

    2. Footstone - Baby (no date)

    3. Capt. William Williams died June 4, 1846 ae 37 yrs. 6 mos.

    4. Baby Hunt died Aug. 5, 1881 (VR: son of George W. and Sarah S. Hunt)

LOT #225 -- 5 Stones

    1. In memory of Capt. Jesse N. Williams lost at sea on board Schooner James Porter on his passage home from the Grand Banks in October 1858 ae 56 years

    2. Mrs. Augusta wife of Jesse N. Williams died Dec. 10, 1845 ae 47 years 10 months 19 days

    3. Lucinda wife of Capt. Jesse N. Williams died April 18, 1886 ae 79 years 9 months 18 days

    4. Hervey Chester son of Jesse N. and Augusta Williams died August 22, 1835 ae 1 year 8 months 24 days

    5. Chylena H. daughter of Jesse and Augusta Williams born July 18, 1838 died Feb. 14, 1853

LOT #226 -- Tomb

    1. Jonathan Cook and Jonathan Cook Jr's Tomb
(VR: Jonathan Cook born 1753 died 1835. Mercy, his wife born 1750 died about 1831. Jonathan Cook Jr. 1780-1862 is buried in Hamilton Cemetery. There are two persons buried in this tomb. See LOT #219 for possible second wife of Jonathan Cook)

CEMETERY NUMBER TWO - OLD SECTION

LOT #227 -- No Stone

LOT #228 -- 4 Stones

1. Mr. Joshua F. Grozer died April 29, 1829 ae 60
   Joshua Grozer son of Mr. J. F. and Martha Grozer was drowned between Boston and Provincetown Dec. 25, 1824 ae 27

2. Mrs. Martha consort of Mr. Joshua F. Grozer died Sept. 26, 1826 ae 52

3. Rebecca Grozier born July 18, 1799 died Nov. 11, 1845

4. Richard Watkins died Aug. 5, 1825 ae 32

LOT #229 -- 1 Monument

1. Helena P. Howes born May 8, 1835 died Jan. 24, 1838

LOT #230 -- 3 Stones - 2 Markers

1. Joshua Nickerson died Nov. 20, 1885 aged 68 years 11 months 14 days

2. Almira wife of Joshua Nickerson died Oct. 21, 1898 aged 77 years 1 month 3 days

3. Eddie P. son of Joshua and Almira Nickerson born Sept. 29, 1854 died July 23, 1866

4. Charles P. son of J. & A. Nickerson died Jan. 25, 1855 ae 2 years 4 months

5. Elmer C. Young 1861-1916
   his wife Effie L. Nickerson 1849-1940

LOT #231 -- 7 Stones

1. Eliza Emerson daughter of Enoch and Rosetta Hall died March 23, 1843 ae 16 months
   Also, Capt. Enoch Hall died at sea Oct. 23, 1843

2. Mrs. Rosetta widow of Capt. Enoch Hall died March 29, 1849 ae 34 years 10 months

3. Mr. David N. (Cook) died May 18, 1856 ae 79 years 8 months

4. Mrs. Salome wife of David N. Cook died March 20, 1845 ae 63

5. Thomas D. son of David N. and Salome Cook died Sept. 6, 1823 ae 6 years 8 months

6. Salome daughter of David N. and Salome Cook died Oct. 2, 1823 ae 14 years 10 months

7. Martha widow of James Stanford died May 12, 1857 ae 53 years 4 months
   James Stanford died at Boston Harbor ae 25 (Died circa 1818 - Stone nearly disintegrated)

CEMETERY NUMBER TWO - OLD SECTION

LOT #232 -- No Stone

LOT #233 -- 1 Stone

1. Edward C. son of Capt. Edward and Dorcas Lewis died May 13, 1827 ae 2 years 6 months 13 days

LOT #234 -- No Stone

LOT #235 -- 2 Stones

1. Harvey Cook died May 27, 1872 ae 39 years 7 months

2. Front: Maria wife of Samuel Cook Jr. born April 13, 1812 died Dec. 23, 1888

    Rear: Samuel Cook Jr. born Aug. 21, 1806 lost at sea Feb. 14, 1841

LOT #236 -- 5 Stones

1. Mr. John Snow born Dec. 5, 1796 died Oct. 8, 1849

2. Sally wife of John Snow born Nov. 20, 1804 died Oct. 12, 1886

3. John Snow Jr. son of John and Sally Snow died May 9, 1843 ae 19 years

4. Benjamin H. Snow March 13, 1835 - July 6, 1904

5. Sarah S. wife of James Young died Aug. 16, 1859 ae 44 yrs.

LOT #237 -- 4 Stones

1. Father - Jonathan Sparrow 1822-1905

2. Mother - Mary A. wife of Jonathan Sparrow 1823-1890

3. Maryetta daughter of Jonathan and Mary Ann Sparrow born July 3, 1847 died August 16, 1848

4. Robert Henry Sparrow 1849-1933
   Elizabeth Rand wife 1855-1897
   Alvin Mears son 1875-1906

LOT #238 -- 2 Stones

1. Mr. Stephen Atkins died October 9, 1850 ae 77

2. Rebecca widow of Stephen Atkins died Jan. 17, 1860 ae 79 years 5 months

LOT #239 -- No Stone

LOT #240 -- 13 Stones

1. Paul Dyer born August 18, 1811 died Feb. 21, 1880 ae 68 years 6 months

2. Mrs. Hannah Lewis wife of Paul Dyer died Jan. 1, 1846

CEMETERY NUMBER TWO - OLD SECTION

LOT #240 (continued)

   ae 31 years 8 months

3. Mary E. daughter of Paul and Hannah Dyer died Sept. 16, 1836 aged 10 months

4. Paul A. son of Paul and Hannah L. Dyer died Sept. 22, 1841 ae 4 days

5. James F. died Aug. 13, 1844 ae 6 years 11 months
   Mary E. died Sept. 2, 1844 ae 11 months
   Children of Paul and Hannah L. Dyer

6. Brother - P. Lester Dyer died March 5, 1884 ae 26 years 17 days

7. Joseph R. son of Paul and Susan J. Dyer died May 28, 1853 ae 18 months 20 days

8. Obie K. son of Paul and Susan Dyer died August 31, 1865 aged 3 years 7 months

9. Hattie C. Dyer Sept. 19, 1864 - Nov. 20, 1903

10. Capt. Henry Dyer died Feb. 25, 1828 ae 63

11. Mrs. Betsey Dyer consort of Henry Dyer died March 23, 1817 aged 54 years

12. Apphia C. Dyer daughter of Henry and Betsey Dyer died June 25, 1825 aged 11 years 9 months

13. Benjamin F. son of Charles A. and Betsey Brown died August 7, 1830 aged 21 months

LOT #241 -- 1 Monument - 4 Stones - 8 Footstones

1. Monument Front: Johnson - 1866 (monument erected 1866)
      Timothy P. Johnson died July 15, 1864
         ae 64 years 8 months 17 days
      Betsey Johnson died Jan. 23, 1892
         ae 92 years 11 days

   Monument Right: William Paine son of Nancy W. P. and
         William May Smith Sept. 1, 1889 - March 21, 1919
      Sarah Maria (Johnson) died Jan. 4, 1843
         ae 2 months
      Rebecca Allen (Johnson) died July 26, 1846
         ae 7 years 6 months 9 days

   Monument Rear: Bethia Grozier (Johnson) died Dec. 1, 1905
      ae 64 years 11 months 26 days

   Monument Left: William W. Smith died Jan. 30, 1892
      ae 66 years 2 months 19 days
      "He had a kind and pleasant word for all"

      March C. Smith died March 29, 1908
      ae 79 years 2 mos. 27 days

-46-

CEMETERY NUMBER TWO - OLD SECTION

LOT #241 (continued)

    2. Front: John Moore son of Arthur and Ellen Moore born Liverpool, England Sept. 7, 1829 died in Provincetown December 8, 1856 ae 29 years 3 months

       Rear: Walter T. Smith 1849-1932

    3. In memory of Mr. John W. Johnson who died Jan. 26, 1829 ae 51

    4. William M. Smith 1857-1943
       his wife Rev. Nancy W. Paine Smith 1859-1940

    5. Infant child of Warren and Susan E. Smith
       (VR: died Feb. 8, 1855 ae 1 day)

    6. Footstone - Sarah Mariah daughter of Timothy P. and Betsey Johnson died Jan. 4, 1843 ae 2 months

    7. Footstone - Rebecca Allen daughter of Timothy P. and Betsey Johnson died July 26, 1846 ae 7 years 6 months 9 days

    8. Footstone - Tye

    9. Footstone - Mother

   10. Footstone - Father

   11. Footstone - William Paine Smith

   12. Footstone - Will

   13. Footstone - Mary

LOT #242 -- 1 Stone

    1. Thomas A. Weeks 1837-1911
       Hattie G. Weeks 1843-1901

LOT #243 -- 1 Stone

    1. Sarah R. daughter of William and Peggy Dyer died July 18, 1825 ae 17 years 7 months

LOT #244 -- No Stone

LOT #245 -- 2 Stones

    1. Isaiah Atkins died August 24, 1872 ae 85 years 10 months

    2. Rebecca wife of Isaiah Atkins died July 15, 1863 ae 74 years 10 months

LOT #246 -- 7 Stones

    1. Mr. Charles Parker died March 17, 1838 aged 56 years

    2. Mrs. Salley wife of Charles Parker died July 19, 1827 aged 49

CEMETERY NUMBER TWO - OLD SECTION

LOT #246 (continued)

    3. Charles E. C. Parker son of Charles and Sally Parker died Oct. 23, 1839 aged 19 years

    4. Two sisters dear - daughters of Charles Parker

        Betsey Collins wife of George C. Leach died Jan. 9, 1848 ae 32 years
        Sarah Maria wife of John Allen died June 8, 1845 ae 27 years
        "They loved and were beloved"

    5. Susan E. E. Parker died July 29, 1832 ae 2 years
       Also an infant died May 21 (VR: died May 20, 1832)
       Children of Mr. Charles and Nancy Parker
       "We would have kept you, but your Savior lov'd you more"

    6. Mary M. Parker daughter of Chas. and Nancy Parker died Jan. 9, 1838 aged 8 months

    7. Mr. Hutty Dyer who departed this life Oct. 24, 1826 aged 26 years, also his father, Joshua Dyer who was drowned in Cape Harbour March 21, 1804 ae 29

LOT #247 -- No Stone

LOT #248 -- 7 Stones

    1. Richard A. Cook died June 25, 1862 aged 57 years 11 months 25 days

    2. Martha A. wife of Richard A. Cook died July 16, 1845 aged 39 years 7 months 7 days

    3. Franklin Willis son of Mr. Richard A. and Mrs. Martha Cook died March 8, 1830 ae 1 year 4 months 24 days

    4. Phebe C. W. daughter of Richard A. and Martha Cook died Sept. 11, 1845 ae 2 months 2 days

    5. Lauretta A. daughter of Richard A. Cook died in Boston March 14, 1875 aged 40 years 4 months 27 days

    6. Sylvanus son of Sylvanus and Betsey Collins died Oct. 22, 1855 aged 16 years 1 month 25 days

    7. Little Josie son of J. R. (Joseph) and M. W. (Martha) Atkins died Feb. 1, 1861 aged 1 year 6 months

LOT #249 -- 1 Monument - 3 Stones - 4 Footstones

    1. Monument Front: Bethiah widow of James T. Cook May 19, 1819 - May 12, 1896

       Monument Right: Wallace J. Cook 1853-1911
                        his wife Susie T. 1855-1924
                        Norman S. 1873-(1873)

       Monument Rear: Norman S. Cook, Lieut. U. S. N. 1879-1918 buried in France

CEMETERY NUMBER TWO - OLD SECTION

LOT #249 (continued)

    Monument Left: Alex R. Thompson 1840-1867
                               his wife Mary W. 1840-1867
                               Charles J. G. Thompson 1841-1867
                               Norman S. Cook 1851-1867
                               lost at sea in whaling Schooner Etta G. Fogg

2. Bethia G. daughter of Alexander and Bethia Thompson died Sept. 14, 1855 ae 16 years 9 months 23 days

3. Samuel Tilton son of James T. and Bethia Cook born Nov. 10, 1854 died Oct. 26, 1855

4. Bethiah G. daughter of James T. and Bethiah Cook died Sept. 8, 1857 ae 18 months

5. Footstone - Mother

6. Footstone - Wife

7. Footstone - Husband

8. Footstone - Norman

LOT #250 -- 3 Stones (2 of these are buried)

1. Mrs. Huldah Elms died Jan. 1828 aged 26 years

2. In memory of Mary Ann D. daughter of Ignatius and Huldah Elmes who died June 14, 1827 aged 20 months 19 days

3. William son of Ignatius and Huldah Elmes died March 14, 1825 ae 5 years 3 months

LOT #251 -- 3 Stones (one of these buried)

1. Ruth wife of John LeCount died May 23, 1855 ae 41 years 5 months

2. Ruth T. LeCount died June 4, 1836 aged 49 years 5 months 9 days
John LeCount drownded (sic) March 5, 1827 aged 46 years
"Religion should our thought engage
Amid the youthful bloom
Twill fit us for declining age
And for the awful tomb"

3. Nancy LeCount daughter of John and Ruth LeCount died August 25, 1825 aged 2 years 8 days

LOT #252 -- 3 Stones

1. Front: Capt. Owen Roberts died June 15, 1894 aged 71 years 10 months 16 days

   Rear: Phoebe P. wife of Owen Roberts Aug. 2, 1838 - Feb. 2, 1901

2. Sarah P. wife of Owen Roberts died July 4, 1850 aged 30 years

CEMETERY NUMBER TWO - OLD SECTION

LOT #252 (continued)

    William O. son of Owen and Sarah P. Roberts born Dec. 31, 1849 died Aug. 31, 1859

  3. Owen L. son of Owen and Phebe P. Roberts died June 24, 1890 ae 22 years 10 months 11 days

LOT #253 -- 1 Stone

  1. In memory of Mr. Obadiah Snow who died Feb. 18, 1825 ae 30 Also Mr. Josiah Snow, his father was drowned at sea, Sept. 9, 1800 ae 42

LOT #254 -- 2 Buried Stones

  1. Gamaliel Collins died March 29, 1839 ae 56
    Also Capt. Nathaniel H. Collins who sailed from Tenneriffe Dec. 28, 1835 ae 27 and has not been heard of since
    Also Solomon Higgins who died Feb. 27, 1823 in Port au Prince ae 23 years 4 months

  2. Mrs. Elizabeth widow of Gamaliel Collins died July 22, 1852 ae 75 years 5 months

LOT #255 -- 1 Buried Stone

  1. Elizabeth wife of Russel Holway died Jan. 10, 1886 ae 74 years 4 months 28 days

LOT #256 -- 1 Stone

  1. Joseph C. Ellis 1815-1908
    Judith B. his wife 1821-1890
    Three infants (no dates)

LOT #257 -- 1 Buried Stone

  1. Amanda C. wife of Justus Doane died Feb. 26, 1881 ae 37 years 8 months 2 days
    "We loved her"

LOT #258 -- 2 Buried Stones

  1. Sally Conant born in Truro April 28, 1788 died March 28, 1878 ae 89 years 11 months

  2. John Wesly 2nd, son of Simeon and Sally Conant died Dec. 29, 1827 aged 3 months 21 days

LOT #259 -- No Stone

LOT #260 -- 1 Monument

  1. Front: Charles F. Fishburn (no date)
    (Ed. note: We could find no record of the death of Charles Fishburn)

CEMETERY NUMBER TWO - OLD SECTION

LOT #260 (continued)

    Right: Elizabeth Jane 1852-1873
        "I praised God with heart and song"

    Left: In Memoriam - James Fishburn born 1815 lost at sea 1855
        his wife Mary A. 1820-1904
        "My dear parents"

LOT #261 -- 5 Stones

1. Capt. Francis Joseph died July 24, 1888 ae 79 years 5 mos.

2. Jarusha (sic) G. wife of Francis Joseph born April 21, 1813 died in Beverly Feb. 19, 1853

3. Mercy M. wife of Francis Joseph died Nov. 11, 1892 ae 63 years 28 days (Initial M. on this stone, and H. on stone #4)

4. Little sister - Luthera C. daughter of Francis and Mercy H. Joseph died Sept. 9, 1856 ae 2 months

5. Lillian A. Joseph 1871-1909
J. (Jerusha) Fannie Joseph 1855-1911

LOT #262 -- 1 Stone

1. Father - Jared Hill died October 26, 1884 aged 76 years 11 months 3 days
Mother - Elizabeth D. Hill died May 9, 1885 aged 66 years 6 months 14 days

LOT #263 -- 2 Stones

1. Serg't. C. H. Holway - Co. I 17 Ill. INF. (no date)
(VR: died April 4, 1902 ae 68 years 9 months 6 days)

2. Abbie R. daughter of Charles H. and Lydia A. Holway died March 23, 1880 ae 6 years 10 months

LOT #264 -- 5 Stones - 1 Marker - 1 Footstone

1. Mother - Sarah C. Cornell died May 21, 1898 aged 67 years 10 months 3 days

   Father - George H. Cornell died Nov. 25, 1888 aged 69 years 7 months

2. Martha Hellen daughter of George H. and Sarah C. Cornell died March 12, 1851 ae 1 year 10 months 6 days

3. Adaline daughter of G. H. and S. C. Cornell 1857-1934

4. Sadie (VR: surname Cornell) 1863-1886

5. Ebed E. Cook 1877-1962
Inda S. Cornell his wife 1866-1950

6. Footstone - Willie (Cornell)

CEMETERY NUMBER TWO - OLD SECTION

LOT #264 (continued)

    7. George H. Cornell Jr. Sept. 21, 1852 - Feb. 19, 1900

LOT #265 -- 1 Stone

    1. John H. Livermore 1850-1904
       Lizzie W. Livermore 1853-1931

LOT #266 -- 5 Stones - 6 Markers on common base

    1. Father - Joseph P. Knowles died Sept. 2, 1885 aged 70 years 4 days

    2. Mother - Delia C. Knowles died July 9, 1899 aged 76 years 11 mos. 8 days

    3. Lucy A. Knowles 1851-1936

       6 Markers on common base:
       Children of Joseph P. & Delia C. Knowles

    4. Marker - Lovias Kibby 1844-1845

    5. Marker - Lovisa Kibby 1849-1855

    6. Marker - Hannah Kidder 1854-1855

    7. Marker - Hannah Kidder 1858-1859

    8. Marker - Willie B. 1861-1861

    9. Marker - Lizzie B. 1861-(VR: died 1863)

    10. Willard Knowles 1807-1880
        Polly K. Knowles 1806-1896
        Angie M. Knowles 1839-1908

    11. Howard F. Hopkins 1864-1928
        his wife Julia C. Knowles 1865-1948

LOT #267 -- 1 Stone

    1. Front: Isaac B. Alexander June 10, 1810 - Jan. 8, 1890
            Elizabeth G. April 2, 1814 - April 10, 1848
            Caroline P. May 2, 1814 - March 12, 1885
            Sarah W. Feb. 24, 1837 - July 6, 1838
            Margreatte S. Feb. 8, 1848 - April 10, 1850 (twin)
            Nancy A. Feb. 8, 1848 - May 17, 1848 (twin)

       Rear: William Palmer Jan. 2, 1775 - April 15, 1848
            Elizabeth A. Palmer Dec. 15, 1779 - June 10, 1848

LOT #268 -- 1 Stone

    1. Amanda M. wife of R. G. Alexander died Nov. 10, 1880
       ae 50 years 2 months 11 days
       "A good woman"

LOT #269 -- 1 Monument - 3 Footstones - 1 Base with no stone

CEMETERY NUMBER TWO - OLD SECTION

LOT #269 (continued)

    1. Monument Front: Ebenezer W. Holway died August 20, 1881
                        ae 67 years 5 months
                        Hannah B. wife of Ebenezer W. Holway died
                        July 28, 1851 ae 31 years 7 months 20
                        days
                        Mary J. wife of E. W. Holway died Aug. 14,
                        1897 ae 72 years 10 months
       Monument Right: John died April 10, 1848 ae 3 months 12 dys.
                        Hannah B. died July 5, 1853 ae 1 year
                        11 months 11 days
                        Children of Ebenezer W. and Hannah B. Hol-
                        way
       Monument Left: William H. son of Ebenezer W. and Mary J.
                        Holway died Jan. 18, 1877 ae 23 years
                        2 months 19 days
                        Hannah B. Holway 1860-1934

    2. Footstone - Mother

    3. Footstone - Father

    4. Footstone - Mother

    5. Base with stone missing

LOT #270 -- 3 Stones

    1. Betsey wife of Capt. Benjamin Fuller died June 15, 1858
       ae 80 years 5 months 14 days

    2. (Broken top of stone) ....aged 20 years 7 months (Unknown)

    3. Mary Thomas daughter of David and Mary Smith died July 13,
       1841 ae 2 years 5 months

LOT #271 -- 1 Monument - 8 Stones - 5 Footstones

    1. Monument Front: Capt. William H. Dyer son of William and
                        Mary S. Dyer lost at sea August 20, 1887
                        ae 30 years 10 months 19 days

       Monument Right: Mary S. Dyer born Feb. 13, 1828 died July
                        6, 1885
                        Charlotte C. Dyer born Dec. 14, 1828 died
                        Oct. 13, 1853

       Monument Rear: Capt. William Dyer 1825-1909

       Monument Left: Hermie Dyer aged 4 years 8 months
                        (VR: died 1860)
                        Charlotte C. (Dyer) 1866-1910

    2. Arthur C. Smith 1870-1950

    3. Christina D. Smith 1869-1945

    4. Footstone - Mother

CEMETERY NUMBER TWO - OLD SECTION

LOT #271 (continued)

 5. Footstone - Father

 6. Footstone - Charlotte C.

 7. Footstone - Hirmie

 8. Footstone - Charlotte

 9. H. C. Holmes 1861-1943

 10. Mary E. Holmes 1862-1940

 11. Rachel daughter of H. C. and M. E. Holmes 1893-1901

 12. James S. Dyer died July 5, 1880 aged 82 years 10 months 3 days

 13. Hannah Cook wife of James S. Dyer died Oct. 15, 1865 aged 63 years

 14. Hannah C. daughter of James and Hannah Dyer died Sept. 12, 1849 ae 2 years

LOT #272 -- 8 Stones

 1. Augustus Mitchell died April 13, 1888 ae 55 years 5 months 21 days

 2. Harriett F. wife of Augustus Mitchell died Jan. 29, 1885 ae 52 years 7 months 24 days

 3. Philip S. Rich died Feb. 15, 1879 ae 73 years 7 months

 4. Sally D. wife of Philip S. Rich died June 12, 1884 ae 73 years 8 months 29 days

 5. Charles S. son of Philip S. and Sally D. Rich died July 3, 1854 ae 8 years 10 months 16 days

 6. Phillip S. son of Phillip S. and Sally D. Rich died Sept. 5, 1850 ae 9 months 7 days

 7. Charles S. son of Phillip S. and Sally D. Rich died Sept. 22, 1838 ae 9 months 22 days

 8. Delia C. daughter of Phillip S. and Sally D. Rich died July 29, 1842 ae 1 year 3 days

LOT #273 -- 5 Stones - 1 Footstone

 1. Ezra Freeman 1797-1830 (the stone is inscribed 1830, but this should be 1839....see stone #3, son Edwin born c. 1836)
  Polly Freeman 1794-1882

 2. Betsy Dyer Freeman 1823-1839

 3. Edwin son of Ezra and Polly Freeman died October 29, 1843 ae 7 years 15 days

 4. Ezra son of Mr. Ezra and Mrs. Polly Freeman died March 22, 1830 ae 2 years 10 months

CEMETERY NUMBER TWO - OLD SECTION

LOT #273 (continued)

    5. Cynthia daughter of Benjamin and Matta Freeman born in Sandwich Jan. 13, 1803 died June 11, 1841

    6. Footstone - C. F.

LOT #274 -- 4 Stones

    1. John Hill died Oct. 8, 1886 aged 75 years

    2. Angeline W. wife of John Hill died Oct. 5, 1874 aged 62 years 6 months

    3. Catherine C. wife of Capt. John Hill born Oct. 25, 1812 died June 10, 1852

    4. Mrs. Hannah Hill wife of Job D. Hill died Sept. 9, 1837 ae 56 years

LOT #275 -- 3 Stones

    1. Silas Harding died October 24, 1838 aged 62 years

    2. Betsy S. daughter of Newcomb and Betsy Cook died March 16, 1838 aged 9 years 5 months

    3. Sarah Elizabeth wife of Phineas Paine died April 29, 1837 in her 32 year

LOT #276 -- 1 Buried Marker

    1. Joshua (Cemetery records list this lot in the name of Ruth P. Pierce. We find no record of a Joshua Pierce, but in the VR's, Ruth P. Pierce, daughter of Eben and Ruth P. Pierce died Aug. 18, 1853 ae 16 years)

LOT #277 -- 1 Stone

    1. Samuel Smith died August 3, 1837 aged 39 son of Samuel and Abigail Smith

LOT #278 -- 4 Stones

    1. Benjamin Smith born May 10, 1822 died June 1, 1855

    2. Sarah L. daughter of Benjamin and Sarah Smith born Aug. 13, 1850 died Jan. 7, 1851

    3. Sarah Smith wife of Jacob Williams died Nov. 20, 1907 aged 82 years 5 months 23 days

    4. Mrs. Sally wife of Mr. Hardin Smith born Aug. 11, 1796 died June 27, 1847

LOT #279 -- 3 Stones

    1. Capt. Stephen Ryder born August 5, 1770 died Oct. 30, 1843

    2. Joanna R. wife of Capt. Stephen Ryder born Dec. 16, 1769 died Feb. 20, 1848

CEMETERY NUMBER TWO - OLD SECTION

LOT #279 (continued)

    3. Mrs. Rebecca R. Adams died Feb. 11, 1836 aged 40 years
John W. Adams lost at sea 1836 aged 18 years

LOT #280 -- 2 Stones

    1. Mr. Richard W. Atkins died July 20, 1848 ae 69 years

    2. Jedidah A. wife of Harvey Cook and daughter of Richard and Phebe Smith died March 23, 1840 in the 23rd year of her age

LOT #281 -- 1 Monument - 4 Stones

    1. John A. Williams aged 38 years
Laura E. Williams aged 30 years 2 months 26 days
Ina E. Williams aged 6 years 18 days

    Lost at sea Nov 25 1883 on board Schooner Westmoreland bound from Portland, Maine to Martinique, W. I.

    2. Enoch Snow died July 21, 1882 ae 69 years 8 months 21 days

    3. Eliza A. wife of Enoch Snow died Dec. 24, 1880 ae 62 years 2 months 6 days

    4. John Swift lost at sea March 1827 aged 43 years
Lydia his wife died March 5, 1873 aged 87 years

    5. Josiah Swift son of Mr. John and Mrs. Lydia Swift died Sept. 14, 1825 in the 7 year of his age

LOT #282 -- Tomb

    1. Marble door - Capt. Thomas Rider's tomb - 1829 (date erected)
Capt. Thomas Rider died Dec. 23, 1830 ae 70
Mrs. Polly Rider his widow died August 25, 1841 ae 83

LOT #283 -- 7 Stones

    1. Samuel Cook who perished on a wreck Feb. 18, 1825 ae 69

    2. Mrs. Jane Cook consort of Capt. Samuel Cook departed this life April 27, 1829 in 72 year

    3. Capt. James T. Cook died March 8, 1871 ae 74 years 4 months

    4. Mrs. Phebe consort of Capt. James T. Cook died Sept. 13, 1834 ae 37

    5. Mrs. Louisa consort of Capt. James T. Cook died Sept. 15, 1846 ae 37 years

    6. Horace Porter Stephens Cook died August 2, 1865 ae 22 years 8 months 11 days

    7. Parker Cook died Sept. 12, 1849 ae 45 years 24 days
(Ed. note: It is possible that this stone is misplaced and should be on LOT #285. Parker Cook was the son of Ephraim

CEMETERY NUMBER TWO - OLD SECTION

LOT #283 (continued)

    and Rebecca Cook)

LOT #284 -- 2 Stones

1. Harvey Nickerson died March 4, 1875 ae 69 years 8 months 29 days

2. Ann C. wife of Harvey Nickerson died November 17, 1887 ae 78 years 10 months 23 days

LOT #285 -- 5 Stones

1. Ephraim Cook born Feb. 4, 1779 died Aug. 27, 1833

2. Rebecca widow of Ephraim Cook born Jan. 4, 1784 died July 13, 1858

3. Aphia daughter of Ephraim and Rebecca Cook born March 27, 1817 died August 22, 1833

4. Sally E. daughter of Ephraim and Rebecca Cook born Jan. 5, 1828 died July 24, 1844

5. Epaphras Kibby Cook June 14, 1824 - July 25, 1905
   Sarah G. Cook Sept. 21, 1826 - April 6, 1897

LOT #285A -- 6 Stones

1. Mr. Zaccheus Atkins born Sept. 18, 1802 died July 12, 1848 ae 46

2. Mrs. Salome wife of Zacheus Atkins died July 28, 1835 ae 30
   Also an infant ae 6 days (VR: infant died 1835)

3. Mother - Sally C. wife of Zaccheus Atkins died Jan. 14, 1866 ae 62 years 7 months

4. Hellen A. daughter of Zacheus and Mrs. Salome Atkins died August 23, 1831 ae 14 months

5. Benjamin D. son of Mr. Zacheus and Mrs. Salome Atkins died Aug. 24, 1832 ae 4 years 2 months

6. Phebe W. daughter of Zacheus and Salome Atkins died July 17, 1835 ae 17 months

LOT #286 -- 7 Stones

1. William T. Pierce born Oct. 25, 1812 died April 20, 1856

2. Sacred to the memory of Sarah wife of William Pierce who died Sept. 10, 1836 ae 23

3. An infant dau. of Wm. and Sarah Pierce died Aug. 16, 1836

4. An infant son of Wm. and Sarah Pierce died May 11, 1839

5. In memory of Harison (sic) Gilman son of William and Sarah Pierce died Sept. 25, 1837 aged 1 year

CEMETERY NUMBER TWO - OLD SECTION

LOT #286 (continued)

6. Marion Wallace daughter of William T. and Eliza A. Pierce died Nov. 10, 1850 ae 15 months

7. Hannah M. daughter of William T. and Eliza A. Pierce died Feb. 10, 1853 ae 6 months

LOT #287 -- 5 Stones

1. Silas S. Young born Nov. 5, 1814 died Sept. 23, 1887

2. Sarah wife of Silas S. Young and daughter of Capt. Stephen and Delia Cook died June 5, 1872 ae 46 years 11 months 10 days

3. Dorinda wife of Silas S. Young and daughter of Capt. Samuel and Tamsin Cook died Oct. 2, 1851 ae 31 years 1 mo. 2 days

4. Hannah L. daughter of Silas S. and Dorinda Young died Oct. 2, 1839 ae 5 months

5. Dorinda C. daughter of Silas S. and Dorinda Young born Sept. 6, 1851 died June 21, 1852

LOT #288 -- 6 Stones

1. Father - Hiram Holmes died Aug. 6, 1888 aged 68 years 10 months 28 days

2. Mrs. Betsey wife of Hiram Holmes died Dec. 14, 1849 ae 27 years 5 months

3. Mother - Nancy Avery wife of Hiram Holmes died March 13, 1892 aged 64 years 11 months 25 days

4. Infant daughter of Hiram and Betsey Holmes died Dec. 26, 1849 ae 16 days

5. Little Wally son of Hiram and Nancy Holmes died Aug. 21, 1860 ae 1 year 10 months

6. Sister - Susie Perry daughter of Hiram and Nancy A. Holmes died May 6, 1892 aged 35 years 10 mos. 22 days

LOT #289 -- 2 Stones

1. Mrs. Polly B. wife of Capt. David Brown Jr. and daughter of Oliver and Eliza Bowley died Sept. 5, 1849 age 48 years

2. Delora daughter of Capt. David Jr. and Polly Brown died June 11, 1840 age 9 months 11 days

LOT #290 -- 3 Stones

1. Mrs. Sally wife of Jesse Rider died May 21, 1842 at 40 years 9 months

2. Miss Sally B. Rider departed this life Oct. 22, 1836 age 15 years 5 months

CEMETERY NUMBER TWO - OLD SECTION

LOT #290 (continued)

    3. Ephraim H. son of Jesse and Sally Rider died April 15, 1843 age 2 years 9 months

LOT #291 -- No Stone

LOT #292 -- 1 Stone

    1. Charles T. Baker Oct. 18, 1833 - Feb. 7, 1883
       Rosa R. his wife Sept. 16, 1852 - Sept. 5, 1936

LOT #293 -- 4 Stones

    1. Isaac Atwood died Nov. 22, 1881 (rest of stone broken)

    2. Eliza wife of Isaac Atwood died Jan. 15, 1879 aged 75 years 11 days

    3. Martha R. Ghen Sept. 19, 1842 - Nov. 11, 1884
       Also an infant (no date)
       Ed. note: Possibly Freddie S. who died July 12, 1872 ae 8 months 12 days)

    4. Elwood F. died Sept. 19, 1862 ae 1 month 5 days
       Clarence O. died Sept. 1, 1864 ae 2 months 6 days
       Children of Stephen F. and Adelia C. Atwood

LOT #294 -- 1 Stone

    1. William H. Kenney Oct. 22, 1843 - April 23, 1902

LOT #295 -- 7 Stones

    1. Capt. Henry Ryder shipwrecked off Long Island March 2, 1849 and is buried here ae 45 years

    2. Mrs. Anna wife of Henry Rider died June 3, 1847 ae 40 years 6 months

    3. Amanda daughter of Henry and Anna Rider died Oct. 21, 1829 ae 11 days

    4. Lorenzo son of Henry and Anna Rider died July 26, 1839 ae 1 year 11 months 16 days

    5. William W. son of Henry and Anna Rider died on his passage from California to Oregon Dec. 26, 1855 aged 21 years 5 months 23 days

    6. Wm. T. L. Ryder son of William and Angeline Ryder died March 2, 1849 ae 18 years 7 months

    7. Henry Rider died at Grand Haven, Michigan March 9, 1866 aged 35 years
       "Here lies the body of a liberal and honest man"

LOT #296 -- 5 Stones

    1. Mrs. Lydia widow of Levi Nickerson died Nov. 19, 1847 ae 56 years

CEMETERY NUMBER TWO - OLD SECTION

LOT #296 (continued)

    2. (Stone disintegrated) (Possibly this is Levi Nickerson. VR: died Oct. 19, 1820 ae 34 years 11 months 17 days husband of Lydia Nickerson)

    3. Levi Nickerson died May 17, 1839 ae 26
       Lydia Nickerson died Oct. 9, 1840 ae 24

    4. Isaiah Nickerson died Nov. 3, 1884 ae 75 years 2 mos. 25 days

    5. Abbie C. Hopkins wife of Isaiah Nickerson Dec. 12, 1822 - Jan. 27, 1893

LOT #297 -- 2 Stones

    1. Mr. John Whare Jr. died May 29, 1840 ae 31

    2. Sarah Frances daughter of John and Mary Wharf died Sept. 4, 1837 ae 1 year 6 months

LOT #298 -- 1 Monument - 1 Boulder - 4 Small Stones - 2 Footstones

    1. Monument: Godfrey Rider born Dec. 31, 1797 died July 22, 1876
              Ruth G. Rider born July 7, 1798 died May 20, 1881

    2. Boulder: Rev. William Henry Rider D. D. born Nov. 13, 1846 Provincetown, Mass. died August 28, 1923, Essex, Mass.

    3. Thomas Lee son of Godfrey Jr. and Phebe N. Rider born Jan. 22, 1857 died at Cambridgeport March 14, 1858

    4. Thomas Lee son of Godfrey Jr. and Phebe N. Rider born Jan. 25, 1859 died at Cambridgeport April 26, 1859

    5. Freddie Collins son of Godfrey Jr. and Phebe N. Rider born July 4, 1860 died at Provincetown August 3, 1862

    6. Freddie Collins son of Godfrey Jr. and Phebe N. Rider born March 3, 1863 died at Provincetown June 7, 1864

    7. Footstone - No inscription

    8. Footstone - No inscription

LOT #299 -- 1 Stone

    1. T. Jefferson Healey 1836-1871

LOT #300 -- 1 Stone

    1. Eliza C. Ridly daughter of John and Hannah Ridly died Dec. 22, 1826 ae 6 years 10 months 15 days

LOT #301 -- 2 Stones

    1. Mr. John Whorf died Dec. 23, 1825 ae 65

CEMETERY NUMBER TWO - OLD SECTION

LOT #301 (continued)

    2. Mrs. Rebeckah Whorf died March 24, 1826 ae 61

LOT #302 -- 2 Stones

    1. Charles Dyer died July 24, 1838 aged 47 years 10 months 20 days

    2. Mrs. Sarah wife of Charles Dyer died Oct. 12, 1835 ae 43

LOT #303 -- 1 Stone - 1 Footstone

    1. In memory of Mrs. Mary Cook who died Feb. 24, 1825 ae 73 yrs.
       Her Husband Capt. John Cook died at Orland, Me. April 27, 1823 ae 74

    2. Footstone - M. C.
       (Ed. note: In the Village Cemetery, Orland, Maine, there is a stone and footstone for Capt. John Cook, "born Dec. 25, 1748, died Orland April 27, 1823". The stone in the Provincetown Cemetery is so badly shattered and pieces buried that we dug up the pieces, screened the soil for all fragments and were able to piece it together well enough to determine the data above. Since the stone could not be repaired, we have carefully reburied the fragments.)

LOT #304 -- 1 Stone

    1. Mrs. Sarah wife of William Sprague died July 7, 1831 ae 28 years
       Sarah Ann died Aug. 5, 1825 ae 1 year 29 days
       William H. died Sept. 22, 1827 ae 2 years 8 days
       John W. died Jan. 24, 1836 ae 6 years 11 mos. 17 days
       Children of William and Sarah Sprague

LOT #305 -- 2 Stones

    1. Mrs. Jemima wife of Mr. William Bush died Oct. 8, 1833 ae 37

    2. Mrs. Lois wife of Mr. William Bush died June 22, 1838 in 30 year of her age (VR: 36 years old)
       Also, Edwin William died Aug. 7, 1838 aged 10 months 17 dys.

LOT #306 -- 1 Stone

    1. George W. Readey Jan. 1, 1833 (VR: died Feb. 20, 1920 ae 88 years 1 month 19 days)
       Mary B. Oct. 20, 1822 (VR: died Feb. 1, 1915)
       "We have no home but Heaven"

LOT #307 -- 1 Stone

    1. Dear Sarah (VR: died 1838 age 11)
       Also three infant children of James and Susan Whorf (no dates)

CEMETERY NUMBER TWO - OLD SECTION

LOT #308 -- 1 Stone

    1. Adeline daughter of Elisha and Sally Cook died July 23, 1828 aged 21 months

LOT #309 -- 2 Stones

    1. Mr. Samuel Chapman died July 8, 1826 age 75, also his son Lewis Lombard Chapman drowned at sea Dec. 10, 1811 ae 18
"Beneath this stone the father lies,
His son in distant seas did die,
He sailed from home in youth,
But death to him was nigh"

    2. Mrs. Elizabeth widow of Samuel Chapman died Feb. 14, 1853 in her 90 year

LOT #310 -- 4 Stones

    1. Reuben Cook died Sept. 3, 1862 ae 73 years 11 months

    2. Mrs. Elizabeth wife of Reuben Cook died Sept. 17, 1856 ae 69 years

    3. George B. Cook son of Capt. Reuben and Elizabeth Cook died July 27, 1825 age 9 years 2 months

    4. Polly B. Cook died Oct. 31, 1838 ae 16 years 2 months
Reuben Cook drowned off Race Point Oct. 19, 1832
    ae 18 years 4 months
Children of Reuben and Elizabeth Cook

LOT #311 -- 7 Stones

    1. Abraham Chapman died Oct. 26, 1865 ae 75 years 3 months 23 days

    2. Mrs. Mercy wife of Abraham Chapman died March 10, 1849 ae 52 years 5 months

    3. Elizabeth wife of Mr. Abraham Chapman died Sept. 12, 1864 ae 72 years

    4. Mercy H. daughter of Abraham and Mercy Chapman died Sept. 13, 1825 ae 1 year 9 days

    5. Elizabeth P. dtr. of Abraham and Mercy Chapman died Dec. 3, 1836 ae 14 years 4 months 10 days

    6. Elizabeth daughter of Abraham and Mercy Chapman died Sept. 15, 1839 ae 15 days

    7. Abraham Chapman born Nov. 27, 1831 died June 15, 1860 (rest of stone broken) (VR: died at the age of 28 yrs. 6 mos. 18 days)

LOT #312 -- 4 Stones

    1. Mr. Peter L. Avery died Oct. 27, 1835 age 42 years 8 months

    2. Betsey Avery died March 18, 1871 age 74 years 10 months

CEMETERY NUMBER TWO - OLD SECTION

LOT #312 (continued)

3. Hannah P. daughter of Peter L. and Betsey Avery died Sept. 14, 1842 ae 18 years

4. Miss Elizabeth Avery died March 4, 1863 aged 74 years 10 months 14 days

LOT #313 -- 10 Stones

1. John Atkins died Sept. 5, 1857 aged 60 years

2. Hannah widow of John Atkins July 30, 1801 - May 8, 1888

3. Sally Ann daughter of John and Hannah Atkins died April 29, 1832 ae 2 years 6 months 4 days

4. Rawlins Thomas son of John and Hannah Atkins died April 14, 1832 ae 4 years 11 months 2 days

5. Rawlins Thomas son of John and Hannah Atkins died Sept. 21, 1834 ae 1 year 6 months 28 days

6. John Edwin son of John and Hannah Atkins died Feb. 18, 1843 ae 2 years 26 days

7. Lucy and John - twin children of John and Hannah Atkins:
Lucy died June 27 ae 10 days
John died Sept. 28, 1844 ae 3 months

8. Lucena Wilder daughter of John and Hannah Atkins died June 15, 1851 ae 13 years 10 months 12 days

9. Hannah C. wife of Paul Wheeler died Aug. 30, 1878 ae 53 years 2 months

10. Lt. Rawlins T. Atkins - Co. H 56 Mass. Inf. (died after 1890)

LOT #314 -- 1 Stone - 4 Footstones

1. Front: Thomas R. Whorf 1815-1887
Alvina Whorf 1818-1890
Philip A. Whorf 1841-1916

   Rear: Thomas R. Whorf 1788-1868
Elizabeth A. Whorf 1788-1869

2. Footstone - T. R. W.

3. Footstone - E. A. W.

4. Footstone - T. R. W.

5. Footstone - A. W.

LOT #315 -- 3 Stones

1. Elisha Rider died Aug. 30, 1858 aged 72 years 3 months

2. Elizabeth wife of Elisha Ryder died Dec. 21, 1873

CEMETERY NUMBER TWO - OLD SECTION

LOT #315 (continued)
　　ae 73 years 3 months 19 days
　3. Sister - Sarah Y. Ryder died Jan. 21, 1891
　　ae 59 years 4 months 9 days

LOT #316 -- 3 Stones
　1. John Whorf died Nov. 22, 1854 ae 69 years 3 months
　2. Rebecca wife of John Wharf died Sept. 10, 1837 ae 52
　3. Susan wife of John Wharf died June 16, 1850 ae 54 years 5 mos.

LOT #317 -- 4 Stones
　1. James S. Welsh 1858-1929
　　Annie O. Welsh 1864-1929
　2. Abbie M. Williams 1883-1910
　3. Alice M. Welsh 1888-1900
　4. Baby - Alice Margaret daughter of Fred and Abbie Williams born July 7, 1905 died Oct. 22, 1905

LOT #318 -- 3 Stones
　1. Mr. Seth Nickerson died June 4, 1837 ae 73
　2. Mrs. Phebe widow of Mr. Seth Nickerson died Nov. 18, 1843 ae 79
　3. Solomon Dyer son of Lewis and Bethiah Nickerson died Jan. 9, 1837 ae 4 months

LOT #319 -- 5 Stones
　1. Capt. Elisha Young died Dec. 5, 1848 in the 73 year of his age
　2. Mrs. Hannah wife of Mr. Elisha Young died Aug. 19, 1836 in the 55 year of her age
　3. Polly widow of Elisha Young died May 16, 1856 in the 69 year of her age
　4. Newcomb C. Young son of Elisha and Hannah Young died March 23, 1832 in the 14 year of his age
　5. Mrs. Emily wife of Mr. Henry Young died Nov. 19, 1840 in the 22 year of her age

LOT #320 -- 1 Monument - 7 Stones - 4 Markers on common base
　1. Monument Front: Thomas Hilliard died April 9, 1879 ae 76 years
　　Monument Left:　Nathaniel L. Nickerson Dec. 5, 1839 lost at sea ae 29 years

CEMETERY NUMBER TWO - OLD SECTION

LOT #320 (continued)

    Monument Right: Rebecca C. wife of Thomas Hilliard born Aug. 29, 1813 died Aug. 14, 1901

2. Pauline wife of Thomas Hilliard died May 17, 1837 ae 28 yrs.

3. Mrs. Abby P. wife of Thomas Hilliard died Dec. 22, 1849 ae 43 years

4. Sally widow of Thomas Hilliard died Aug. 28, 1860 aged 82 years

5. Thomas Hilliard died April 18, 1832 aged 56 years

6. Mrs. Lucy H. wife of Richard W. Hilliard died Oct. 18, 1849 ae 28 years 11 months

7. Rebecca L. Nickerson 1837-1915 (dtr. of Nathaniel & Rebecca Nickerson)
Rebecca C. Hilliard 1813-1901 (widow of Nathaniel Nickerson, married 2nd Thomas Hilliard)

8. In memory of Sally wife of Elisha Cook born Oct. 28, 1804 died July 7, 1838 aged 34 years

    4 Markers on common base: Children of R. W. and C. Nickerson

9. Marker - Baby (VR: infant male died March 30, 1853 ae 28 days)

10. Marker - Eddie (VR: died Oct. 13, 1863 ae 5 months)

11. Marker - Charlie (VR: died Sept. 25, 1864 ae 3 months 4 days)

12. Marker - Carrie (No record)

LOT #321 -- 3 Stones

1. Father - Elisha Cook July 10, 1799 - March 23, 1874
Mother - Ann Cook Sept. 1, 1808 - Sept. 25, 1886
Adiline H. Cook 1852-1929

2. Sarah A. daughter of Elisha and Ann Cook died Sept. 4, 1845 ae 23 months

3. S. (Solomon) Thomas Cook was drowned Sept. 29, 1858 age 28 y. 8 m.

LOT #322 -- 3 Stones

1. In memory of Capt. Parron C. Cook who died Oct. 18, 1834 at 74 years 9 months

2. In memory of Mrs. Hannah wife of Capt. Parron Cook who died Aug. 28, 1836 at 80 years 5 months

3. In memory of Miss Rebecca Cook who died April 19, 1832 age 34 years 6 months

CEMETERY NUMBER TWO - OLD SECTION

LOT #323 -- 1 Stone

   1. Mrs. Paulina wife of Micah Sherman died Feb. 18, 1836 ae 26

LOT #324 -- 2 Stones

   1. Mrs. Jane B. wife of Elishua Nickerson Jr. died June 28, 1843 age 19 years 8 months

   2. George B. son of Solomon and Sarah Cook lost at sea Sept. 16, 1846 age 20 years 9 months

LOT #325 -- 2 Stones

   1. George H. Hurlbert Jr. 1854-1904
      Lexie Kelley 1863-1924 (VR: maiden name McDonald)
      Cora B. (Hurlbert) 1893-1899

   2. Alonzo W. Hurlbert - Mass. MM1 USNRF WWI
      Jan. 3, 1895 - July 4, 1956

LOT #326 -- 2 Stones

   1. Asa son of Asa and Rachel Atkins died March 24, 1838 aged 5 years

   2. Asa 2nd, son of Asa and Rachel Atkins died Sept. 8, 1844 aged 6 years

LOT #327 -- 2 Stones

   1. Mother - Elizabeth Strachauer 1841-1903

   2. Claude Strachauer Dec. 7, 1871 - Sept. 24, 1898

LOT #328 -- 2 Stones

   1. Mrs. Joanna widow of Ebenezer Higgins died June 22, 1849 ae 71 years 9 months

   2. Stephen son of George W. and Frances Spalding died April 1, 1842 ae 1 year 9 months

LOT #329 -- 4 Stones

   1. Deacon Silas Atkins died Feb. 4, 1840 ae 81

   2. Mrs. Lydia widow of Deacon Silas Atkins died Feb. 13, 1849 ae 86 years 6 months

   3. Silas Atkins died July 25, 1875 aged 84 years 8 months 29 days

   4. Rebecca wife of Silas Atkins died Nov. 7, 1871 aged 74 years 4 months 26 days

LOT #330 -- 5 Stones

   1. Capt. Joshua Cook born Oct. 17, 1774 died Sept. 20, 1852

CEMETERY NUMBER TWO - OLD SECTION

LOT #330 (continued)

    2. Mrs. Elizabeth wife of Joshua Cook died July 13, 1845 age 69

    3. Father - Joshua Cook 2nd died March 10, 1867 at 67 years 6 months 15 days
       Mother - Joanna wife of Joshua Cook 2nd died August 30, 1865 at 61 years 11 months 18 days

    4. Eliza Paine daughter of Mr. Joshua Jr. and Mrs. Joanna Cook died Aug. 4, 1830 at 1 year 10 months

    5. (Broken stone) (VR: Possibly Joshua, son of Joshua 2nd and Joanna Cook born Jan. 7, 1834 died Feb. 20, 1836)

LOT #331 -- 2 Stones

    1. In memory of Capt. Solomon Cook who died March 21, 1840 at 75 years 8 months

    2. Susannah widow of Solomon Cook died Sept. 6, 1860 at 93 years

LOT #332 -- No Stone

LOT #333 -- 4 Stones

    1. Father - James Cook died Dec. 26, 1881 ae 84 years 3 months 25 days

    2. Mrs. Sally wife of Mr. James Cook died April 8, 1827 ae 28 years

    3. Mother - Anna wife of James Cook died Sept. 15, 1885 ae 88 years 7 months 25 days

    4. In memory of our deceased children:
       Rachel W. died July 11, 1823 ae 1 year 11 months 16 days
       Rachel W. died Dec. 27, 1826 ae 1 year 10 days
       Children of James and Sally Cook

       James died Feb. 27, 1829 aged 1 month 10 days
       James F. Cook lost at sea Sept. 16, 1846 aged 16 years
       Children of James and Anna Cook

LOT #334 -- No Stone

LOT #335 -- 5 Stones

    1. Lemuel Paine born at East Harbor, Truro Jan. 12, 1797 died Sept. 1, 1876

    2. (Top of stone missing) born Sept. 15 (broken) died Sept. 17, 1828 (VR: Elizabeth (Cook) Paine born Sept. 15, 1801 died Sept. 17, 1828 first wife of Lemuel Paine)

    3. Huldah C. Nickerson wife of Lemuel Paine born Nov. 30, 1802 died October 1839

CEMETERY NUMBER TWO - OLD SECTION

LOT #335 (continued)

    4. Sarah B. wife of Lemuel Paine born Dec. 6, 1819 died May 23, 1889

    5. Harvey Cook Paine died Sept. 27, 1826 - 1 year 11 months 10 days
       An infant of 4 days died in Sept. 1828 (VR: Sept. 18)
       Children of Lemuel and Elizabeth Paine

LOT #336 -- 1 Monument - 1 Stone

    1. Capt. Jacob Cook born Sept. 9, 1797 died Dec. 25, 1871

    2. Vergenia (sic) S. died Aug. 3, 1851 at 11 years 7 months
       Mary G. died July 22, 1836 at 1 year 11 months 16 days
       Children of Jacob and Polly Cook

LOT #337 -- 2 Stones

    1. Mrs. Sally wife of Mr. Charles Brown died March 20, 1839 ae 37 years

    2. Mrs. Sophila (sic) wife of Mr. Ezra C. Small died March 6, 1833 ae 25

LOT #338 -- 2 Stones

    1. William H. son of Mr. Hiram and Rebecca Prior died Nov. 30, 1831 ae 4 years

    2. Hellen M. daughter of Mr. Hiram and Rebecca Prior died Sept. 4, 1832 ae 1 year 8 months

LOT #339 -- 1 Stone

    1. Mary wife of Enoch Hall died April 26, 1839 aged 23 years

LOT #340 -- 1 Stone

    1. Front: Capt. Joseph Cross 1814-1894
       Right: Jonathan K. 1843-1844
             Joseph 1841-1867
             Jonathan K. 1847-1867

LOT #341 -- 4 Stones

    1. Joseph Atkins born June 28, 1789 died Aug. 8, 1872

    2. Henrietta wife of Joseph Atkins born Liverpool, Nova Scotia Oct. 16, 1785 died Nov. 12, 1863 aged 78 years 29 days

    3. Josephine dtr. of John and Susan P. Eldridge died Sept. 11, 1842 aged 3 years 9 months 14 days

    4. Hannah H. daughter of Freeman M. and Joanna S. Bowley died Oct. 21, 1884 age 38 years
       Abbie B. daughter of Solomon D. and Sarah P. Pierce died Nov. 5, 1898 age 51 years 2 months 16 days

CEMETERY NUMBER TWO - OLD SECTION

LOT #341 (continued)

(Ed. note: The parents of Hannah H. Bowley are buried in the lot next to this one - LOT #342)

LOT #342 -- 3 Stones

1. Capt. Freeman M. Bowley born Provincetown Oct. 7, 1819 died June 1. 1902

2. Joanna S. wife of Freeman M. Bowly died Dec. 6, 1853 age 31 years 2 months

3. Sarah P. wife of Freeman M. Bowley died Oct. 15, 1880 age 61 years 9 months 4 days
(Ed, note: See LOT #341 for Hannah H. Bowley daughter of Freeman M. Bowley)

LOT #343 -- 3 Stones

1. Olive wife of Zenas W. Crocker died April 11, 1878 aged 51 years 9 months

2. Mrs. Hannah wife of Samuel C. Elliott died March 14, 1842 age 25

3. Hannah A. dtr. of Samuel C. and Hannah Elliott died March 25, 1842 age 3 months 20 days

LOT #344 -- 3 Stones

1. Samuel W. Atkins died April 24, 1859 age 74 years 6 months

2. Hannah widow of Samuel W. Atkins died April 12, 1869 age 72 years 8 months

3. Benjamin O. Elliott Aug. 1, 1839 - May 27, 1903

LOT #345 -- 1 Stone

1. William T. born Nov. 24, 1844 died Nov. 28, 1850
Catherine I. born May 21, 1852 died Nov. 10, 1852
Children of William and Mary J. Wheldin

LOT #346 -- 1 Stone - 1 Footstone

1. Capt. Hezekiah Galacar died April 19, 1864 ae 49 years 2 months

2. Footstone - M. B. - 1839 (VR: Possibly Mary Galacar who died June 3, 1839 age 31)

LOT #347 -- 2 Stones

1. Capt. Gamaliel S. Bowly died May 13, 1836 ae 60

2. Mrs. Temperance widow of Gamaliel S. Bowly died May 13, 1844 ae 63

CEMETERY NUMBER TWO - OLD SECTION

LOT #348 -- 5 Stones

1. Martin W. Cornell died July 25, 1882 aged 72 years 9 months

2. Edna B. wife of Martin W. Cornell died March 31, 1890 aged 74 years 2 months 9 days

3. Eliza H. daughter of Martin W. and Edna Cornell died April 30, 1839 ae 1 year 5 months 7 days

4. Martin L. son of Martin W. and Edna Cornell died Aug. 30, 1846 ae 1 year 14 days

5. Mary H. died March 31, 1848 aged 1 year
   Martin W. died May 25, 1850 aged 8 months
   Sabra C. died July 1, 1857 aged 2 years 9 months
   Children of Martin W. and Edna Cornell

LOT #349 -- 1 Stone

1. Father - James V. Bowley born Feb. 11, 1845 died May 6, 1909
   Mother - His wife Rosa W. Churchill born April 6, 1851 died Oct. 5, 1907

LOT #350 -- 2 Stones - 2 Footstones

1. Joseph C. Small son of Silas and Susannah Small died April 30, 1852 ae 29 years 8 months
   Also his father Silas Small who was lost at sea Feb. 1846 ae 50 years

2. Mrs. Susannah wife of Silas Small died Jan. 12, 1842

3. Footstone - J. C. S. and S. S.

4. Footstone - S. S.

LOT #351 -- 5 Stones - 1 Marker

1. Michael A. Parker Dec. 20, 1826 - Oct. 16, 1906
   Eliza Ann Parker April 3, 1833 - Dec. 7, 1904

2. Sadie-Sarah E. Parker May 31, 1853 - Sept. 13, 1854

3. Brother - S. A. P. (VR: Probably Samuel A. Parker, born Sept. 1, 1848 died Sept. 21, 1849)

4. Lina-Lavina J. Parker June 15, 1873 - March 27, 1877

5. John P. son of Frank A. and Jennie B. Jennings died May 9, 1888 aged 7 months 27 days

6. Marker - Jennings (no dates)

LOT #352 -- 4 Stones

1. Mrs. Clarissa wife of Stephen Atwood died Oct. 9, 1854 at 45 yrs. 11 months

2. Abigail Atwood died Sept. 13, 1886 aged 74 years

CEMETERY NUMBER TWO - OLD SECTION

LOT #352 (continued)

    3. Mary A. daughter of Stephen and Clarissa Atwood died May 16, 1856 at 15 years

    4. Capt. Joseph A. Lavender died Sept. 22, 1870 at 45 years 9 months

LOT #353 -- 4 Stones

    1. Capt. John Adams died April 20, 1847 ae 53 years 10 months

    2. Mrs. Sally wife of Capt. John Adams died July 3, 1835 ae 39

    3. Levina Adams wife of Capt. John Adams died June 25, 1839 aged 23 years

    4. Sarah M. daughter of John and Sarah Adams died Aug. 3, 1848 ae 16 years 7 months

LOT #354 -- No Stone

LOT #355 - 3 Markers

    1. Lucy L. Rider 1785-1870

    2. Hannah G. Holway 1825-1900

    3. John W. Holway 1861-1918

LOT #356 -- 1 Stone

    1. Olive wife of John Stone born Oct. 27, 1806 died May 27, 1860
       Ann wife of John Stone born in the year 1824 died Jan. 24, 1868

LOT #357 -- 1 Stone

    1. Infant son and daughter of Luther and Lucretia Chapman (no dates) (VR: Infant male died Aug. 25, 1855 ae 1 day and infant female not listed in VR)

LOT #358 -- 1 Stone

    1. Front: Russell Atkins 1805-1890
            Martha D. Atkins 1818-1880
            Anna 1852-1884

       Left: Mary A. (Atkins) 1837-1838
            An infant -1839-
            William T. 1848-1849

       Rear: Salome C. Hawes 1856-1934
            Frank L. Hawes 1878-1901

LOT #359 -- 4 Stones

    1. Joseph S. Tuck, our Father, died June 29, 1846 at 65 years
       Mary Elizabeth (no date)

CEMETERY NUMBER TWO - OLD SECTION

LOT #359 (continued)

    2. Sophronia Tuck, our Mother, died Sept. 10, 1836 at 33 years
       Sophronia (no date)
       Mary Susan (no date)

    3. Front: Joseph W. Tuck Sept. 8, 1824 - Jan. 11, 1902
            Maria C. Tuck June 9, 1827 - March 22, 1909

       Rear: (same as stone #1 and #2)
            Joseph Tuck 1781-1846
            Sophronia Tuck 1803-1836

    4. Josey S. Tuck only son of Joseph W. and Maria C. Tuck died March 17, 1863 ae 7 years 11 months 8 days

LOT #360 -- 1 Stone

    1. In memory of Mr. Jona. Atwood who died Jan. 15, 1837 at 67, also Henry D. son of Mr. Jonathan and Mrs. Nabby Atwood drowned at sea Sept. 12, 1837 ae 17

LOT #361 -- 2 Stones

    1. Capt. William Galicar died Aug. 24, 1849 ae 74

    2. Mrs. Mary wife of William Galacar died July 25, 1853 ae 74 years

LOT #362 -- 4 Stones

    1. Alfred Adams born Dec. 27, 1824 died March 7, 1853

    2. Zilpha A. Adams born Sept, 8, 1829 died Sept. 19, 1867

    3. Sarah Adaline daughter of Alfred and Zilpha Ann Adams born Jan. 16, 1848 died Jan. 20, 1852

    4. Alfred W. Adams son of Alfred and Zilpha Ann Adams born May 17, 1851 died April 23, 1875

LOT #363 -- 1 Stone

    1. Eugene W. son of Elisha and Ann M. Freeman Jr. died June 27, 1852 at 4 years 6 months 20 days

LOT #364 -- 5 Stones

    1. Reuel Atkins died Oct. 21, 1884 aged 78 years 6 months 20 days

    2. Rebekah wife of Reuel died Oct. 5, 1862 ae 53 years 2 mos.

    3. Sarah Jane B. daughter of Reuel and Rebekah Atkins died April 21, 1845 ae 1 year 6 months 8 days

    4. Reuel son of Reuel and Rebekah Atkins died July 28, 1850 ae 18 years 9 months

    5. Paulina F. Wiggins daughter of Reuel and Rebekah (Atkins) died Sept. 8, 1853 ae 23 years 2 months

CEMETERY NUMBER TWO - OLD SECTION

LOT #365 -- Infant son of Amos and Lucy M. Pratt died Nov. 6, 1843

LOT #366 -- 3 Stones - 1 Marker - 1 Footstone

1. Mrs. Amanda M. L. Standish died June 21, 1852 ae 32

2. Father - Isaiah Young 1807-1846
   Mother - Hannah Young 1815-1855

3. Nehemiah H. Young died 1844 aged 45
   (see LOT #158 - Footstone N. Y. probably belongs on this lot)

4. J. S. Young - Ensign U. S. Navy (no date) (VR: Probably Joseph S. Young born Nov. 22, 1832 - no date of death found)

5. Footstone - Baby (This is next to the J. S. Young marker)

LOT #367 - 2 Stones

1. Isaac Small 1796-1875
   Augusta P. his wife 1818-1901
   Hannah his wife 1806-1840

2. Ella A. Small 1845-1923
   Abraham Small 1770-1846
   Polly his wife 1770-1855

LOT #368 -- 2 Stones

1. Mr. Moses Paine died Dec. 4, 1843 ae 77

2. Mrs. Priscilla widow of Moses Paine died Feb. 28, 1845 ae 77

LOT #369 -- 1 Stone

1. Mary E. twin daughter of William and Evelina Shed died Oct. 29, 1840 ae 1 year 10 months

LOT #370 -- 2 Markers

1. Harry J. Coleman 1876-1939

2. Nellie F. Coleman (no date)
   James E. (no date)
   Andrew T. (VR: born 1889, died 1922)

LOT #371 -- 4 Stones

1. Jeremiah Mayo died at sea Feb. 19, 1867 ae 39 years

2. Mrs. Deborah widow of Joseph Mayo died June 20, 1862 ae 73

3. Mr. Joseph Mayo died Jan. 15, 1848 ae 56

4. Mrs. Martha widow of Joshua A. Mayo died May 7, 1844 ae 85

CEMETERY NUMBER TWO - OLD SECTION

LOT #372 - 6 Stones

1. Henry R. son of Henry R. and Sophia Pierce born Feb. 24, 1839 died Sept. 6, 1839

2. Sophia daughter of Henry R. and Sophia Pierce born Dec. 31, 1845 died April 1, 1846

3. Isaac N. son of Henry R. and Sophia Pierce born Jan. 2, 1848 died June 14, 1849

4. Sophia daughter of Henry R. and Sophia Pierce born April 9, 1851 died Aug. 19, 1851 (twin)

5. Isaac N. son of Henry R. and Sophia Pierce born April 9, 1851 died Oct. 31, 1851 (twin)

6. William F. son of William and Martha M. Whalen died Sept. 7, 1849 ae 10 months

LOT #373 -- 8 Stones

1. Capt. James Sparks died Sept. 10, 1849 at 78 years 8 months 10 days

2. Abigail wife of Capt. James Sparks died June 18, 1854 at 76 years

3. Harvey Sparks died April 8, 1886 aged 68 years 10 months 9 days

4. Clarissa M. wife of Harvey Sparks died July 4, 1854 aged 34 years 10 months 12 days

5. Chloe B. wife of Harvey Sparks died June 22, 1894 aged 62 years 3 months 28 days

6. Benjamin F. son of Harvey and Clarissa Sparks died Feb. 4, 1848 aged 1 year 6 months 24 days

7. Eddie (no date) (VR: James E. born Sept. 19, 1861 died Sept. 16, 1862)

8. Angie (no date) (VR: born Oct. 10, 1855 died April 25, 1864)

LOT #374 -- 3 Stones

1. Father - David Sparks March 16, 1814 - Aug. 6, 1897
   Mother - Martha D. Sparks June 5, 1822 - May 17, 1892

2. Mrs. Rebekah wife of David Sparks died Feb. 5, 1845 at 27 years 4 months 6 days
   Also Rebekah their daughter died Sept. 5, 1844 at 2 months

3. Frank son of David and Martha D. Sparks Oct. 13, 1854 - Dec. 8, 1872

LOT #375 -- 2 Stones

1. Capt. Alexander Grose died Oct. 24, 1849 ae 49 years
   Jonah Grose died at sea Sept. 28, 1823 ae 20 years 8 months

CEMETERY NUMBER TWO - OLD SECTION

LOT #375 (continued)

    2. Mrs. Ann widow of Alexander Grose died Nov. 20, 1849 ae 42 years 11 months

LOT #376 -- 2 Stones

    1. Jule M. Silva (no date) (VR: died May 26, 1913 ae 27 years 5 months)

    2. Aurelia M. Alexander 1897-1973

LOT #377 -- No Stone

LOT #378 -- 7 Stones - 1 Base with no stone

    1. Base - (Possibly Amasa T. Smith died March 22, 1888 ae 78 years 7 months 17 days)

    2. Rebecca E. wife of Amasa T. Smith died Jan. 15, 1863 at 41 years

    3. Mary L. wife of Amasa T. Smith died Aug. 2, 1875 age 54 years 10 months

    4. Mary E. dtr. of Amasa T. and Rebeccah Smith born Nov. 22, 1850 died July 22, 1851

    5. Mary E. dtr. of Amasa T. and Rebeccah E. Smith born May 22, 1852 died July 22, 1852

    6. Lothrop H. son of Amasa T. and Rebecca E. Smith born March 4, died May 11, 1854

    7. Judith M. beloved wife of Albert W. Lavender died Aug. 23, 1869 aged 21 years 6 months

    8. Mary Snow 1797-1883

LOT #379 -- 10 Stones

    1. Mr. Benjamin Dyer died April 3, 1826 age 46

    2. Salome Dyer widow of Benjamin Dyer died Jan. 8, 1867 at 81 years 5 mos.

    3. Benjamin Dyer died March 13, 1882 aged 70 years 8 months 21 days

    4. Thankful L. wife of Benjamin Dyer died April 10, 1876 aged 62 years 1 month

    5. Georgianna dtr. of Benjamin and Thankful L. Dyer died Oct. 20, 1840 at 1 year 23 days

    6. Joshua P. Atkins died March 2, 1884 aged 48 years 2 months 18 days

    7. Carrie F. wife of Joshua P. Atkins died Aug. 7, 1872 aged 35 years 23 days

    8. Benjamin R. son of Joshua P. and Carrie F. Atkins died Oct. 7, 1863 at 14 days

CEMETERY NUMBER TWO - OLD SECTION

LOT #379 (continued)

    9. George O. Knowles 1842-1909
       Georgie M. Knowles 1843-1946

   10. Mabel Osborne dtr. of George O. and Georgie M. Knowles died Jan. 27, 1884 at 4 years 2 months 29 days

LOT #380 -- 2 Stones - 1 Footstone

    1. John Small died May 29, 1872 aged 77 years 8 months

    2. Rebecca wife of John Small born July 24, 1795 died Sept. 29, 1864 at 69 years

    3. Unknown Footstone - M. - J.

LOT #381 -- 13 Stones

    1. Mr. William Dyer died Sept. 19, 1851 ae 56 years

    2. Mrs. Phebe Dyer wife of William Dyer died July 27, 1851 ae 53 years

    3. William Dyer died Sept. 17, 1830 ae 1 year 5 months

    4. Emily J. Dyer died Jan. 21, 1831 ae 3 years 5 months

    5. Melville W. Dyer died June 17, 1843 ae 1 year 5 months

    6. William L. Dyer drowned Nov. 25, 1852 ae 21 years 8 months

    7. Nathaniel A. Couilliard Jan. 16, 1825 - July 17, 1899
       Sarah D. his wife 1826-1914

    8. Melville W. son of Nathaniel A. and Sarah Couillyard died July 31, 1851 ae 1 year 10 months 14 days

    9. Phebe D. died March 29, 1856 ae 3 years 3 months 4 days
       Lee died Aug. 27, 1866 ae 6 months
       Mary M. died March 27, 1856 ae 1 year 6 months 14 days
       Baby died Feb. 14, 1870 ae 1 day
       Children of Nathaniel A. and Sarah D. Couilliard

   10. Shattered stone - nearest the Couilliard stones

   11. Clara L. daughter of Nathaniel A. and Sarah D. Couilliard died June 25, 1884 ae 23 years 4 months 25 days

   12. Amasa D. Couilliard born 1862 Provincetown died March 15, 1941

   13. Mary S. wife of Horace H. Vinton died Oct. 1850 aged 27 years

LOT #382 -- No Stone

LOT #383 -- 1 Monument - 12 Stones - 3 Footstones

    1. Monument Front: Clara T. wife of Amos Chapman died June 24, 1873 ae 35 years 10 months

CEMETERY NUMBER TWO - OLD SECTION

LOT #383 (continued)

    Monument Right: Infant of Amos and Clara T. Chapman
                   (VR: died Sept. 23, 1857 ae 1 day)
                 Amie C. son of Amos and Clara T. Chapman
                 died March 1, 1878 ae 5 years 1 month
                 8 days

    Monument Rear: Amos Chapman died May 7, 1904 ae 89 years 8 months

2. Footstone - Father
3. Footstone - Clara
4. Footstone - Infant
5. Father - Samuel Chapman died May 4, 1868 ae 75 years
6. Mother - Mary Chapman wife of Smauel Chapman died March 20, 1875 ae 77 years
7. Abram son of Samuel and Mary Chapman born Sept. 19, 1823 died Aug. 8, 1825
8. Sarah L. Chapman 1832-1922
9. William N. Chapman born Sept. 16, 1819 died June 5, 1895
   Phebe N. Chapman born Feb. 11, 1817 died Aug. 21, 1892
10. Samuel Chapman died June 27, 1889 ae 67 years 9 months
11. Lizzie-Elizabeth E. wife of Samuel Chapman died May 13, 1880 ae 52 years 5 months
12. My husband - Abram Chapman died March 3, 1878 aged 52 years
13. Mrs. Lucinda wife of Abram Chapman died May 28, 1891 ae 63 years
14. Abbie S. daughter of Abram and Lucinda Chapman born Sept. 6, 1849 died Nov. 14, 1869
15. Mrs. Abby N. wife of Thomas D. Stanford born March 15, 1827 died Oct. 28, 1849
    Also their daughter Abby C. born Oct. 20, 1849 died May 20, 1850
16. William H. Crowell 1822-1872
    Mary E. Crowell 1830-1917

LOT #384 -- 1 Stone

1. Bethiah R. wife of Coleman Cook died July 6, 1861 ae 43 years

LOT #385 -- 1 Stone

1. Lucy Parks May 2, 1787 - April 5, 1880
   Rufus Williams May 20, 1815 - April 13, 1884

CEMETERY NUMBER TWO - OLD SECTION

LOT #386 -- 1 Stone

    1. Danie A. son of Alex and Annie McLeod died July 25, 1884 ae 2 years 6 months

LOT #387 -- 1 Stone - 1 Marker

    1. Ralph I. Cobb 1899-1968

    2. Thomas J. Carrigan Sept. 1, 1835 - Sept. 6, 1897
       Mary Carrigan June 15, 1837 - July 14, 1904

LOT #388 - 3 Stones - 1 Footstone

    1. Father - Charles F. Doeble died May 25, 1903 ae 69 years 5 months 18 days

    2. Mother - Olive N. Doeble died Aug. 29, 1889
        ae 49 years 11 months 18 days
       Fredie (sic) died June 10, 1873 ae 8 years 4 months 3 days
       John A. died Feb. 1, 1867 ae 10 days
       Lillian C. died Nov. 10, 1863 ae 2 months 10 days
       Children of Charles F. and Olive N. Doeble

    3. Footstone - Freddie

    4. Mother - Hannah Howard died Jan. 4, 1890 ae 74 years 7 months 7 days
       John Howard born Jan. 14, 1807 lost at sea 1852
       David N. Howard born Dec. 11, 1835 lost at sea 1852

LOT #389 -- 5 Stones

    1. Nabby B. wife of Michael Whelden died Nov. 3, 1866 ae 70 years 2 months

    2. Susannah daughter of Michael and Abby Whilding born Jan. 8, 1836 died Aug. 24, 1837
       Michael son of Michael and Abby Whilding who was lost at sea Sept. 1839 aged 14 years 11 months

    3. Catherine A. wife of John Whilding and daughter of Michael and Abigail Whilding died Dec. 22, 1848 ae 17 years 5 months 22 days

    4. Michael T. son of John and Catherine Whilding died Dec. 28, 1848 ae 14 days

    5. Michael T. son of John and Abigail Whilding born Dec. 22, 1841 died Feb. 15, 1851

LOT #390 -- 5 Stones

    1. Mr. John Pirce died Dec. 20, 1831 ae 40 years
       "My husband died, I am left alone,
       With six children for to mourn;
       And may they all prepare to die,
       And meet him there above the sky"

    2. Susannah widow of Lewis L. Smith died April 14, 1868

CEMETERY NUMBER TWO - OLD SECTION

LOT #390 (continued)

  ae 74 years 8 months (Also, wodow of John Pirce-Stone #1)

 3. William Pierce died Feb. 25, 1853 ae 85 years 8 months

 4. Mrs. Sally wife of William Pirce died Nov. 6, 1847 ae 78

 5. James Fitch died Sept. 3, 1840 ae 10 months 18 days
   His father James Fitch who was lost at sea 1839 ae 27 years

LOT #391 -- 4 Stones

 1. Father - Levi B. Kelley Acting Engisn U. S. N. Nov. 10, 1827 - Sept. 4, 1895

 2. Mother - Laura A. wife of Levi B. Kelley Dec. 7, 1828 - May 13, 1898

 3. Jasie died Aug. 11, 1883 ae 10 years 8 months 11 days son of Levi B. and Laura Kelley

 4. Levi A. Kelley 1862-1941
   Leonora B. Kelley 1874-1967
   Albion E. Kelley 1900-1970

LOT #392 -- 2 Stones

 1. James E. Kelley 1859-1919

 2. Catherine 1908-1914

LOT #393 -- 2 Stones

 1. Wife - Abbie C. Talon Dec. 25, 1852 - July 16, 1889

 2. Clara A. Talon 1880-1928

LOT #394 -- 1 Stone

 1. Front: John E. Collins 1847-1894
     Ella F. Collins 1850-1882
     Richard F. Collins 1837-1894

   Rear: Capt. William R. Clapp - 22 Mass. Vols. 1839-1927
     Bessie L. Clapp 1869-1945
     Louise R. -1898-

LOT #395 -- 4 Stones - 2 Footstones

 1. Newcomb Pierce died Feb. 29, 1876 ae 64 years 6 months 18 days

 2. Asenath wife of Newcomb Pierce died Oct. 27, 1872 ae 58 years 8 months

 3. Henry F. Pierce 1838-1883
   Mary F. Pierce 1838-1925

 4. Asenath Pierce 1846-1922
   Thomas C. 1842-1870
   Esther 1839-1877

CEMETERY NUMBER TWO - OLD SECTION

LOT #395 (continued)

    5. Footstone - Thomas

    6. Footstone - Esther

LOT #396 -- 6 Stones

    1. Stephen A. Mayo died Jan. 16, 1876 ae 79 years 9 months 15 days

    2. Jerusha wife of Stephen A. Mayo died June 11, 1863 ae 58 years 10 months

    3. Stephen A. son of Mr. Stephen and Jerusha Mayo died Jan. 9, 1829 ae 11 months

    4. Stephen A. son of Stepehn A. and Jerusha Mayo born May 5, 1833 died Sept. 12, 1852

    5. Elmira F. daughter of Stephen A. and Jerusha Mayo died May 2, 1850 ae 20 years 3 months

    6. Reuben A. Mayo 1840-1916
       Selina S. Mayo 1846-1914
       Ida F. 1867-1868
       Albert S. 1870-1911 lost at sea

LOT #397 -- No Stone

LOT #398 -- 1 Stone

    1. Curtis Doane died Feb. 10, 1880 ae 71 years 9 months 20 days
       Ruth H. Doane died May 23, 1893 ae 80 years 6 months 26 days

LOT #399 -- 2 Stones

    1. William Pirce Jr. died July 25, 1850 ae 66 years

    2. Mrs. Betsey wife of William Pirce Jr. died April 6, 1845 ae 44

LOT #400 -- 2 Stones

    1. Neil McMillan lost at sea on passage to Newfoundland Nov. 14, 1883 ae 41
       Sarah wife of Neil McMillan died March 31, 1886 aged 37 years

    2. Jessie McMillan Jan. 26, 1877 - Feb. 20, 1929
       Eva McMillan 1879-1948

LOT #401 -- 1 Stone

    1. Mr. Daniel Smith died Oct. 26, 1848 ae 84 years 8 months

CEMETERY NUMBER TWO - OLD SECTION

LOT #402 -- 4 Stones

    1. Lewis L. Smith died March 31, 1862 ae 72 years 5 months

    2. Polly wife of Lewis L. Smith born May 2, 1791 died Jan. 12, 1852

    3. Lucinda died April 12, 1832 ae 2 years 9 months
       Jesse D. lost at sea Sept. 1839 ae 22
       Children of Lewis L. and Polly Smith

    4. Melissa Jane daughter of Lewis and Jane Smith born Aug. 24, 1832 died June 15, 1835

LOT #403 -- 2 Stones - 1 Wood Cross

    1. Sophia R. wife of Joseph Thomas died Nov. 26, 1876
        ae 52 years 11 months 25 days
       John B. son of Joseph and Sophia R. Thomas died at sea May 30, 1859 ae 14 years 8 months

    2. Infant daughter of William and Rebecca Cook died March 23, 1831 ae 3 weeks, also Edward (Cook) died April 2, 1836 ae 1 year 2 months

    3. Wood Cross - Walter and Harriet Cook (VR: James Walter Cook died May 25, 1967 ae 78; Harriet died Nov. 22, 1973)

LOT #404 -- 1 Stone

    1. Solomon Higgins 1824-1859
       Betsey C. Higgins 1826-1919
       Louisa S. 1847-1847

LOT #405 -- 1 Stone

    1. Heman C. Sparks 1811-1895
       Betsey Sparks 1813-1846
       Eliza R. Sparks 1819-1903
       Heman Sparks 1852-1889
       and children of Heman C. and Eliza R. Sparks
       (VR: George W. born April 20, 1851 died Aug. 25, 1851
       James A. born Jan. 20, 1861 died Sept. 8, 1861
       Infant son born Aug. 9, 1862 died Aug. 10, 1862)

LOT #406 -- 1 Stone

    1. Henry Kneeland was drowned in Provincetown Harbor Aug. 18, 1867 aged 49 years

LOT #407 -- 8 Stones

    1. Capt. Barzillai Higgins died July 15, 1852 ae 58 years

    2. Abigail wife of Barzillai Higgins (stone broken) died Feb. 23, 1877 ae 75 years 5 months 3 days

    3. Josiah C. son of Barzillai and Abigail Higgins born Sept. 11, 1819 died Jan. 26, 1825

CEMETERY NUMBER TWO - OLD SECTION

LOT #407 (continued)

    4. Abigail C. daughter of Barzillai and Abigail Higgins born Nov. 13, 1827 died April 13, 1832

    5. Isaac H. son of Barzillai and Abigail Higgins born Jan. 20, 1831 died April 19, 1832

    6. Nathaniel C. son of Barzillai and Abigail Higgins born Oct. 18, 1835 died May 9, 1836

    7. Nathaniel C. son of Barzillai and Abigail Higgins born Feb. 6, 1837 died Sept. 25, 1843

    8. Mother - Mrs. Elizabeth T. Case died Oct. 18, 1867 ae 46 years 28 days

LOT #408 -- 1 Stone

    1. William Frizzell died Sept. 11, 1853 ae 30 years "Erected by his wife"

LOT #409 -- 2 Stones

    1. J. George Nixon died Oct. 19, 1850 ae 26 years

    2. Elizabeth daughter of Joseph and Ann Butler died March 23, 1852 ae 4 years 8 months

LOT #410 -- 1 Stone

    1. Solomon D. Pierce died Nov. 22, 1850 ae 32 years
Eliphlet W. son of Solomon D. and Sarah Pierce died Sept. 9, 1850 ae 9 months 15 days

LOT #411 -- 2 Monuments - 11 Stones - 4 Footstones

    1. Monument - Nathaniel Lewis died Dec. 1, 1864 aged 69 years 2 mos.
Azubah Lewis died Sept. 12, 1873 aged 71 years 9 mos.

    2. Monument - Nathaniel Lewis Jr. died June 26, 1875 aged 53 years 9 months 28 days
Ruth H. his wife born Sept. 14, 1822 died July 4, 1897

    3. Mrs. Lucinda S. wife of Nathaniel Lewis Jr. died Sept. 1, 1846 age 21 years daughter of Jesse and Azubah G. Wiley of Wellfleet

    4. Mrs. Betsey G. wife of Nathaniel Lewis Jr. died Sept. 6, 1853 aged 23 years 11 months daughter of Jesse and Azubah Wiley of Wellfleet

    5. George son of Mr. Nathaniel and Azubah Lewis died March 1, 1828 ae 4 months 23 days

    6. John A. son of Nathaniel and Azubah Lewis died Sept. 17, 1845 age 4 months 5 days

CEMETERY NUMBER TWO - OLD SECTION

LOT #411 (continued)

    7. Mary dtr. of Nathaniel and Azubah Lewis died Sept. 3, 1846 at 22 years 11 months 19 days

    8. John A. son of Nathaniel and Lucinda S. Lewis Jr. died April 12, 1856 age 10 years 5 months 15 days

    9. Eugene W. son of Nathaniel and Betsey G. Lewis died Sept. 5, 1853 age 1 year

    10. Jesse F. daughter of Nathaniel and Betsey Lewis died Dec. 10, 1853 aged 4 years

    11. Nathaniel E. Lewis died June 30, 1882 age 24 years 10 months 15 days

    12. Infant daughter of Nathaniel and Ruth H. Lewis Jr. died Oct. 28, 1855

    13. Emma F. daughter of Nathaniel and Ruth H. died Sept. 4, 1862 age 2 years 6 months 14 days

    14. Footstone - Father

    15. Footstone - Mother

    16. Footstone - Father

    17. Footstone - Mother

LOT #412 -- 4 Stones

    1. Husband - David S. Kelley Jr. died March 24, 1881 age 38 years 10 months 20 days

    2. Evelina V. wife of D. S. Kelley died Nov. 10, 1889 age 76 years 7 months

    3. Mary G. dtr. of David S. and Evelina Kelley died July 15, 1877 at 37 years 5 months 25 days

    4. Gershom D. son of David S. and Jessie A. Kelley died Oct. 10, 1881 at 2 years 10 months 9 days

LOT #413 -- 7 Stones

    1. Capt. Reuben Ryder died April 11, 1868 age 65 years 7 mos.

    2. Lucinda wife of Capt. Reuben Ryder died Aug. 4, 1877 age 71 years 7 months 21 days

    3. Polly A. dtr. of Reuben and Lucinda died May 19, 1829 at 20 mos. 21 days

    4. Rebecca Whorf dau. of Reuben and Lucinda Ryder died Aug. 21, 1836 aged 21 mo. 3 dys.

    5. Charles Francis son of Reuben and Lucinda Ryder died July 28, 1849 ae 4 years 2 months 14 days

    6. Mary Emma dtr. of Benjamin and Lucinda H. Cole died Sept. 2, 1855 at 3 months 3 days

CEMETERY NUMBER TWO - OLD SECTION

LOT #413 (continued)

    7. George W. Carson May 9, 1824 - April 11, 1895
       Mary A. Carson April 26, 1830 - Nov. 11, 1907

LOT #414 -- 4 Stones

    1. Hannah wife of John Atwood died Nov. 12, 1878 ae 85 yr. 1 m. 27 days

    2. Reuben Wareham died Jan. 23, 1901 age 84 years 4 months 29 days

    3. Ruth wife of Reuben Wareham died May 23, 1884 age 64 years 7 months 29 days

    4. Lizzie (no date)

LOT #415 -- 1 Stone

    1. Mother - Loies E. Handy June 7, 1869 - April 21, 1918
       Father - Moses H. March 26, 1857 - Nov. 16, 1929

LOT #416 -- 1 Stone

    1. Bertha A. wife of John A. Edwards 1878-1910

LOT #417 -- 1 Stone - 2 Markers

    1. Joseph F. (Souza) 1886-1938
       Kate B. 1886-1947

    2. Joseph E. (Souza) 1919-1972

    3. Francis Souza - Mass. Pvt. Quartermaster Corp. World War II Aug. 3, 1926 - Dec. 27, 1967

LOT #417B -- 1 Stone

    1. Joseph Borges 1884-1959
       Mary P. 1892-(not cut)

LOT #418 -- 1 Stone - 1 Marker

    1. Peter Morrill 1830-1901
       Catherine Myles Morrill 1837-1909

    2. Joseph L. Morrill died March 8, 1918

LOT #418A - New Lot - No Stone

LOT #419 -- 1 Stone

    1. Front: Charles W. Burkett 1844-1916 Co. C 56th Mass. Vol.
            GAR
          Mary 1845-1918

      Rear: James W. Allen 1864-1931
             Alice A. 1875-1943
             Charles W. 1902-1914

CEMETERY NUMBER TWO - OLD SECTION

LOT #419 (continued)

   James B. 1905-1977
   his wife Jane J. 1905-1976

LOT #419A - New Lot - No Stone

LOT #419B -- 1 Stone

 1. Jose B. Alemany Feb. 13, 1895 - July 15, 1951

LOT #420 -- 1 Stone

 1. James H. Blake 1831-1907
  Reliance P. Blake 1830-1902

LOT #420A -- 2 Stones

 1. Joshua A. Hopkins 1835-1901
  Betsey Hopkins 1836-1927

 2. Lottie M. Hopkins 1869-1914

LOT #421 -- 1 Stone - 1 Marker

 1. Robert N. Fisher 1868-1923

 2. Robert Newton 1923-1928

LOT #422 -- 1 Stone - 1 Marker

 1. Reuben N. Freeman 1871-1943

 2. Leroy L. twin son of Reuben and Bertha Freeman born July 30, 1899 (died) ae 2 months

LOT #423 -- No Stone

LOT #424 -- 1 Stone

 1. William Welch (no date) (VR: died May 26, 1876 ae 56 years)
  Mary A. Welch (no date) (VR: died Jan. 31, 1907 ae 74 yrs.)
  Mary A. Bowley (no date) (VR: died Dec. 21, 1929 ae 77 yrs.)
  Annie S. Bemis (no date) (VR: died Sept. 11, 1952 ae 84 yrs)

LOT #425 -- 1 Stone - 2 Markers

 1. John T. Logan 1846-1886
  Margaret his wife 1845-1916

 2. Father - John Adam Logan 1873-1916
  Mother - Katie May 1876-1950

 3. Agnes F. Foster 1877-1945
  Leonard J. Foster 1879-1942

LOT #426 -- 1 Boulder - 1 Footstone

 1. PINCKNEY (VR: Lewis B. Pinckney died Nov. 10, 1932 ae 72 years 8 mos. 16 days and his son Lawrence Bates

CEMETERY NUMBER TWO - OLD SECTION

LOT #426 (continued)

    Pinckney died Sept. 10, 1962 ae 78 yrs. 3 mos. 5 days. Both buried this lot)

  2. Footstone - Mother and Sister
    (VR: Nora Dolliver Pinckney widow of Lewis Pinckney died Nov. 7, 1952 ae 94 yrs. 3 mos. 9 days. Adda H. Pinckney Day sister of Lewis B. Pinckney born Sept. 23, 1860 - no death record found)

LOT #427 -- 1 Stone

  1. Father - Charles Freeman Jan. 21, 1816 - Oct. 7, 1888
    Mother - Sally Freeman July 10, 1822 - April 7, 1899

LOT #428 -- No Stone

LOT #429 -- 1 Stone

  1. Walter Osborne son of J. (John) W. and C. (Catherine) L. Lee died July 2, 1880 aged 23 years 10 months 18 days

LOT #430 -- No Stone

LOT #431 -- 1 Stone - 1 Marker

  1. Capt. George R. O'Neil 1843-1916
    Margaret A. S. O'Neil 1852-1938
    Martha E. Tasha 1884-1959
    James Tasha 1879-1963

  2. Leroy C. Tasha 1912-1916

LOT #432 -- 10 Stones

  1. Father - James Cowing died Feb. 15, 1873 ae 75 years 28 days
    Mother - Rebecca wife of James Cowing died Jan. 9, 1881 ae 78 years 5 months 21 days

  2. Joseph A. son of James and Rebecca Cowing died Nov. 1, 1837 aged 1 year

  3. Rebecca daughter of James and Rebecca Cowing died Oct. 20, 1841 age 19

  4. Joseph E. died Sept. 1, 1842 son of James and Rebecca Cowing age 8 months 14 days

  5. James E. son of James and Rebecca Cowing died Aug. 13, 1848 aged 19 years

  6. Henry W. Cowing died Jan. 3, 1893 aged 59 years 10 months 20 days

  7. Betsey W. wife of Henry W. Cowing Aug. 12, 1834 - March 2, 1913

  8. Mary wife of William E. Cowing June 4, 1865 - June 21, 1892

CEMETERY NUMBER TWO - OLD SECTION

LOT #432 (continued)

    9. Carrie A. Cowing 1862-1956

   10. Maybelle Jan. 8, 1906 - Feb. 12, 1908 daughter of William D. and Bessie W. Birge

LOT #433 -- 1 Stone - 3 Markers - 3 Footstones

    1. Capt. Antone J. Silva 1866-1911 lost at sea
       Mary L. his wife 1873-1935
       Albert L. 1892-1912
       Infant (no date) (VR: died 1889)

    2. Footstone - Mother

    3. Footstone - Albert

    4. Footstone - Baby

    5. Joseph A. Pacheco Dec. 5, 1910 - March 11, 1975

    6. Marjorie F. Pacheco March 31, 1914 - (not cut)

    7. Frank Silva - Mass. Surf. U. S. C. G. WWI & WWII
       Sept. 28, 1894 - July 11, 1955

LOT #434 -- No Stone

LOT #435 -- 1 Stone

    1. Jos. P. Bickers - Co. 50 Mass. Mil, Inf. (no date)
      (VR: died Dec. 30, 1924 ae 89 years 2 months 11 days)

LOT #436 -- 1 Stone - 2 Markers

    1. Daniel L. Suker born Dec. 12, 1862 died March 31, 1929
       Annie E. Suker born Aug. 12, 1862 died Nov. 19, 1963

    2. Hilda (no date) (VR: died June 19, 1973 ae 79 years 4 months 21 days)

    3. Olive (no date)

LOT #437 -- 1 Stone

    1. Archibald McCurdy 1828-1904
       Hannah M. his wife 1827-1910

LOT #438 -- 2 Stones

    1. Father - Samuel S. Smith died Aug. 6, 1888 age 71

    2. Charles W. Dyer 1866-1924
       his wife Gertrude R. 1867-1909
       Her sister Louise B. Smith 1863-1922

LOT #439 -- 2 Stones

    1. Sarah D. Pennock 1829-1911

CEMETERY NUMBER TWO - OLD SECTION

LOT #439 (continued)

    2. John M. Carnes 1818-1911
       Eunice M. Carnes 1818-1898

LOT #440 -- 3 Stones - 4 Markers

    1. Amasa Taylor 1824-1901

    2. Rebecca wife of Amasa Taylor died July 1, 1854 aged 30 years 7 mos. 20 das.

    3. Hannah M. Taylor 1824-1913

    4. Rebecca A. wife of Benjamin F. Smith born 1857 died 1884

    5. S. (Stephen) Churchill Smith 1884-1913

    6. Lucinda T. Fisher 1867-1952

    7. Louise A. Ullian 1902-1938

LOT #441 -- 2 Stones - 2 Footstones

    1. Front: Caleb Fisher 1823-1906
            Ann J. Fisher 1826-1887
            Jane M. Fisher 1885-1971

       Rear: Spencer V. Fisher 1853-1934
            Annie C. Fisher 1861-1936
            Irving S. Fisher 1895-1952

    2. Footstone - Mother

    3. Footstone - Father

    4. Mother - Ann J. wife of Caleb Fisher died Oct. 8, 1887 at 61 years 9 months 2 days

LOT #442 -- 2 Stones - 1 Marker

    1. W. L. (William L.) Baker - Ensign U. S. Navy (no date) (VR: died Feb. 8, 1880 ae 39 years 11 months 4 days)

    2. Anna Baker Brown 1858-1934

    3. Emma Baker Keyes died Oct. 26, 1918

LOT #443 -- No Stone

LOT #444 -- No Stone

LOT #445 -- 1 Stone

    1. Frank Poulsen - Mass. CHF Bos'n Mate USNRF (died Nov. 22, 1925)

LOT #446 -- 3 Markers

    1. #11 (VR: Nov. 27, 1898, Unknown, age 33, frozen to death in rigging of Schooner Lester A. Lewis, Provincetown Harbor)

CEMETERY NUMBER TWO - OLD SECTION

LOT #446 (continued)

    2. #32 (VR: Nov. 27, 1898, Unknown, age 35 years, drowned off Cape Cod from Steamer Portland. Body found in Herring Cove)

    3. #33 (VR: Nov. 27, 1898, Unknown, no age given, drowned off Cape Cod from Steamer Portland)

LOT #447 -- 3 Stones

    1. Anthony (surname)

    2. Grandma (VR: Mary Anthony Sears died March 4, 1924 ae 84 years 5 months 4 days)

    3. Aunt (VR: Robenia Florence Anthony died Sept. 29, 1968 ae 89 years 3 months 24 days)

LOT #448 -- 1 Stone

    1. John Randall died June 26, 1850 aged 32 years
       John Cady died Jan. 26, 1883 aged 76 years

LOT #449 -- Tomb (4 Plaques inside)

    1. Left Top: Edwin Atkins Grozier born Sept. 12, 1859 died May 9, 1924

    2. Left Middle: Alice Goodell Grozier born July 14, 1864 died Jan. 26, 1943

    3. Right Top: Richard Grozier born Jan. 12, 1887 died June 19, 1946

    4. Right Middle: Margaret Murphy Grozier b. 1899 d. 1933

LOT #450 -- Tomb - 1 Stone over tomb

    1. John Young 1811-1855
       Maria Young 1816-1889
       Enos N. Young 1836-1914
       Lydia A. Young 1839-1914
       Nathaniel L. Young 1840-1899
       Nellie Young 1846-1902
       John Young Jr. 1847-1872
       Seviah S. Young 1855-1855

LOT #451 -- Tomb - Inscribed on front

    1. Lewis Jerauld 1818-1873
       His wife Hannah Small 1817-1893
       Faustina A. (Jerauld) 1847-1866

    (Ed. note: Since there are 4 coffins in the tomb it is possible that Lewis Jerauld's first wife, Tabitha Higgins Jerauld who died Sept. 1, 1841, is interred here)

CEMETERY NUMBER TWO - OLD SECTION

LOT #452 -- Tomb - Inscribed front - 1 Stone above

1. Front of Tomb: Capt. Jonathan Nickerson Aug. 19, 1781 - Jan. 25, 1871
    Sally (Miller) Nickerson his wife Sept. 22, 1785 - Feb. 4, 1876
    Their Children:
    Amos Oct. 1, 1804 lost at sea Oct. 29, 1823
    Jonathan Dec. 27, 1807 - Feb. 3, 1873
    Franklin March 22, 1810 - Nov. 11, 1828
    Stephen Peck Feb. 26, 1816 - Jan. 6, 1843
    Josiah March 18, 1821 - April 24, 1849

    Rebecca Dyer (Watkins) wife of Jonathan Jr. July 2, 1810 - Jan. 11, 1873

    Children of Jonathan Jr. and Rebecca
    Rebecca Franklin first wife of Seth Lewis Nickerson Oct. 26, 1829 - Jan. 11, 1853

    Franklin May 5, 1833 - June 18, 1835
    John Lothrop July 13, 1839 - Jan. 18, 1845

    Sarah Nickerson daughter of John L. and Sarah (Nickerson) Lothrop Jan. 19, 1843 - Jan. 24, 1847

2. Stone Front: Rebecca F. wife of Seth L. Nickerson died Jan. 11, 1853 aged 23 years 2 months 15 days

   Stone Right: Franklin died June 18, 1835 aged 2 years 1 month
                  John L. died Jan. 15, 1845 aged 5 years 6 months
                  Sons of Jonathan and Rebecca D. Nickerson Jr

LOT #453 -- Tomb - 2 Stones in front of tomb

1. Front: Betsey N. Cook Jan. 30, 1885 aged 66 years 4 months 6 days
          Philip Cook March 9, 1893 aged 82 years 10 months 11 days
          Eliza Cook Smith Jan. 26, 1914 aged 70 years 14 days

   Rear: Elisha F. Cook Nov. 29, 1928 aged 82 years 6 months 7 days
          Hannah R. Cook May 27, 1942 aged 87 years 9 months 12 days
          daughter Annie E. Snow born Jan. 1, 1882 died April 23, 1966 aged 84 years 4 months 23 days

CEMETERY NUMBER TWO - OLD SECTION

LOT #453 (continued)

    2. Front: Eben S. Smith Aug. 8, 1873 aged 66 years 5 months 8 days
              Adeline Smith Feb. 11, 1880 aged 73 years 8 months 16 days
              A. Eloise Gurney March 20, 1862 aged 26 years 10 months 9 days
              Eben S. Smith Nov. 4, 1833 aged $28\frac{1}{2}$ months
              Eben H. Smith March 22, 1849 aged 23 months

       Right: Cynthia P. C. Smith Aug. 10, 1876 aged 42 years 27 days
              Amasa Smith 1832-1902
              Fred Walton Smith Feb. 24, 1864 aged 6 years 3 months

       Rear: Infant son of L. H. & A. Eloise Gurney March 12, 1862
             Infant dtr. of Isaac N. and Eliza F. Keith Oct. 9, 1866
             Infant son of Raymond and Susan S. Ellington December 2, 1870

       Left: Raymond Ellington Adj't 3rd Mass. Cav. Vols. March 5, 1892 aged 51 years 4 months 9 days
            Susan S. Ellington Feb. 7, 1908 - 69 years 19 days

LOT #454 -- 1 Stone

    1. Front: Ephraim Ryder 1818-1891
              Sally H. 1822-1856
              Mehitable 1829-1907

       Right: George F. Johnson 1853-1922
              Sarah Ney 1860-1944
              Carrie R. Walker 1864-1923

       Rear: Ephraim T. 1849 (VR: ae 2 years 2 months 13 days)
             Infant 1849 (VR: ae 1 day)
             Allie 1858 (VR: ae 1 year)
             Mary E. 1862-1864
             Willie M. 1867 (VR: ae 8 mos. 9 days)
             Mabel 1873 (VR: ae 9 mos. 23 days)
             Infant 1875 (VR: ae 2 days)
             Lena B. 1868-1905
             (Children of Ephraim Ryder)

       Left: Nathaniel Ryder 1774-1850
            Martha 1775-1847
            Alphena C. 1859-1925

LOT #455 -- 1 Stone

    1. Priscilla Maria died May 14, 1843 ae 2 years 3 months 7 days
       Nancy Ellen died March 10, 1848 ae 4 days

CEMETERY NUMBER TWO - OLD SECTION

LOT #455 (continued)

    Children of Heman M. and Priscilla F. Smith

LOT #456 -- 3 Stones - 1 Footstone

1. Capt. Isaiah Young died on his passage from Cuba to N. Y. April 2, 1847 ae 43 years 8 months

2. Mary Young born March 3, 1808 died April 15, 1892

3. Louisa daughter of Isaiah and Mary Young died April 26, 1833 ae 3½ months

4. I. Y.

LOT #457 -- 3 Stones

1. Elisha Young died March 19, 1873 aged 67 years 9 months 16 days

2. Betsy Young died April 14, 1873 aged 65 years 4 months 27 days

3. Henry Young son of Elisha and Betsy Young died Dec. 7, 1869 aged 25 years 10 months 17 days

LOT #458 -- 2 Stones

1. Jonathan E. Smith 1807-1870
   Clarissa D. Smith 1815-1876

2. Clara Osborn died Aug. 12, 1849 ae 2 yrs. 5 mos.
   An infant son died Sept. 10, 1848 aged 2 weeks
   An infant son born and died Dec. 15, 1849
   An infant daughter died Aug. 20, 1851 aged 8 days
   Children of Jona. E. and Clarissa Smith

LOT #459 -- 3 Stones

1. Mr. Aquilla Higgins died Jan. 3, 1847 ae 78 years

2. Mrs. Tamsin wife of Aquila (sic) died May 3, 1844 ae 74 years

3. Mrs. Lydia A. wife of Haskel P. Higgins died June 13, 1850 ae 25 years 4 months

LOT #460 -- 4 Stones

1. Alexander Manuel died Nov. 11, 1880 (rest of stone broken)

2. Mrs. Philena wife of Alexander Manuel died July 25, 1846 ae 34 years

3. Mrs. Tamsin wife of Alexander Manuel died Nov. 27, 1872 ae 73 years 1 month

4. Alexander son of Alexander and Philena Manuel died Jan. 6, 1849 ae 3 years 6½ months

CEMETERY NUMBER TWO - OLD SECTION

LOT #461 -- 1 Stone

    1. Mr. Levi Lurton died Sept. 24, 1847 ae 63 years 6 months

LOT #462 -- 1 Stone

    1. Jesse Forrest died March 4, 1850 aged 25 years 3 mos. 9 days

LOT #463 -- 1 Monument - 2 Stones - 7 Footstones

    1. Monument Front: Solomon Bangs died July 4, 1874 ae 83 years 22 days
                        Betsy wife of Solomon Bangs died Oct. 10, 1849 ae 59 years
                        Patty wife of Solomon Bangs died Sept. 4, 1872 ae 83 years 1 month 15 days

       Monument Right: Perez Bangs April 18, 1847 - Aug. 30, 1899
                       Julia Bangs Dec. 25, 1848 - Oct. 4, 1907

       Monument Rear: Solomon Bangs Sept. 2, 1821 - Nov. 19, 1905
                      Rosilla Bangs Oct. 27, 1823 - Aug. 5, 1908

       Monument Left: Perez Bangs died Jan. 15, 1848 on board Brig Samuel Cook, buried on Mono Island, West Indies aged 23 years

    2. Footstone - Father - Solomon ae 83 yrs.

    3. Footstone - Mother - Patty ae 83 yrs.

    4. Footstone - Mother - Betsy ae 59 yrs.

    5. Footstone - Perez ae 52 yrs.

    6. Footstone - Julia

    7. Footstone - Solomon

    8. Footstone - Rosilla

    9. Husband - William B. Bangs 1866-1923

    10. Wife - Jane M. Bangs 1874-1935

LOT #464 -- 2 Stones

    1. Mr. Eldredge Smith died August 18, 1849 ae 65 years

    2. Mrs. Experience wife of Eldredge Smith died August 8, 1849 ae 65 years

LOT #465 -- 1 Stone

    1. Daniel W. Atwood 1846-1914
       Lydia A. his wife 1846-1914
       Freddie M. 1873-1876

LOT #466 -- 1 Stone

    1. John R. Smith 1833-1864 GAR Veteran buried in Phila.

CEMETERY NUMBER TWO - OLD SECTION

LOT #466 (continued)
    Deborah P. 1839-1934
    John R. Jr. 1859-1945

LOT #467 -- No Stone

LOT #468 -- 1 Stone - 2 Footstones

1. Mr. Lewis P. Morgan died Feb. 19, 1875 aged 72 years 3 months 20 days

2. Lewis

3. Mother (VR: Possibly Rebeckah Atkins Morgan, wife of Lewis P. Morgan - no date of death)

LOT #469 -- 1 Stone

1. Colin MacDonald 1846-1887
Isabel his wife 1844-1916
John C. 1884-1885
Annie J. Campbell 1868-1903
Katherine I. (Campbell) (no date) (VR: died Dec. 3, 1903 ae 1 yr. 8 mos. 10 dys.)
Mary C. Corrigan 1873-1913

LOT #470 -- 3 Stones

1. Sally wife of James Sparks died Jan. 4, 1873 ae 70 years 4 days

2. Reuben G. Sparks died March 5, 1888 ae 65 years 7 months 6 days

3. Cynthia H. wife of Capt. James T. Sparks died Nov. 4, 1852 aged 24 years 4 months 11 days

LOT #471 -- 4 Stones

1. Mr. Washington Case died Sept. 20, 1843 ae 66 years

2. Mrs. Susan widow of Washington Case died March 22, 1848 ae 70 years 7 months

3. Mr. Jesse S. Case died April 30, 1848 ae 28 years 6 months

4. Washington Case died Dec. 4, 1880 aged 64 years 1 mo. 19 days

LOT #472 -- 8 Stones - 2 Footstones

1. Joseph Swarez (Fisher), Grand Canaria 1841-1910 his wife Mary S. Atkins 1852-1915

2. Footstone - Joseph

3. Footstone - Mary

4. Father - Elisha B. Atkins Nov. 6, 1812 - Nov. 27, 1870

CEMETERY NUMBER TWO - OLD SECTION

LOT #472 (continued)

5. Mother - Mary wife of Elisha B. Atkins June 9, 1812 - Dec. 28, 1870

6. Alzina E. Atkins Nov. 1, 1837 - Dec. 6, 1907

7. Alfred L. Mayo died May 25, 1872 ae 34 years

8. Mother - Elizabeth D. wife of Alfred L. Mayo July 8, 1840 - Feb. 25, 1898

9. Alfred A. Mayo 1870-1957

10. Henry P. son of Ellis H. and Clarissa Holmes died March 20, 1845 ae 5 wks. 4 ds. (Ed. note: Parents of Henry P. are buried at Hamilton Cemetery)

LOT #473 -- 1 Monument - 3 Stones - 2 Footstones

1. Monument Front: Jona. C. Kilburn died 1861 ae 72
   Pricilla wife of Jona. C. Kilburn died 1837 ae 45 years
   Cinderella H. 1837-1839

   Monument Right: Levi A. Kilburn ae 30 years
   Wm. G. Kilburn ae 28 years
   Charles H. Kilburn ae 17 years 9 months
   Were lost at sea Oct. 1858

   Monument Left: E. (Edward) J. Kilburn 1820-1897
   Abby H. his wife 1820-1848

2. Edward H. son of Edward J. and Abby H. Kilburn died Sept. 29, 1848 ae 16½ months

3. James H. son of Edward J. and Mary S. Kilburn died Aug. 31, 1855 ae 3 months

4. Mary S. Kilburn 1831-1910

5. Footstone - Mother

6. Footstone - Father

LOT #474 -- 9 Stones

1. Father - John C. P. Harvender died March 31, 1897 ae 81 years 5 months 29 days
   Mother - Sarah A. wife of John C. P. Harvender died July 31, 1891 ae 68 years 8 months 4 days

2. Sarah Y. daughter of John C. P. and Sarah A. Harvender died SEpt. 23, 1842 ae 13 months

3. Lucy A. daughter of John C. P. and Sarah A. Harvender died Nov. 8, 1847 ae 4 years 5 months 14 days

4. George S. H. son of John C. P. and Sarah A. Harvender died Nov. 13, 1861 ae 17 mos. 10 days

5. William T. son of John C. P. and Sarah A. Harvender

CEMETERY NUMBER TWO - OLD SECTION

LOT #474 (continued)

    died August 30, 1851 ae 2 yrs. 2 mos.

  6. Hatty W. daughter of John C. P. and Sarah A. Harvender died Feb. 26, 1858 ae 4 years 2 months 10 days

  7. Father - John H. Harvender died May 20, 1857 aged 67 years 1 month 9 days
    Mother - Deborah C. Harvender died Dec. 31, 1861 ae 64 years 8 months 19 days

  8. Mr. William W. Harvender died April 27, 1848 ae 21 years 6 months

  9. William W. son of Wm. W. and Sophronia Harvender died Aug. 24, 1848 ae 3 weeks

LOT #475 -- 1 Stone - 3 Footstones

  1. Front: Capt. Elisha S. Burch died Nov. 21, 1893 aged 70 years 11 months 15 days
    Elizabeth W. Burch died Sept. 23, 1905 ae 74 years 7 days

    Right: Lizzie daughter of Elisha S. and Elizabeth Burch died Jan. 30, 1858 ae 3 years 6 months

  2. Footstone - Mother

  3. Footstone - Father

  4. Lizzie daughter of Elisha and Elizabeth Burch died Jan. 30, 1858 ae 3 yrs. 6 ms.

LOT #476 -- 2 Stones

  1. William A. Doyle 1828-1903
    Lydia F. Doyle 1835-1912
    Laura May 1880-1912

  2. Maria S. daughter of William A. and Lydia T. (sic) Doyle died Sept. 30, 1854 ae 3 months

LOT #477 -- 2 Stones

  1. Jonathan H. Little 1838-1907

  2. Mary A. wife of George H. Little born Nov. 1, 1817 died Aug. 16, 1848
    George H. Little died March 14, 1858 aged 51 years

LOT #478 -- 1 Stone

  1. Susan E. daughter of Jonathan H. and Susan Hill died Feb. 3, 1844 ae 1 year 6 mos. 11 days

LOT #479 -- 1 Stone

  1. Samuel A. only son of William and Jerusha Howe died March 22, 1842 ae 1 year 6 mos. 22 days

CEMETERY NUMBER TWO - OLD SECTION

LOT #480 -- 7 Stones

    1. Capt. David Brown died Oct. 2, 1850 ae 75

    2. Atkins Brown died July 3, 1878 aged 71 years 6 months 21 days

    3. Lydia K. Brown 1810-1906

    4. Eunice H. dtr. of Atkins and Sally Brown born July 17, 1833 died July 28, 1834

    5. Hannah S. daughter of Atkins and Lydia Brown died Aug. 24, 1848 ae 2 years 15 days

    6. Martha E. daughter of Atkins and Lydia Brown born Jan. 17, 1851 died Aug. 25, 1853

    7. Hannah S. daughter of Atkins and Lydia Brown died July 28, 1861 ae 12 years 11 months 6 days

LOT #481 -- No Stone

LOT #482 -- 2 Stones - 1 Footstone

    1. Father - Capt. Atkins Smith died Dec. 20, 1876 ae 52 yrs. 5 mos. 24 days

    2. Mother - Sabra C. wife of Capt. Atkins Smith died May 19, 1870 ae 46 years 10 months 9 days

    3. Footstone - Maria (no date)

LOT #483 -- 2 Stones - 1 Burial no stone

    1. Jesse Gaspar 1858-1929
       Rosa 1858-1925
       Jesse 1886-1926
       Joseph (no date)
       Louis (no date) (VR: died 1900)

    2. William J. Gaspie Mass. Pvt. 1cl. 301 Engrs. 76 Div. Oct. 19, 1938

    3. (no stone) John Joseph Gaspie died July 3, 1961 ae 76 years 10 months 25 days

LOT #484 -- Tomb - Inscribed on front

    Left: William Matheson 1828-1896
         Mary 1833-1926
         Murdock 1869-1869
         Lizzie W. 1872-1957
         Jessie T. 1865-1962
         Harold F. Van Ummerson 1896-1963
         Jessie P. 1892-1968

    Right: Rufus M. Paine 1885-1953
          Clara B. 1874-1948
          Oren O. 1851-1891 Lost at sea

CEMETERY NUMBER TWO - OLD SECTION

LOT #484 (continued)

        Georgie D. 1859-1931
        Robert MacMurray 1858-1899
        Mary S. 1862-1913

LOT #485 -- No Stone

LOT #486 -- 1 Stone

  1. Mother - Rebecca Cook Aug. 29, 1805 - Sept. 5, 1896
    (VR: widow of Charles Reed, married (2) Elisha Cook)

    Charles Reed lost at sea April 1837

LOT #487 -- 1 Stone

  1. Moses S. Turner 1840-1925
    Nora Costelloe his wife 1839-1888
    Daniel C. 1871-1893
    Georgie (no date)
    Bessie (no date) (VR: died April 21, 1881 ae 8 mos. 24 dys.)
    Nora (no date) (VR: died May 18, 1874 ae 7 yrs. 9 mos. 8 ds)

LOT #488 -- 1 Stone - 1 Marker - 1 Footstone

  1. Edward B. Cook died at sea July 11, 1868
    ae 23 years 8 months 28 days

  2. John C. son of Myrick S. and Elizabeth Cook died
    June 23, 1843 aged 13 months 12 days

  3. Footstone - C. H. S. (Unidentified)

LOT #489 -- 2 Stones

  1. Isaac D. Knowles born in Barrington, Nova Scotia, Nov. 11,
    1829 died in Provincetown Sept. 10, 1853

  2. Rebecca H. daughter of John and Rebecca Small died
    Jan. 26, 1859 ae 28 years

LOT #490 -- 1 Stone

  1. Front: William Clarke 1799-1875
          Tabitha his wife 1800-1842
          Mary P. 1822-1839

     Right: Daisy Anne wife of I. A. Small (no date)

     Rear: William Clarke Jr. 1827-1869
           Sabrina S. his wife 1833-1914
           Willie P. 1858-1860
           Willie W. 1862-1863
           Mamie M. 1853-1878

     Left: Isaiah A. Small 1868-1945
           Carrie W. Small 1865-1929
           Isaiah A. Small Jr. 1904-1924

CEMETERY NUMBER TWO - OLD SECTION

LOT #491 -- 1 Stone

    1. Mary J. Hudson died Jan. 6, 1872 aged 36 years 3 months 11 days

LOT #492 -- 1 Stone

    1. Rover (Unknown - no date)

LOT #493 -- 3 Stones

    1. Mother - Louise Morris 1863-1943

    2. Wife - Mary G. Brazil 1862-1927

    3. Husband - Joseph Gomes 1851-1899

LOT #494 -- No Stone

    (Cemetery records indicate William P. Connor owner of this lot)

LOT #495 -- No Stone

LOT #496 -- 1 Stone

    1. James T. Jordan 1816-1880
       Johanna H. his wife 1816-1896
       James T. Jordan Jr. 1854-1899
       Annie J. his wife 1855-1899

LOT #497 -- 1 Stone

    1. Mary daughter of Michael and Mary Ready died Aug. 16, 1863 aged 6 weeks

LOT #498 -- 11 Stones

    1. Father - Joseph F. Smith died Dec. 13, 1863 ae 45 years
       Mother - Tamsin wife of Joseph F. Smith died June 1, 1887 ae 62 years

    2. Elizabeth daughter of Joseph F. and Mary Smith died Aug. 11, 1853 ae 10 months 10 days

    3. George son of Joseph F. and Mary Smith died Oct. 21, 1855 ae 8 months 17 days

    4. Phebe E. daughter of Joseph F. and Tamsin Smith died Nov. 12, 1886 aged 24 years

    5. Maria daughter of Joseph and Maria Silva born May 21, 1853 died Aug. 29, 1853

    6. Cinnie dtr. of John C. and Mary J. Silva died Feb. 6, 1889 ae 21 years 7 months

    7. Mother - Mary Julia Sylva 1850-1936

    8. Hannah E. wife of Manuel E. Edmunds died March 11, 1887 ae 30 years 3 months 26 days

CEMETERY NUMBER TWO - OLD SECTION

LOT #498 (continued)

    9. Lillie died Nov. 2, 1891 ae 13 years 2 months daughter of Hannah and M. E. Edmunds
       M. E. Edmunds died at sea 1888

    10. Mary daughter of John and Mary Murry died March 14, 1853 ae 2 years 9 months 4 days

    11. Frank A. Rogers 1870-1946
       Olivia S. Rogers 1872-1954

LOT #499 -- 2 Stones

    1. Joseph Brown 1829-1914
       Rose 1837-1905
       Edward 1870-1936
       Joseph 1864-(no date)
       Frank 1866-(no date) (VR: Frank Brown son of Joseph and Rose Brown died Jan. 20, 1954 ae 89 years 1 month 13 days - Surfman U.S.C.G.)

    2. Thomas son of Thomas and Christina Converse died Sept. 12, 1853 ae 13 months 12 days

LOT #500 -- No Stone

LOT #501 -- 1 Stone

    1. Father - Richard Barnett died Jan. 18, 1885 aged 75 yrs. 5 mos. 17 days
       Mother - Hannah Barnett 1828-1918

LOT #502 -- 1 Stone

    1. Capt. John Pettingill lost at sea Sept. 1857 aged 35 years 3 months
       also, Belinda N. his wife age 31 years
       also, Two children - Thomas I. aged 8 years 7 months and Marshall C. aged 4 years 2 months
       (Ed. note: All lost at sea Sept. 1857)

LOT #503 -- 2 Stones

    1. Capt. John W. Iverson born Oct. 27, 1823 died Dec. 28, 1850

    2. My wife - Susan F. wife of Capt. Thatcher Rich died Aug. 11, 1862 aged 29 years 7 months

LOT #504 -- 2 Stones

    1. In memory of John Small who died April 19, 1861 aged 71 years 8 months 21 days

    2. Mercy wife of John Small died Aug. 18, 1873 ae 76 years 2 months 28 days

CEMETERY NUMBER TWO - OLD SECTION

LOT #505 -- 2 Stones

1. Almira wife of Elisha Cook born June 27, 1804 died March 9, 1848

2. Thomas S. son of Elisha and Almira Cook died July 22, 1825 ae 10 months 22 days

LOT #506 -- 1 Stone

1. Our Brother - William H. Carr born Sept. 9, 1858 died Sept. 3, 1905

LOT #507 -- 8 Stones

1. Isaiah G. Ward died May 12, 1880 ae 69 years 5 months 7 days

2. Betsey Ward died Jan. 22, 1894 ae 80 years 11 months 5 days

3. Isaiah H. son of Isaiah G. and Betsey Ward died April 20, 1859 ae 7 years 21 days

4. Henry F. son of Isaiah G. and Jerusha Ward died April 14, 1859 aged 18 years 2 months 9 days

5. Jacob C. Williams died March 2, 1866 aged 61 years 6 months 23 days

6. Mrs. Mary wife of Jacob C. Williams died Dec. 25, 1855 ae 46 years 11 months

7. Andrew T. (Williams) died Aug. 20, 1834 ae 3 years 4 months
Laura A. Cook (Williams) died May 8, 1843 ae 3 years 6 months

8. Abigail Rich died April 25, 1855 age 84 years 7 months
David Rich lost at sea April 1819 ae 51 years
David Rich Jr. son of David and Abigail Rich lost at sea April 1819 ae 17 years 7 months

LOT #508 -- Tomb

1. "In sweet remembrance of 'Little Pet', Annie F., child of Edward E. and Zerrie A. Small, who fell asleep June 4, 1882, aged 9 years 8 months 21 days"

LOT #509 -- No Stone

(Cemetery records indicate the owner of this lot to be Nettie C. Dutra)

LOT #510 -- No Stone

LOT #511 -- 1 Stone

1. Manuel Francis Silva born in 1852 died March 17, 1871

CEMETERY NUMBER TWO - OLD SECTION

LOT #512 -- 2 Stones

    1. Peter Bennett (no date) (VR: died Oct. 15, 1912 ae 77 yrs.) his wife Honora and family (no dates) (VR: Honora died Sept. 11, 1896 ae 66 years)

    2. Mary Louisa Bennett died Aug. 7, 1858 ae 3 yrs. 7 mos.

LOT #513 -- No Stone

LOT #514 -- 2 Stones - 5 Markers

    1. Thomas J. Lopes 1840-1924
       His wife Louisa A. Lopes 1844-1926

    2. Harold E. Cowing 1886-1922 (VR: Husband of Olivia Lopes)

    3. Rita (Lopes) (VR: died 1946 ae 77 yrs. 1 month 12 days)

    4. Tom (Thomas J. Lopes Jr.) (VR: died 1965 ae 82 yrs. 1 mo. 26 days)

    5. Elizabeth (Lopes) (VR: died 1961 ae 90 years 8 days)

    6. Julia (Lopes) 1866-1916

    7. Julia A. (Lopes) (VR: 1873-1959)

LOT #515 -- 1 Stone

    1. Dennis Scannell Co. F 3rd Mass. Cavalry (no date)

LOT #516 -- 1 Stone

    1. Edward Sweeney March 16, 1813 - June 16, 1889
       Catherine Sweeney Jan. 18, 1809 - Jan. 18, 1894

LOT #517 -- 7 Stones

    1. Michael Welch died Nov. 16, 1881 ae 50 years 6 mos. 20 dys. Mary E. dtr. of Michael & Ellen Welch died Nov. 7, 1875 ae 21 years 2 mos. 7 days

    2. Ellen Barry wife of Michael Welch 1833-1906

    3. James son of Michael and Ellen Welch died March 15, 1863 ae 17 months

    4. Ella daughter of Michael and Ellen Welch died April 1, 1863 ae 6 years 5 months 8 days

    5. Jeney daughter of Michael and Ellen Welch died April 24, 1864 ae 5 yrs. 1 month 12 days

    6. Margaret daughter of Michael and Ellen Welch died May 5, 1864 ae 11 years 2 mos. 9 days

    7. John W. Welch son of Michael Welch 1866-1944

LOT #518 -- No Stone

CEMETERY NUMBER TWO - OLD SECTION

LOT #519 -- 1 Stone - 1 Footstone

1. Thomas Nympha of Liverpool, England, lost back of Provincetown from Schooner Narcissa of Cold Spring, N.Y. March 4, 1853 ae about 45

2. Footstone - T. N.

LOT #520 -- 2 Stones - 1 Footstone

1. Joseph son of Frank and Hannah Sears died Jan. 9, 1864 ae 1 year

2. Jesse son of Francis and Hannah Sears died Jan. 15, 1860 ae 18 months

3. Footstone - J. S.

LOT #521 -- No Stone

(Cemetery records indicate owner of lot to be Mary Silvey)

LOT #522 -- 1 Stone - 1 Footstone

1. John Mayhew died Nov. 16, 1868 aged 17 years

2. Footstone - J. M.

LOT #523 -- 1 Marker

1. Joseph Pimental 1850-1918

LOT #524 -- No Stone

LOT #525 -- 1 Stone

1. John Anthony 1867-1936
his wife Grace 1863-1915
Lucinda E. 1889-1973
Vilena M. Woods 1888-(living 1979)
Ann Mae Gove 1897-1964

LOT #526 -- 6 Stones - 7 Footstones

1. Ida Perie Avellar 1894-1931

2. Footstone - Baby (VR: John Bradshaw Avellar died May 28, 1927 ae 9 months 16 days)

3. Frank Perie died Jan. 26, 1920 age 60 years 3 months 10 days

4. Matilda wife of Frank Perie died May 2, 1911 age 45 years 8 mos. 4 days

5. Augustus S. Perie died Aug. 25, 1883 age 3 months

6. Emanuel Jones husband of Hannah Jones died Feb. 17, 1905 age 65 yrs.

7. Hannah wife of Emanuel Jones died Dec. 29, 1910 age 72 yrs.

CEMETERY NUMBER TWO - OLD SECTION

LOT #526 (continued)

    8. Footstone - M. P.

    9. Footstone - E. J.

   10. Footstone - H. J.

   11. Footstone - Baby (VR: Stephen Jones died Jan. 10, 1877 ae 2 months 3 days)

   12. Footstone - Baby (VR: Abbie Jones died April 7, 1872 ae 3 months 12 days)

   13. Footstone - Baby (VR: Stephen Jones died April 26, 1871 ae 2 years 11 months)

LOT #526A -- 3 Stones

    1. John S. Jones Jan. 18, 1873 - March 13, 1954

    2. Angie B. Jones May 22, 1876 - July 16, 1949

    3. Warren Edward Jones - Mass. Mach. Mate 2 Cl. U.S.N.R.F. Sept. 26, 1918

LOT #527 -- No Stone

LOT #527A -- 2 Markers

    1. Manuel S. Perry 1877-1958

    2. Lucy V. Perry 1877-1958

LOT #528 -- 1 Stone

    1. Lawrence Segura 1883-1949

LOT #528A -- 1 Stone - 2 Markers - 1 Footstone

    1. Capt. Antone Gaspar 1863-1950
       his wife Rita Gaspar 1863-1932

    2. Olga (Gaspar) (VR: died July 27, 1934 age 22)

    3. Mamie (Gaspar) (VR: died Feb. 13, 1892 ae 1 year 6 months 6 days)

    4. Footstone - Mother

LOT #529 -- 1 Stone - 1 Marker - 3 Footstones

    1. Joseph DeCosta died at sea Aug. 10, 1917
       his wife Amelia April 23, 1873 - Dec. 1, 1949
       Manuel July 10, 1906 - Nov. 24, 1955
       Josephine DeCosta Ferreira Sept. 9, 1912 - April 5, 1958

    2. Footstone - Mother

    3. Footstone - Brother

    4. Footstone - Josephine

CEMETERY NUMBER TWO - OLD SECTION

LOT #529 (continued)

    5. Joseph DeCosta - Mass. Cox. U.S.N.R.F. WWI Aug. 13, 1898 - July 30, 1969

LOT #530 -- 1 Monument - 3 Stones - 4 Footstones

    1. Monument Front: E. C. Parker 1871 (date Mon. erected)

        Monument Right: Edward C. Parker died May 4, 1867
                      aged 58 years 4 months 21 days
                Sarah wife of Edward C. Parker died
                      Aug. 22, 1869 aged 53 years 6 months

        Monument Left: Solomon Cook died July 24, 1868
                      aged 77 years 10 months 17 days
                Sally wife of Solomon Cook died Oct. 12,
                1871 ae 77 years 4 months

    2. Footstone - Mother

    3. Footstone - Father

    4. Footstone - Edward

    5. Footstone - Sarah

    6. Nathaniel Covell died July 8, 1867 aged 44 years 3 months 4 days

    7. Rachel W. Covell died March 5, 1889 aged 60 years 7 months 4 days

    8. Joshua D. son of Nathaniel and Rachel W. Covell died Nov. 1, 1866 aged 16 years 26 days

LOT #531 -- 4 Stones

    1. Mrs. Salome wife of Isaiah Atkins 2nd died Oct. 17, 1838 ae 33

    2. Caleb U. Atkins died March 29, 1907 aged 79 years 4 months 14 days

    3. Sophronie E. wife of Caleb U. Atkins died May 17, 1891 aged 57 years 11 months 17 days

    4. Frankie, Atherton, Charlie, children of Caleb U. and Sophronie E. Atkins (No record of deaths found)

LOT #532 -- Tomb

    1. Town of Provincetown

LOT #533 -- 2 Stones

    1. Charles H. Critchett died Feb. 27, 1887 ae 79 years 9 months 5 days

    2. Martha S. wife of Charles H. Critchett died March 25, 1870 ae 46 years 6 months 22 days

CEMETERY NUMBER TWO - OLD SECTION

LOT #534 -- Tomb

    1. Over Entrance: C. (Charles) B. Snow 1833-1903

        Left Side: Anna C. Lancy (Snow) 1836-1913
                          Charlena (Snow) 1857-1863
                          Charles H. (Snow) 1862-1863
                          Charlena (Snow) 1864-1880
                          A. Elnora (Snow) wife of D. B. Paine
                              1859-1882
                          D. B. Paine 1852-1927
                          Charles B. (Paine) 1873-1914

        Right Side: Effie Y. (Snow) Watson 1866-1886
                          E. (Emanuel) A. DeWager 1878-1953
                          Gertrude (Snow) his wife 1871-1948

LOT #535 -- Tomb

    1. Over Entrance: Capt. Samuel C. Small died March 10, 1882
                            aged 44 years

        Right Side: In memory of Capt. James Small aged 43 years
                          and sons, Joshua D. P. age 21 years; James
                          H. age 14 years who were lost at sea Sept.
                          16, 1846. The wife and mother, Betsey
                          Small died April 14, 1847 aged 42 years -
                          Broken hearted at her loss

        Left Side: Capt. Reuben G. Case died April 25, 1856
                            aged 46 years
                          Joan Hilliard wife of Reuben G. Case died
                          Jan. 10, 1881 aged 65 years

LOT #536 -- Tomb

    1. Over Entrance: J. Fuller
                            (VR: James Fuller died June 26, 1906 aged
                            84 years 3 months. Maria Frances Fuller
                            died May 11, 1906 aged 76 years 9 months
                            28 days, wife of James Fuller)

LOT #537 -- Tomb

    1. Over Entrance: Small - 1903
                            (VR: John W. Small died May 25, 1863
                            ae 53 years 5 months. His widow Rachel S.
                            Small died May 16, 1903 ae 86 years 1 month
                            16 days)

LOT #538 -- 1 Stone

    1. Mary wife of James Gorman died June 25, 1863 ae 35 years
       Michael son of Jas. and Mary Gorman died Sept. 1864
          ae 4 years

CEMETERY NUMBER TWO - OLD SECTION

LOTS #539
THRU #600 -- Numbers not assigned to lots

LOT #601 -- 1 Stone

    1. James Wingate Parr - "Painter" (no date)
       (VR: died at Eastham, Mass. June 22, 1969 age 46 years
       3 months 24 days)

LOTS #602
AND #603 -- 1 Marker with sculpture

    1. Nanno De Groot 1913-1963
       (Cem. records: died Dec. 26, 1963 ae 50 years 9 months
       3 days)

LOTS #604
AND #605 -- Numbers not assigned to lots

LOTS #606
#607-#608
AND #609 -- 1 Stone

    1. Kenneth Stubbs 1907-1967

INDEX TO PART ONE

PERSONS, PLACES & SHIPS BY LOT NUMBER

CEMETERY NUMBER TWO - OLD SECTION

ABBOT/ABBOTT Achsah S 202 Etta R 202 Frances M R 202 Francis 202 Francis O 202 George R 202 John W 202 Lawrence E 202 Melinda 202 Walter R 202
ADAMS Alfred 362 Alfred W 362 Clara J 181 Infant son 80 John 353 John W 279 Levina 353 Nathan 181 Rebecca R 279 Reuben A 160 Sally 353 Sarah Adaline 362 Sarah M 353 Zilpha 362
ALEMANY Jose B 419B
ALEXANDER Amanda M 268 Aurelia M 376 Caroline P 267 Elizabeth G 267 Isaac B 267 Margreatte S 267 Nancy A 267 Sarah W 267
ALLEN (see also ALLINE) Alice A 419 Charles W 419 James B 419 James W 419 Jane J 419 Sarah Maria (Parker) 246
ALLINE (see also ALLEN) Jane 172
ALLSTRUM Benjamin 175 Charles 175 Lizzie B 175 Tamsin 175
ANTHONY Frank J 203 Grace 525 John 525 Lucinda E 525 Mary 447 Robenia Florence 447
ATKINS Alzina E 472 Anna 358 Asa 326 Asa 2nd 326 Atherton 531 Benjamin D 285A Benjamin R 379 Bethia 94 Betsey 74 Caleb U 531 Carrie F 379 Charlie 531 Elisha B 472 Emily C 103 Experience E 103 Frankie 531 Freeman 187 Genie G 145 George A 94 Hannah 313 344 Hellen A 285A Henrietta 341 Infant 285A 358 Isaiah 94 103 245 Isaiah M 103 Jane M 94 John 94 313 John Edwin 313 Joseph 119 341 Joshua F 145 Joshua P 379 Josie 248 Lucena Wilder 313 Lucy 313 Lydia 329 Maria S 94 Martha D 358 Mary 472 Mary A 358 Mary S 472 Miriam (Gross) 187 Nathaniel 74 Olive 119 Paulina 364 Phebe W 285A Rachel C (Brown) 156 Rawlins T 313 Rawlins Thomas 313 Rebecca 238 245 329 Rebeckah 468 Rebekah 364 Reuel 364 Richard W 280 Russell 358 Sally Ann 313 Sally C 285A Salome 285A 531 Samuel W 344 Sarah F 94 Sarah Jane B 364 Silas 94 329 Sophronie E 531 Stephen 238 Thomas Gross 156 William T 358 Zaccheus 285A
ATWOOD Abigail 352 Anna 196 Arthur C 77 Clara F 131 Clarence O 293 Clarissa 352 Daniel W 465 Eleanor D 210 Eliza 293 Elwood F 293 Eugene F 77 Freddie M 465 Hannah 414 Henry 77 Henry D 360 Isaac 293 Jabez W 210 Jona (Jonathan) 360 Laura E 131 Lydia A 465 Mary A 352 Mary E (Nye) 131 Mary N 131 Rodolphus 131 Samuel 196 Urania T 77 Wallace H 77
AVELLAR Ida (Perie) 526 John Bradshaw 526
AVERY Austine 104 Betsey 312 Elizabeth 312 Emmie 104 Hannah P 312 Infant 104 Nancy 288 Peter 104 Peter L 312
AYERS Benjamin B 201 Clara P 201 Nathaniel W 201 N (Nathaniel) W 201 William H 201

BAILEY Daniel F 36 Marilla S 36 Mary 36 Oliver E 36 Ruth W 36
BAKER Anna 442 Charles T 292 Emma 442 Rosa R 292 W (William) L 442
BANGS Betsy 463 Jane M 463 Julia 463 Patty 463 Perez 463 Rosilla 463 Solomon 463 William B 463
BARNES Antone 62 Frank 62 Lillian 62 Manuel Joseph 62 Rose 62
BARNETT Hannah 501 Richard 501
BARRY Ellen 517
BELCHER Jane S 176
BEMIS Annie S 424
BENNETT Eliza A 193 George B 193 Honora 512 Lonnie 193 Mary Louisa 512 Peter 512 Walter Russell 193
BERRY Horace G 35 Patty S 35
BICKERS Jos P 435

CEMETERY NUMBER TWO - OLD SECTION

BIDWELL Newton Church 162
  William McKendree 162
BIRGE Maybelle 432
BLAKE James H 420 Reliance P 420
  Sophia Clark 162
BLANCHARD Isabelle 56
BORGES Joseph 417B Mary P 417B
BOSWORTH Flora F 162
BOWLEY/BOWLY Asa S 216 Cynthia
  216 Eliza 168 Freeman M 342
  Gamaliel S 347 Gideon 168
  Hannah H 341 James V 349
  Joanna S 342 Mary A 424
  Mary Ann 168 Mary W 168 Mary
  Y 168 Polly 289 Rosa W
  (Churchill) 349 Sarah P 342
  Temperance 347
BRAZIL Mary G 493
BROWN (see also BROWNE) Almira
  218 Anna (Baker) 442 Anthony
  218 Atkins 480 Benjamin F 240
  David 480 Delora 289 Edward
  499 Eunice H 480 Frank 499
  Hannah S 480 Joseph 499
  Lydia K 480 Martha E 480
  Polly (Bowley) 289 Rachel C
  156 Rose 499 Sally 337
BROWNE (see also BROWN) Obadiah
  S 3 Wilhelmina R 3
BRUNDAGE Mary L 34
BURCH Alexander T 60 Alice M
  123 Catherine 70 Charles W
  123 Cyrus C 102 Elisha S 475
  Elizabeth 60 Elizabeth S 123
  Elizabeth W 475 Enos S 50 70
  Eva H 50 George B 60 Infant
  50 Lizzie 475 Lizzie B 60
  Lizzie Brewer 60 Mary A 70
  Nathaniel T 70 Nellie T 123
  Sarah A 50
BURDEN Christie A 194 Eugene
  194 Mary L 194 Nellie M 194
BURKETT Charles W 419 Mary 419
BURT Alma P (Nickerson) 185
  Clarence F 41 Cora 41 Edward
  C 177 Edward G 177 Esther A
  (Hull) 185 John 185 John S
  185 M Elizabeth (Chase) 41
  Mathias W 185 Rosetta (Small)
  185 Ruth L 177 Sarah L 177
BUSH Edwin William 305 Jemima
  305 Lois 305
BUTLER Ann 54 Anna E 198 Elizabeth 409 Joseph H 198 William
  H 54

CADY John 448
CAMPBELL Annie J 469 Katherine I
  469
CARNES Eunice M 439 John M 439
CARR William H 506
CARRIGAN Mary 387 Thomas J 387
CARSON George W 413 Mary A 413
CASE Elizabeth T 407 Jesse S 471
  Joan (Hilliard) 535 Reuben G
  535 Susan 471 Washington 471
CASHMAN James 43 Nancy E 43
CATON Bertha M 86 John F 137
  Justine S 137 Manuel F 86
  Stella 86 Winthrop C 86
CHAPMAN Abbie S 383 Abraham 311
  Abram 383 Amie C 383 Amos 383
  Anastasia 25 Austin F 134
  Clara T 383 Elizabeth 309 311
  Elizabeth E 383 Elizabeth P
  311 Ellen M 25 Fannie R 134
  Infant 383 Infant son 357
  Lewis L 25 Lewis Lombard 309
  Lucinda 383 Mary 383 Mercy 311
  Mercy H 311 Nathan 134 Nathaniel P 134 Phebe N 383 Samuel
  309 383 Sarah L 383 William
  N 383
CHASE Cathrine 41 Francis 41
  Frank 40 Laura P 40 M Elizabeth 41
CHURCHILL Rosa W 349
CLAPP Bessie L 394 Louise R 394
  William R 394
CLARKE Mamie N 490 Mary P 490
  Sabrina S 490 Tabitha 490
  William 490 William Jr 490
  Willie P 490 Willie W 490
COBB Abbott L 195 Etta S 195
  Harold W 195 Lawrence W 195
  Ralph I 387
COBURN Charles A 4
COLE Mary Emma 413
COLEMAN Andrew T 370 Harry J 370
  James E 370 Nellie F 370
COLLINS Elizabeth 254 Ella F 394
  Gamaliel 254 John E 394
  Nathaniel H 254 Richard F 394
  Sylvanus 248
CONANT John Wesly 2nd 258 Sally
  258

CEMETERY NUMBER TWO - OLD SECTION

CONNOR William P 494
CONVERSE Thomas 499
CONWELL A Frank 183 Almira (Taylor) 183 David 183 David S 183 Edith M 168 Eleanor 183 Hattie B 183
COOEY Elizabeth T 34 John G 34 Tommie 34
COOK Adeline 308 Adiline H 321 Albert M 180 Almira 505 Ann 321 Anna 333 Anna H 218 Annie E 453 Aphia 285 Aphia L 157 B Lombard 180 Belinda 157 Bethiah 249 Bethiah G 249 Bethiah R 384 Betsey N 453 Betsy S 275 Caleb 173 David N 231 Dorinda 287 Ebed E 264 Edward 403 Edward B 488 Elisha 321 Elisha F 453 Eliza 453 Eliza A 157 Eliza G 173 Eliza Paine 330 Elizabeth 310 330 335 Elizabeth B 12 Ellen S 37 Emerson D 180 Epaphras Kibby 285 Ephraim 285 Francis W 12 Frank A 12 Franklin Willis 248 George B 310 324 Hannah 271 322 Hannah R 453 Harriet 403 Harvey 235 Horace Porter Stephens 283 Inda S (Cornell) 264 Infant 180 Infant dau 173 403 Infant son 173 Jacob 336 James 333 James F 333 James T 283 Jane 283 Jedidah A (Smith) 280 Joanna 330 John 303 John C 488 Jonathan 226 Jonathan Jr 226 Joshua 164 330 Joshua 2nd 330 Kathleen O 180 Lauretta A 248 Lemuel 157 180 Lemuel F 157 Louisa 283 Maria 235 Martha A 248 Martha S 180 Mary 219 303 Mary G 336 Mary J 180 Mercy 226 Mercy P 164 Norman S 249 Parker 283 Parron C 322 Phebe 283 Phebe C W 248 Philip 453 Phillip 218 Polly 170 Polly B 310 Rachel W 333 Rebecca 164 285 322 486 Reuben 310 Richard A 248 Sally 320 333 530 Sally E 285 Salome 231 Samuel 283 Samuel Jr 235 Samuel Tilton 249 Sarah 287 Sarah A 321 Sarah G 285 Solomon 331 530

S (Solomon) Thomas 321 Susannah 331 Susie T 249 Thomas D 231 Thomas S 505 Vergenia S 336 Wallace J 249 Walter 403
CORNELL Adaline 264 Edna B 348 Eliza H 348 George H 264 George H Jr 264 Inda S 264 Martha Hellen 264 Martin L 348 Martin W 348 Mary H 348 Sabra C 348 Sadie 264 Sarah C 264 Willie 264
CORRIGAN Mary C 469
COSTELLOE Nora 487
COUILLIARD/COUILLYARD Amasa D 381 Clara L 381 Infant 381 Lee 381 Mary M 381 Melville W 381 Nathaniel A 381 Phebe D 381 Sarah D 381 Unknown 381
COVELL Joshua D 530 Nathaniel 530 Rachel W 530
COWING Betsey W 432 Carrie A 432 Harold E 514 Henry W 432 James 432 James E 432 Joseph A 432 Joseph E 432 Mary 432 Rebecca 432
CRITCHETT Charles H 533 Martha S 533
CROCKER Olive 343
CROSBY Eliza A 46 George 46 George W 46
CROSS Jonathan K 340 Joseph 340 Marietta F 31
CROWELL Addie S 95 Albert F 95 Amaziah 95 Ansel 208 Avis J 95 Infant son 208 Lewis H 208 Mary E 383 William H 383
CUTTER Ardelle J 186 Josiah 186 Rebecca G 186

DAVIS Rosetta 202
DAY (see also DAYS) Adda H (Pinckney) 426
DAYS (see also DAY) Annie 73 Charles E 73 Frank N 73 Olive C 73
DECOSTA Amelia 529 Joseph 529 Josephine 529 Manuel 529
DE GROOT Nanno 602/3
DERBY Elizabeth P 219 Henry Willard 219
DEWAGER Emanuel A 534 Gertrude

CEMETERY NUMBER TWO - OLD SECTION

(Snow) 534
DEWOLF Abby L 190 George 190 Mary L 190 William Sanborn 190
DOANE Amanda C 257 Curtis 398 Elijah 139 Lydia A 139 Philip S 139 Ruth H 398
DOEBLE Charles F 388 Fredie 388 John A 388 Lillian C 388 Olive N 388
DOLLIVER Nora 426
DOYLE Laura May 476 Lydia F 476 Maria S 476 William A 476
DUNLAP Almira 143 John 143
DUTRA Nettie C 509
DYER Apphia C 240 Benjamin 379 Betsey 240 Charles 302 Charles W 438 Charlotte C 271 Clarissa 220 Elijah 161 Elisha M 158 Elizabeth D 158 Ella M 198 Emily J 381 Georgianna 379 Gertrude R 438 Hannah B 220 Hannah C 271 Hannah (Cook) 271 Hannah Lewis 240 Hattie C 240 Henry 240 Hermie 271 Hutty 246 James F 240 James S 271 John 220 Jonathan 198 Joseph B 198 Joseph R 240 Joshua 158 246 Joshua Thomas 158 Joshua Walter 158 Jottie L 198 Laura A 158 Laura Elizabeth 158 Mary A 198 Mary E 240 Mary E 240 Mary Hersey 158 Mary S 271 Melville W 381 Millie Frances 158 Milly T 158 Obie K 240 P Lester 240 Paul 240 Paul A 240 Phebe 381 Rebecca A 158 Rebeckah 161 Reuben 158 Salome 379 Sarah 302 Sarah R 243 Thankful L 379 Vashti 198 William 381 271 William H 271 William L 381

EDMUNDS Hannah E 498 Lillie 498 M (Manuel) E 498
EDWARDS Bertha A 416 Mary Elsa 205
ELDRIDGE Josephine 341
ELLINGTON Infant son 453 Raymond 453 Susan S 453
ELLIOT/ELLIOTT Anna 155 Benjamin O 344 Hannah 343 Hannah A 343 Richard 155
ELLIS Infants 256 Joseph C 256 Judith B 256
ELMES/ELMS Huldah 250 Mary Ann D 250 William 250
EMERY Cushing H 199 Lurana A 199

FARNSWORTH Chas F A 42
FARRIN Robert H 8
FARWELL James E 126
FERGUSON Jane 10
FERREIRA Josephine (DeCosta) 529
FISHBURN Charles F 260 Elizabeth Jane 260 James 260 Mary A 260
FISHER (see also SWAREZ) Ann J 441 Annie C 441 Caleb 203 441 Irving S 441 Jane M 441 Joseph (Swarez) 472 Lucinda T 440 Mary K 203 Mary S (Atkins) (Swarez) 472 Robert N 421 Spencer V 441
FITCH James 390 Susan 170
FORREST Jesse 462
FOSTER Agnes F 425 Leonard J 425
FREEMAN Abbie L 151 Alsey P 30 Aphia 161 Aphia C 167 Benjamin F 167 Betsy Dyer 273 Charles 427 Cynthia 273 Edwin 273 Elijah 161 Eliza A 40 Eugene W 363 Ezra 273 Helen 167 Leroy L 422 Louise Russell 167 Mary 167 Mary H 167 Michael 151 Nathan 167 Nathan D 167 Polly 273 Prince 40 Reuben N 422 Sally 427 Sarah B 167 Sibyl H 161 Sylvester 167 Unknown 167 William E 151 Willie L 40
FRIZZELL William 408
FULLER Betsey 270 James 536 Maria Frances 536

GALACAR/GALICAR Hezekiah 346 Mary 361 M (Mary) B 346 William 361
GASPAR/GASPIE Antone 528A Jesse 483 John Joseph 483 Joseph 483 Louis 483 Mamie 528A Olga 528A Rita 528A Rosa 483 William J 483

CEMETERY NUMBER TWO - OLD SECTION

GHEN Adelaide L 11 Delia 122 Ephraim S 11 Freddie S 293 Groce 143 John 122 John Gordon 122 Josiah 52 Martha R 293 Mary 11 Rebecca 52 Suvina L 122
GOMES Joseph 493
GOODELL Alice 449
GOODSPEED Reuben 135
GORMAN Mary 538 Michael 538
GOVE Ann Mae 525
GROSE/GROSS Alexander 375 Ann 375 Cora (Burt) 41 Jonah 375 Miriam 187
GROZER/GROZIER Alice (Goodell) 449 Bethiah P 155 Edwin Atkins 449 Joshua 228 Joshua F 228 Margaret (Murphy) 449 Martha 228 Rebecca 228 Richard 449
GRUCHIE Betsey 10
GURNEY A Eloise 453 Infant son 453

HALL Eliza Emerson 231 Enoch 231 Louisa F 28 Mary 339 Rosetta 231
HAMMOND Hattie M 8 John W 8 Lizzie F 8 William H 8
HANDY Loies E 415 Moses H 415
HARDING Silas 275
HARVENDER Deborah C 474 George S H 474 Hatty W 474 Heman 106 Henrietta S 106 John C P 474 John H 474 Lucy A 474 Saphronia G 106 Sarah A 474 Sarah Y 474 William T 474 William W 474
HAWES Frank L 358 Salome C 358
HEALEY T Jefferson 299
HIGGINS Abbie 16 Abigail 16 407 Abigail C 407 Aqilla 16 Aquilla 459 Barzillai 407 Betsey C 404 Freddie S 16 Icena A 163 Isaac H 407 Joanna 328 Josiah C 407 Louisa S 404 Lydia A 459 Nathaniel C 407 Philena 16 Sarah N 16 Solomon 254 404 Solomon R 16 Tabitha 451 Tamsin 459 Willis 163 Zetta F 163
HILL Angeline W 274 Catherine C 274 Elizabeth D 262 Hannah 274 Jared 262 John 274 Margaret 102 Susan E 478
HILLIARD/HILLYARD Abby P 320 Carrie 320 Charlie 320 Cordelia Holmes 166 Eddie 320 Edward Cook 166 Infant son 320 Joan 535 Lucy H 320 Pauline 320 Rebecca C 320 Sally 320 Sarah 166 Sarah G 166 Stephen 166 Stephen A 166 Thomas 320
HODGDON Bessie G 22 Charles H 22
HOLMES Betsey 288 H C 271 Henry P 472 Hiram 288 Infant dau 288 Mary E 271 Nancy (Avery) 288 Rachel 271 Susie Perry 288 Wally 288
HOLWAY Abbie R 263 Angeline 146 C H 263 Charles 146 Ebenezer W 269 Elizabeth 255 Hannah B 269 Hannah G 355 Henry 89 John 269 John W 355 Mary J 269 Unknown 269 William H 269
HOPKINS Abbie C 296 Betsey 96 420A Charles E 109 Eliza C 199 Howard F 266 Jonathan 96 Joshua A 420A Julia A 203 Julia A C 203 Julia C (Knowles) 266 Lottie M 420A Maria L 109 Rufus 203 Rufus H 197 Ruth L 197
HOWARD David N 388 Eliza (Bowly) 168 Hannah 388 John 388 Warren 168
HOWE/HOWES Helena P 229 Samuel A 479
HOWLAND Emma A 63
HUDSON Elizabeth A 56 George W 56 Mary J 491 Nathan S 56
HULL Esther A 185
HUNT Charlotte M 58 Clarissa J 58 Infant son 224 James G 58 James G Jr 58
HURLBERT Alonzo W 325 Cora B 325 George H Jr 325 Lexie (McDonald) 325

IVERSON John W 503

JENNINGS Charles A 191 Hannah M 191 Heman 191 Herman A 191

-115-

CEMETERY NUMBER TWO - OLD SECTION

John P 351 Nathaniel 191 Unknown 191 351
JERAULD Faustina A 451 Hannah (Small) 451 Lewis 451 Tabitha (Higgins) 451
JOHNSON Ann 98 Arthur Clarence 170 Bethia Grozier 241 Betsey 241 Carrie (Ryder) 454 Clarissa 207 Frank L 98 George F 454 Isaac Thomas 170 Jerusha Parker 170 John B Dods 207 John W 241 Joseph Hall 170 Joseph P 170 Josephine P 170 Lemuel Cook 170 Mary (Whorf) 170 Polly (Cook) 170 Polly Cook 170 Rebecca Allen 241 Sarah Maria 241 Sarah (Ryder) 454 Susan (Fitch) 170 Timothy P 241 Timothy Parker 170
JONES Abbie 526 Angie B 526A Emanuel 526 Hannah 526 John S 526A Stephen 526 Warren Edward 526A
JORDAN Annie J 496 James T 496 James T Jr 496 Johanna H 496
JOSEPH Alex 211 Amelia F 3 Avis M 211 C A J (Unknown) 211 Ellen F 3 Eloise G 3 Frances 3 Francis 261 Frank 3 J B D J (Unknown) 211 Jarusha G 261 Jerusha Fannie 261 John F 3 Lillian A 261 Luthera C 261 Mercy M 261

KEITH Infant dau 453
KELLEY Albion E 391 Catherine 392 David S Jr 412 Evelina V 412 Gershom D 412 James E 392 Jasie 391 Laura A 391 Lenora B 391 Levi A 391 Levi B 391 Lexie (McDonald) 325 Mary G 412
KENDALL Eliza P 91 Jesse 220
KENNEY James T 199 P Tillinghast 162 Tamzain 199 William H 294
KEYES Emma (Baker) 442
KILBURN Abby H 473 Charles H 473 Cinderella H 473 Edward H 473 Edward J 473 James H 473 Jona (Jonathan) C 473 Levi A 473 Mary S 473 Pricilla 473 William G 473
KNEELAND Henry 406
KNOWLES Angie M 266 Carrie E 145 Delia C 266 Elizabeth D 172 George O 379 Georgie M 379 Hannah E 145 Hannah Kidder 266 Harbeck 172 Isaac D 489 Joseph P 266 Julia C 266 Lizzie B 266 Lovisa Kibby 266 Lucy A 266 Mabel Osborne 379 Mary J 172 Mary William 172 Mercy Ann 172 Polly K 266 Robert 172 Samuel 145 Willard 172 266 Willie B 266

LANCY Anna C 534
LAVENDER Ann B 172 John Adams 171 John R 171 Joseph A 352 Joseph Henry 171 Judith M 378 Lewis C 172 Mary 171 Robert 172 Robert Jr 171 Sally Mayo 171 Simeon L 171 Susan E 171 William R 171
LEACH Betsey Collins (Parker) 246
LECOUNT John 251 Nancy 251 Ruth 251 Ruth T 251
LEE Walter Osborne 429
LEWIS Albert F 112 Arozana 112 Azubah 411 Betsey G (Wiley) 411 Carrie A 24 Edward C 233 Emma F 411 Eugene W 411 Flora A 24 Freddie E 21 George 112 113 411 George H 21 Hopey R 112 Infant 112 Infant dau 411 Jerusha A 30 Jesse F 411 John A 411 John W 112 Joseph 30 Joseph H 30 Joshua M 113 Lucinda S (Wiley) 411 Mary 113 411 Mary 2nd 113 Mary H 21 Mattie E 21 Nathaniel 411 Nathaniel E 411 Nathaniel Jr 411 Nettie H 24 Olin M 113 Ruth H 411 Sophronia B 113 Thomas 24 Thomas J 24
LITTLE George H 477 Jonathan H 477 Mary A 477
LIVERMORE John H 265 Lizzie W 265
LOGAN John Adam 425 John T 425 Katie May 425 Margaret 425
LOPES Elizabeth 514 Julia 514

CEMETERY NUMBER TWO - OLD SECTION

Julia A 514 Louisa A 514 Rita 514 Thomas J 514 Thomas J Jr 514
LORD Edmund B 108 Sarah A C 108
LOTHROP Sarah Nickerson 452
LOVERING Charles O 49 Otis R 49
LUCE Mary N (Atwood) 131
LURTEN/LURTON John C 63 Levi 461 William J 63

McCURDY Archibald 437 Hannah M 437
McDONALD (see also MACDONALD) Archibald 10 Charles D 10 Duncan 10 Isabella 10 Jane (Ferguson) 10 Joseph W 10 Lexie 325 Walter S 10
MACDONALD (see also McDONALD) Colin 469 Isabel 469 John C 469
McINTYRE Betsey (Gruchie) 10 Jennie Lee 10 John 10 Katherine I 10
McLEOD Danie A 386 John 200 Mary A 200 Wallace E 200
McMILLAN Eva 400 Jessie 400 Neil 400 Sarah 400
MACMURRAY Mary S 484 Robert 484
MANUEL Alexander 460 Catherine K 140 Philena 460 Tamsin 460 Wm Otis 140
MARSTON Adelia 125 Charles S 125 Edward 125 Edward S 125 Henry W 125 Julia D 125 Lydia 125
MATHESON Jessie T 484 Lizzie W 484 Mary 484 Murdock 484 William 484
MAYHEW John 522
MAYO Albert S 396 Alfred A 472 Alfred L 472 Anna 97 David Atkins 213 Deborah 371 Elizabeth D 472 Elmira F 396 Herbert F 213 Ida F 396 Jeremiah 371 Jerusha 396 Joseph 371 Joshua 97 Joshua Jr 97 Margaret A 213 Martha 371 Mary Lizzie 97 Mary T 97 Reuben N 396 Selina S 396 Stephen A 396
MESSER Lillian N (Rich) 44
MILLER Charles H 153 Eliza Y 211

Francis C 152 Francis S 152 George H 211 Hicks S 152 Isabel F 153 Lucinda A 152 Patty 152 Polly S 152 Robert S 152 Sally 452
MITCHELL Augustus 272 Harriett F 272
MOORE John 241
MORGAN Lewis P 468 Rebeckah 468
MORRILL Bessie 64 Catherine (Myles) 418 Joseph L 418 Mary Elizabeth 64 Peter 418
MORRIS Louise 493
MORRISON Helen J 132 John R 132
MOTT Edward P 159 Jane B 159 Silas C 159 Wallace C 159
MULLINS Freeman V 130 Mary J 130 Thomas V 130
MURPHY Margaret 449
MURRY Mary 498
MYLES Catherine 418

NEWCOMB Elisha S 19 Hattie W 19
NEWTON Robert 421
NICHOLS Martha O 114
NICHOLSON Jane N 129 John 129 Mary 129
NICKERSON Abbie C (Hopkins) 296 Albert H 188 Albert S 188 Albertina L 136 Alma P 185 Almira 230 Amanda 188 Amos 452 Angelia B 188 Ann C 284 Annie 140 Annie A 140 Bessie Wyman 31 Blanche L 188 Byron 188 Cecelia G 75 Charles P 230 Charles Vernon 31 Cinderella K 13 Eddie P 230 Effie L 230 Emorie F 37 Francis 31 Franklin 452 George H 165 H B 165 Harvey 284 Helen Page 188 Henry 136 Huldah C 335 Isaac 37 Isaac H 37 Isaiah 296 Jane B 324 John Lothrop 452 Jonathan 452 Joshua 188 230 Joshua S 188 Josiah 452 Lemuel F 13 Levi 296 Lucia 140 Lucia S 7 Lydia 296 Martha M 165 Mary B 37 Mary F 31 Mary G 165 Matilda 75 Melvina F 164 Nathaniel L 320 Nellie F 7 Phebe 318 Rebecca Dyer (Watkins) 452 Rebecca Franklin 452 Rebecca L 320 Reuben 7 Sally (Miller) 452

CEMETERY NUMBER TWO - OLD SECTION

Seth 318 Solomon Dyer 318
Sparrow 75 Stephen Peck 452
Surmentha 136 Theodore 37
Wm K 140
NIXON J George 409
NYE Mary E 131
NYMPHA Thomas 519

O'DONNELL Elmer W 19
O'NEIL George R 431 Margaret A S 431

PACHECO Joseph A 433 Marjorie F 433
PAINE (see also PAYNE) A Elnora (Snow) 534 Addie A 169 Ann S 169 Charles B 534 Clara B 484 D B 534 Elizabeth (Cook) 335 Elkanah 209 Fanny 134 Francis A 169 Georgie D 484 Harvey Cook 335 Huldah C (Nickerson) 335 Infant 335 Joshua 169 Lemuel 335 Martha F 169 Moses 368 Nancy 169 Nancy W 169 241 Nathaniel 134 Oren O 484 Priscilla 368 Rufus M 484 Sarah B 335 Sarah Elizabeth 275 Solomon Dyer 169
PALLAM Bertha G 66 Camelu 66 Infant 66 Nancy T 66
PALMER Elizabeth A 267 William 267
PARKER Betsey Collins 246 Charles 246 Charles E C 246 Edward C 530 Eliza Ann 351 Infant 246 Lavina 351 Mary M 246 Michael A 351 Salley 246 S (Samuel) A 351 Sarah 530 Sarah E 351 Sarah Maria 246 Susan E E 246
PARKS Lucy 385
PARR James Wingate 601
PAYNE (see also PAINE) Hannah D 28 Nathaniel 28 Sally 28
PEIRCE (see also PIERCE/PIRCE) Elizabeth 204
PENNOCK Sarah D 439
PERIE Augustus S 526 Frank 526 Ida 526 Matilda 526
PERRY Lucy V 527A Manuel S 527A
PETTINGILL Belinda N 502 John 502 Marshall C 502 Thomas I 502

PIERCE (see also PEIRCE/PIRCE)
Abbie B 341 Abram 204 Asenath 395 Betsey N 204 Eliphlet W 410 Esther 395 Eva M 33 Gamaliel T 91 George Warren 204 Hannah M 286 Harison Gilman 286 Henry F 395 Henry K 91 Henry R 372 Infant dau 286 Infant son 286 Ira H 204 Isaac N 372 James W 33 John 33 Joshua 276 Marion Wallace 286 Mary F 395 Mary W 33 Newcomb 395 Reuben 206 Ruth P 276 Sarah 286 Solomon D 410 Sophia 372 Thomas C 395 William 390 William T 286
PIMENTEL Joseph 523
PINCKNEY Adda H 426 Lawrence Bates 426 Lewis B 426 Nora Dolliver 426
PIRCE (see also PEIRCE/PIERCE) Betsey 399 John 390 Sally 390 William Jr 399
PLACES <u>California</u> 295; <u>Canary Islands</u> Grand Canaria 472 Tenneriffe 254; <u>China</u> Hankow 133; <u>England</u> Liverpool 241 519; <u>France</u> 249; <u>Grand Banks</u> 225; <u>Japan</u> Hiogo 136; <u>Maine</u> Orland 303 Portland 281; <u>Massachusetts</u> Beverly 261 Billerica 58 Boston 54 58 167 183 218 221 228 248 Boston Harbor 231 Cambridgeport 298 Cape Cod 446 Cape Harbour 246 Cohasset 211 Eastham 164 601 Essex 298 Provincetown 54 58 164 228 241 298 342 381 489 519 Provincetown, Hamilton Cemetery 226 472 Provincetown Harbor 406 446 Provincetown Herring Cove 446 Provincetown Long Point 174 Provincetown Race Point 310 Provincetown Tomb 532 Sandwich 89 273 Truro 258 Truro East Harbor 335 Wellfleet 411; <u>Michigan</u> Grand Haven 295; <u>Newfoundland</u> 400; <u>New York</u> Cold Spring 519 Long Island 295 New York 456; <u>Nova Scotia</u> Barrington 489 Liverpool 341 Old Canso 204; <u>Oregon</u> 295; <u>Pennsylvania</u>

-118-

CEMETERY NUMBER TWO - OLD SECTION

Philadelphia 466; <u>Spanish Main</u> 189 <u>West Indies</u> Auxcayes 221 Cienfuegas, Cuba 167 Cuba 456 Martinique 281 Miragoane 171 Mona I 463 Port Au Prince, Haiti 218 221 254 St Thomas 183 Turk's Island 168
PLAISTED Minnie (Smith) 114
POND Elizabeth C 84
PORTER Henry K 90
POULSEN Frank 445
PRATT Infant son 365
PRIOR Hellen M 338 William H 338

QUINN Vashti L 197

RAEDY (see also READEY) Mary 497
RAND Elizabeth 237
RANDALL John 448
RAUTIO John 29
READEY (see also RAEDY) George W 306 Mary B 306
REED Charles 486
RICE Hattie B 183
RICH Abigail 507 Alvin F 118 Ansel L 118 Charles S 272 David 507 David Jr 507 Delia C 272 Fred L 32 George R 118 Hannah 32 Henry 32 Ida L 118 Jennie 44 Leonard B 32 Lillian N 44 Lottie B 32 Mary S N 118 Olive 119 Philip S 272 Phillip S 272 Ruben (sic) W 118 Sally D 272 Samuel Jones 44 Sarah E (Smith) 44 Sarah L 32 Susan F 503 Xenophen 119
RICKER Eliza A 6 Jessie May 6
RIDER (see also RYDER) Amanda 295 Anna 295 Elisha 315 Ephraim H 290 Freddie Collins 298 Godfrey 298 Henry 295 Lorenzo 295 Lucy L 355 Polly 282 Ruth G 298 Sally 290 Sally B 290 Thomas 282 Thomas Lee 298 William Henry 298 William W 295
RIDLY Eliza C 300
ROBERTS Owen 252 Owen L 252 Phoebe P 252 Sarah P 252 William O 252

RODGERS (see also ROGERS) Adelaide (Williams) 55 Charles 55 Elijah 55 Zipporah 55
ROGERS (see also RODGERS) Charles P 61 Frank A 498 Mary 61 Olivia S 498
ROVER Unknown 492
RUSSELL Elizabeth 177 Israel 177 Martha W 202
RYDER (see also RIDER) Allie 454 Alphena C 454 Asaph S 141 Carrie 454 Charles B 141 Charles Francis 413 David 149 Ephraim 454 Ephraim T 454 Elizabeth 315 Georgie W 141 Henry 295 Infant 454 Joanna R 279 Lena B 454 Lucinda 413 Mabel 454 Martha 454 Mary E 454 Mehitable 454 Nathaniel 454 Polly A 413 Rebecca Whorf 413 Reuben 174 413 Reuben Jr 174 Sally H 454 Sarah 454 Sarah Y 315 Stephen 279 Susannah (Swift) 174 Wally C 141 William T L 295 Willie M 454

SANFORD George E 61 Loretta E 61
SAUNDERS Amy N 13 Ernest W 13
SAVAGE Betsey 8 Robert 8
SAWTELE Joseph 213 Joseph Jr 213 Sabra 213
SCANNELL Dennis 515
SEARS Jesse 520 Joseph 520 Mary (Anthony) 447 Nellie 164
SEGURA Lawrence 528
SETTES George A 64
SHED Mary E 369
SHEPARD Edward 37 Nellie H 37
SHERMAN Paulina 323
SHIPS Etta G Fogg 249 James Porter 225 Lester A Lewis 446 Narcissa 519 Portland 446 Rienza 223 Samuel Cook 463 U S S San Francisco 2 Westmoreland 281
SILVA/SYLVA Albert L 433 Antone J 433 Bessie M 211 Cinnie 498 Frank 433 Infant son 433 Jule M 376 Manuel Francis 511 Maria 498 Mary Julia 498

Mary L 433
SILVEY Mary 521
SMALL (see also SMALLEY) Abraham 367 Alexander G 177 Ann C 34 Annie F 508 Annie W 117 Augusta P 367 Betsey 535 Carrie W 490 Charles Edwin 184 Daisy Anne 490 Daniel 214 Daniel L 82 Daniel S 34 Ella A 367 Freddie 124 Hannah 367 451 Ida Bernette 124 Isaac 367 Isaiah A 124 490 Isaiah A Jr 490 James 535 James H 535 Jesse 92 Joanna 214 John 380 504 John W 537 Joseph C 350 Joshua D P 535 Lucy A 124 Lucy Idella 124 Mary H 34 Mercy 504 Nancy L 184 Nath H 117 Nathaniel H 117 Peggy 117 Polly 367 Rachel 537 Rebecca 380 Rebecca H 489 Rosetta 185 Rosetta S 177 Ruth C 34 Ruth S 34 Samuel 184 Samuel C 535 Samuel D 184 Silas 350 Sophila 337 Susan J 34 Susannah 350 Uriah 117
SMALLEY (see also SMALL) Hannah 221 Isaac 221 Sally 221 Thomas 221
SMITH Addie Louise 93 Adeline 453 Alonzo Jr 211 Alsey P 30 Amasa 453 Amasa T 378 Arthur C 271 Atkins 482 Benjamin 278 Benjamin J 114 Caleb D 58 Charles A 14 Charlotte M (Hunt) 58 Christina D 271 Clara 211 Clara H 58 Clara Osborn 458 Clarissa D 458 Cynthia P C 453 Daisy 58 Daniel 401 David 30 Deborah P 466 Eben H 453 Eben S 453 Eddie Elmer 30 Edmun T 45 Eldredge 464 Eldredge F 127 Elizabeth 5 498 Eliza (Cook) 453 Experience 464 Fannie C 16 Fred Walton 453 Freeman 44 Freeman A 189 George 498 George O 189 George W 211 Grandma Smith 198 Heman S 5 Infant 241 Infant dau 30 458 Infant son 458 Isaiah H 30 Jane Wood 5 Jedidah A 280 Jerusha A 30 Jesse 5 Jesse D 402 John M 189 John R 466 John R Jr 466 John S 199 Jonathan D 114 Jonathan E 458 Joseph F 498 Joseph H 199 Joshua 211 Lewis L 402 Lothrop H 378 Louisa W 93 Louise B 438 Lucinda 199 402 Lucy 30 Lurana C 30 Maria 482 Maria L 189 Marinda (Stubbs) 114 Mary A 14 Mary C 241 Mary E 378 Mary F 114 Mary J 189 Mary L 378 Mary O 189 Mary Osborne 189 Mary S 14 Mary Thomas 270 Melissa Jane 402 Mercie Knowles 5 Minnie 114 Nancy Ellen 455 Nancy P 211 Nancy W (Paine) 241 Pearl 58 Phebe E 498 Philip R 14 Polly 402 Priscilla Maria 455 Rachel A 127 Rebecca A 440 Rebecca E 378 Rebecca L 110 Richard C 30 Robert C 58 Sabra C 482 Sally 278 Samuel 277 Samuel S 438 Sarah 278 Sarah E 44 Sarah L 278 Seth 14 16 Sophronia D 110 S (Stephen) Churchill 440 Susannah 390 Tamsin 498 Truman 14 Walter T 241 William M 241 William Paine 241 William W 241
SNOW A Elnora 534 Anna C (Lancy) 534 Annie E (Cook) 453 Benjamin H 236 Charlena 534 C (Charles) B 534 Charles H 534 Eliza A 281 Elizabeth 178 Enoch 281 Gertrude 534 Hannah D (Payne) 28 John 236 John Jr 236 Joseph Willis 178 Josiah 178 253 Mary 378 Obadiah 253 Reuben S 28 Ruth 178 Sally 236 Sarah E 178
SOUZA Francis 417 Frank A 29 Joseph E 417 Joseph F 417 Kate B 417
SPALDING Stephen 328
SPARKS Abigail 373 Angie 373 Benjamin F 373 Betsey 405 Chloe B 373 Clarissa M 373 Cynthia H 470 David 374 Eddie 373 Eliza R 405 Frank 374 George W 405 Harvey 373 Heman 405 Heman C 405 Infant son 405 James 373

CEMETERY NUMBER TWO - OLD SECTION

James A 405 James E (Eddie) 373 Martha D 374 Rebekah 374 Reuben G 470 Sally 470
SPARROW Alvin Mears 237 Elizabeth (Rand) 237 Jonathan 237 Mary A 237 Maryetta 237 Robert Henry 237
SPENCER Alfred J 87 Mary E 87
SPILMUN Anna 97
SPRAGUE John W 304 Sarah 304 Sarah Ann 304 William H 304
STANDISH Amanda M L 366
STANFORD Abby C 383 Abby N 383 James 231 Martha 231
STARR Edward T 215 Sarah H 215 Sarah Lizzie 215
STONE Ann 356 Olive 356
STRACHAUER Claude 327 Elizabeth 327
STUBBS Kenneth 606-9 Marinda 114
STULL Eliza P 183 George 212 George Jr 183 212 Infants 183 Lydia 212
SUKER Annie E 436 Daniel L 436 Hilda 436 Olive 436
SULLIVAN James 46 Polly 46
SWAREZ (see also FISHER) Joseph (Fisher) 472 Mary S (Atkins) (Fisher) 472
SWEENEY Catherine 516 Edward 516
SWIFT John 281 Josiah 281 Lydia 281 Susannah 174
SYLVA (see SILVA)

TALON Abbie C 393 Clara A 393
TARRANT Ann M 53 Eva Agnes 53 Phoebe S 53 Richard G 53 Ruth A 53 Susan A 53
TASHA James 431 Leroy C 431 Martha E 431
TAYLOR Almira 183 Amasa 440 Hannah M 440 Rebecca 440
THOMAS John B 403 Sophia R 403
THOMPSON Adelia H 8 Alex R 249 Bethia G 249 Charles J G 249 Elnora 8 Mary W 249
TUCK Joseph S 359 Joseph W 359 Josey S 359 Maria C 359 Mary Elizabeth 359 Mary Susan 359 Sophronia 359
TURNER Bessie 487 Daniel C 487 Georgie 487 James M 15 Moses

S 487 Nora 487 Nora (Costelloe) 487 Rhoda 101 William 101
TWOMBLEY Hannah A 144

ULLIAN Louise A 440
UNIDENTIFIED Bodies Unknown 446; Footstones C A J 211 C H S 488 J B D J 211 Joshua 276 M J 380 Rover 492 Smith, Grandma 198; No Stones or Empty Lots 9 17 18 27 38 39 48 49 57 65 67 68 69 71 72 76 79 81 83 99 100 105 107 111 115 116 120 121 128 135 138 144 148 150 154 182 192 208 217 222 227 232 234 239 244 247 259 291 332 334 354 377 382 397 418A 419A 423 428 430 434 443 444 467 481 485 494 495 500 509 510 513 518 521 524 527; Stones/Base Only Freeman lot 167 Holway lot 269 Jennings lot 351 Wareham lot 78 Williams lot 133

VAN UMMERSON Harold F 484 Jessie P 484
VESTY George L 47
VINTON Mary S 381

WALKER Chas H 51 Nancy S 51
WARD Betsey 507 Henry F 507 Isaiah G 507 Isaiah H 507
WAREHAM Alice 78 Jedidah 78 Lizzie 414 Reuben 414 Ruth 414 Unknown 78 William 78 William W 78
WATKINS Rebecca Dyer 452 Richard 228
WATSON Effie Y (Snow) 534
WEEKS Betsy S 23 Celestia A 23 Edward 223 Hattie G 242 Joseph 23 Judith E 223 Thomas A 242
WELCH (see also WELSH) Ella 517 Ellen (Barry) 517 James 517 Jeney 517 John W 517 Margaret 517 Mary A 424 Mary E 517 Michael 517 William 424

CEMETERY NUMBER TWO - OLD SECTION

WELSH (see also WELCH) Alice M 317 Annie O 317 James S 317
WESSELS Klaas D 2
WEST Infant son 85 Walter H 85
WHALEN William F 372
WRIGHT Charles R 1
WHARF (see WHORF)
WHEELER Hannah C 313
WHELDEN (see also WHELDIN/ WHILDING) Ann S 88 Freddie H 88 George N 88 Johnnie T 88 Mamie A 88 Mary F 88 Nabby B 389
WHELDIN (see also WHELDEN/ WHILDING) Catherine I 345 William T 345
WHILDING (see also WHELDEN/ WHELDIN) Catherine A 389 Michael 389 Michael T 389 Susannah 389
WHITE George W 177 Hephzibah 204 John W 204 Lizzie S 177 Nicholas 204 Richard S 177
WHITNEY Charles H 179 Electa 179 Felicia 179 Hannah E 179 Henrietta 179 Henrietta A 179 Isaiah 179 Joseph M 198 Lauretta 179 Sarah P 179 Vashti O 198
WHORF (see WHARF) Alvina 314 Elizabeth A 314 Infants 307 John 301 316 John Jr 297 Mary 170 Philip A 314 Rebecca 316 Rebeckah 301 Sarah 307 Sarah Frances 297 Susan 316 Thomas R 314
WIGGINS Paulina (Atkins) 364
WILEY Austin A 20 Azubah S 20 Betsey C 411 Jesse 20 Jesse W 20 Lucinda S 411
WILLIAMS Abbie M 317 Adelaide 55 Alice Margaret 317 Andrew N 224 Andrew T 507 Ann T 133 Anna 133 224 Augusta 225 Bethiah H 133 Betsey W 133 Charles F 84 Chylena H 225 Clara Anna 133 Emma L 26 Frederick E 26 George V 31 Georgie E 4 84 Hervey Chester 225 Ina E 281 Infant 224 Jacob C 507 Jesse N 225 John 84 John A 281 John T 133 Laura A Cook 507 Laura E 281

Lillian 84 Lucinda 225 Mary 507 Rufus 385 Sarah (Smith) 278 Unknown 133 William 224
WILSON Betsey A 139
WOODS Joan 63 John A 63 Phares L 63 Vilena M 525

YOUNG Arthur C 142 Bessie C 142 Betsy 457 Charles A 59 Charles L 59 Dorinda C 287 Dorinda (Cook) 287 Edith C 46 Effie L (Nickerson) 230 Elisha 319 457 Elmer C 230 Emily 319 Enos N 450 Fannie 59 Hannah 164 165 319 366 Hannah L 287 Henry 457 Infant 366 Isaiah 366 456 John 450 John Jr 450 John W 203 J (Joseph) S 366 Laura A 136 Louisa 456 Lydia A 450 Maria 450 Mary 165 456 Mary F 203 Moses 2nd 164 Nathan 147 Nathaniel L 450 Nehemiah H 366 Nellie 450 Nellie (Sears) 164 Newcomb C 319 Paron C 142 Polly 319 Priscilla B 59 Priscilla P 165 Reuben 165 Sally 147 Sarah (Cook) 287 Sarah L 136 Sarah S 236 Seviah S 450 Silas S 287 Susan E 142

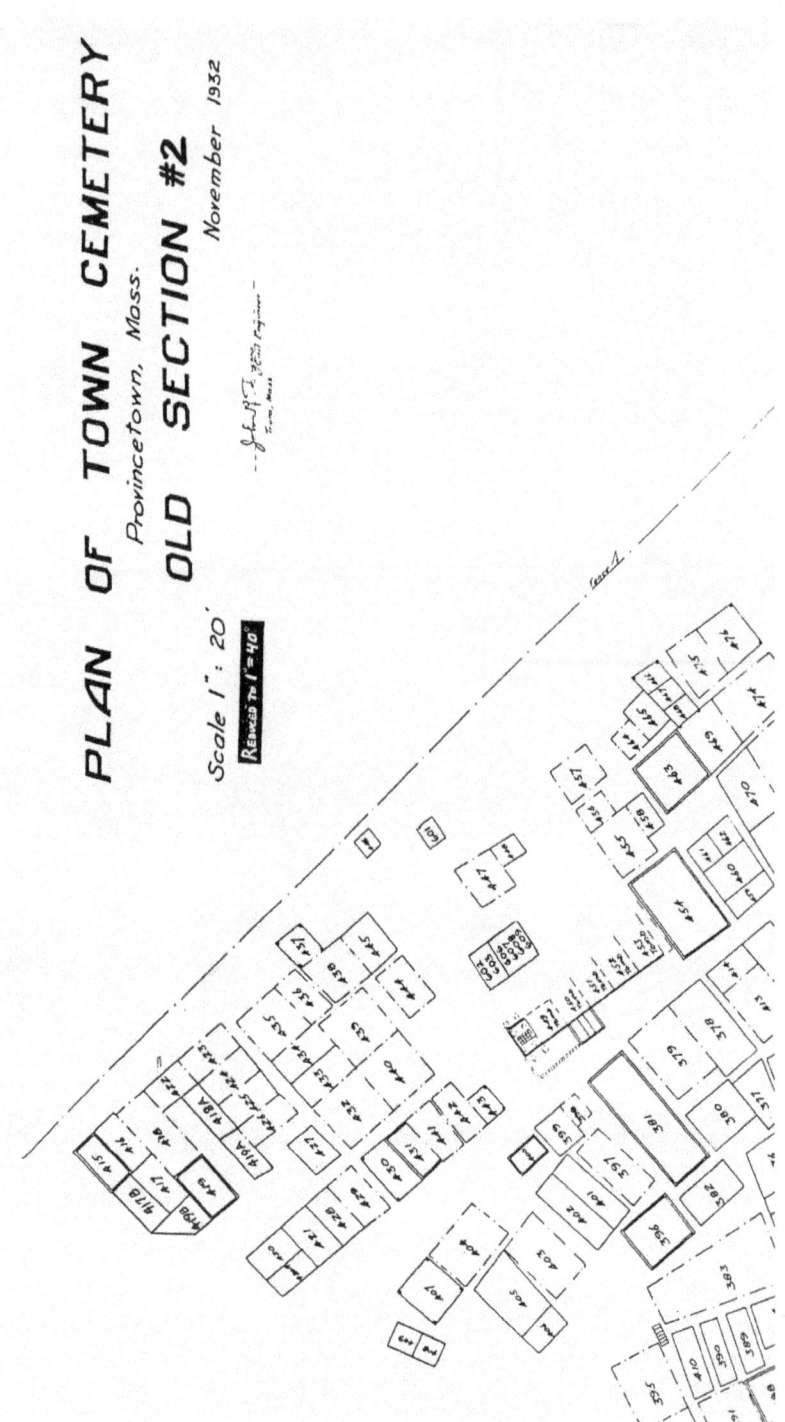

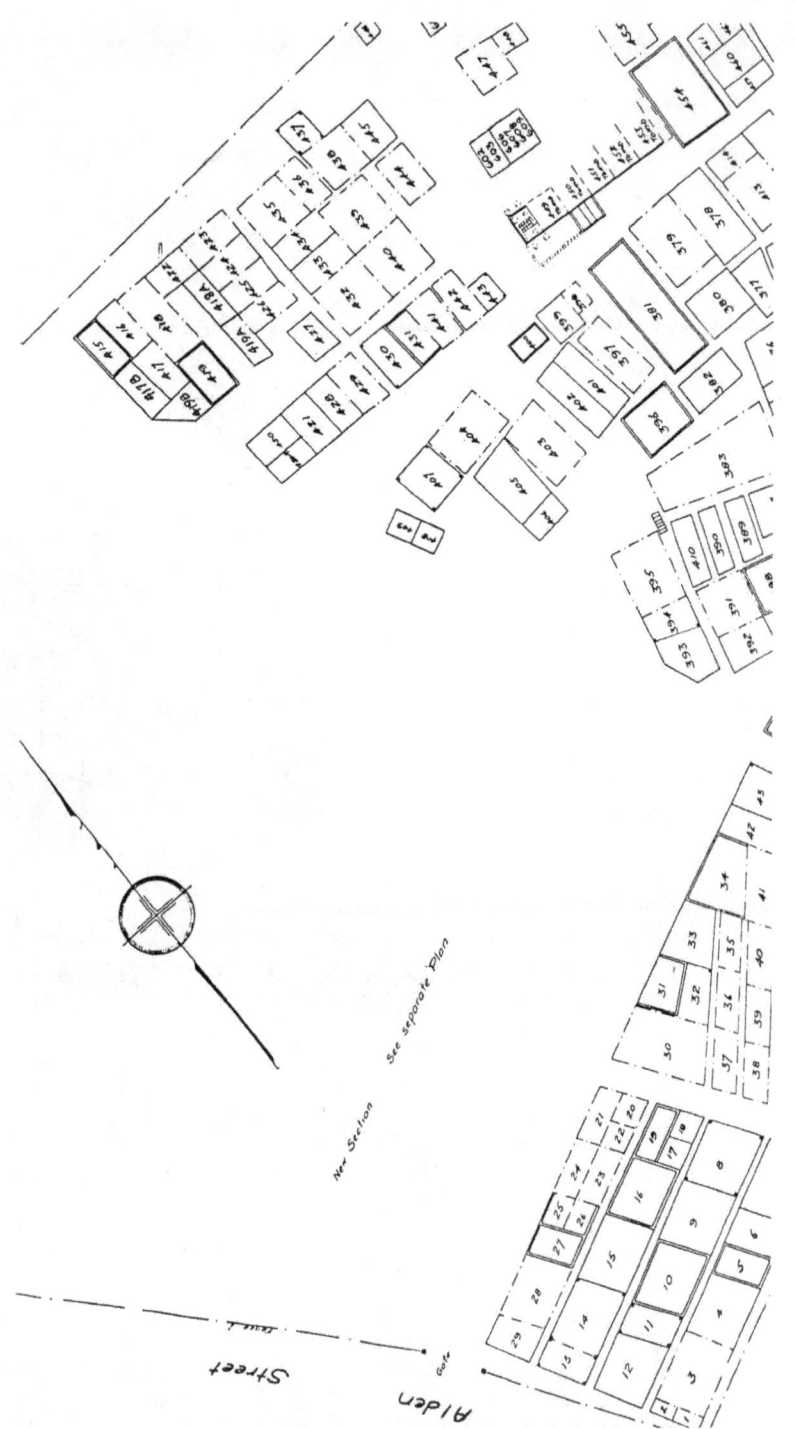

PART TWO

GIFFORD CEMETERY

GIFFORD CEMETERY

LOT #1 -- 1 Monument - 3 Footstones

   1. Monument Front: Capt. Chas. H. Bannister 1824-1899
                       Emina C. Bannister 1826-1910
                       Children
                       Charlie 1861-1863

     Monument Right: Chas. F. Bannister 1865-1953

     Monument Rear: Capt. Alex. Dowling 1843-1889
                      Children
                      Archie F 1878-1881

   2. Footstone - Mother

   3. Footstone - Father

   4. Footstone - Charles

LOT #2 -- 1 Stone - 1 Marker

   1. Manuel Sears 1864-1907
      Emma F Sears 1864-1922
      J. Emmons Winslow 1890-1949

   2. Marker - Baby

LOT #3 -- 2 Stones

   1. Front: John Wells Small 1851-1929
          Susan A Holway Sept. 21, 1849 - Oct. 27, 1901

     Right: Gilbert H. Fifield 1875-1935
          Susie W Fifield 1877-1956

     Rear: Capt. John W. Small Dec. 1, 1810 - May 25, 1863
          Rachel S. Small Apr. 1, 1817 - May 16, 1903

   2. Mary E wife of Amasa S. Dyer Mar. 14, 1835 - Sept. 12, 1898
     Amasa S. Dyer Nov. 9, 1837 - May 9, 1922

LOT #4 -- 1 Stone

   1. Rear: Rev. Porter Monroe Vinton 1833-1913

GIFFORD CEMETERY

LOT #4 (continued)

    Rebecca Sparks Vinton 1847-1920
    William M. 1865-1893
    Isaac Atkins Dyer 1836-1915
    Lorena Sparks Dyer 1841-1923

 Left: Albert J. Vinton 1874-(no date)

 Right: Sherman E. Vinton 1862-1923

LOT #5 -- 1 Stone - 1 Marker

 1. Front: John P. Harvender 1845-1933
     His wife Neoma 1853-1928

  Right: Jacob Diggdon 1852-1881
     Mary Diggdon 1827-1894

  Left: Ada B. (Harvender) 1873-1874
     Sadie E (Harvender) 1876-1900
     Fred M. (Harvender) 1878-1901

 2. Henry B. Harvender, Mass. PVT. Co. K 73 Infantry World War I Feb. 14, 1889 - Sept. 14, 1966

LOT #6 -- 1 Stone - 3 Footstones - 1 Base, no stone

 1. Front: Capt. Isaac B. Lewis Oct. 10, 1831 - Aug. 15, 1912
     Olive A Aug. 9, 1835 - Aug. 24, 1869
     Elizabeth A Dec. 6, 1840 - not cut

  Right: Betsey W Dec. 18, 1854 - Jan. 5, 1856
     Betsey W Oct. 23, 1864 - Oct. 23, 1864

  Left: Charles H. Giles (born) Manchester N.H., Oct. 1, 1859 (died) Sept. 18, 1889
     "A kind brother and a faithful friend"

 2. Footstone - Olive A.

 3. Footstone - Isaac B.

 4. Footstone - Betsey W.

 5. Base - no stone

LOT #7 -- 7 Stones

 1. Bangs A. Lewis 1839-1913
  Emma R. Lewis 1842-1916

 2. James E. Worth 1861-1918
  Nellie P. Worth 1866-1940

 3. Susie Warren, twin daughter of B. A. & Emma R. Lewis died April 22, 1871 ae 9 ms. 24 ds.

 4. Ethel -1889- (surname Worth)

 5. Georgie 1890-1899 (surname Worth)

 6. Henry Blundell 1816-1884

GIFFORD CEMETERY

LOT #7 (continued)

    Mary Blundell 1813-1899

    7. Willie F. son of Henry & Mary Blundell died March 19, 1857 ae 2 ys. 5 mos. 18 ds.

LOT #8 -- 4 Stones

    1. Charles A. Cook 1850-1939
       Marion F. his wife 1854-1940

    2. Capt. William Williams 1858-1914
       Louise B. his wife 1859-1912

    3. Herbert A. Ford 1863-1920
       Lillian M. Cook wife of Herbert A. Ford 1873-1906

    4. Herbert Woodbury Rich 1876-1951
       His wife Grace Elliott Cook 1877-1949

LOT #9 -- 1 Stone - 4 Foorstones

    1. Front: Charles A. Fuller 1854-1922
             Sarah D. Fuller 1856-1911
             Charles P. Kelley 1850-1915
             Hannah C. Kelley 1854-1911

       Rear: Edmund Graham 1828-1875
              Rachel S. Graham 1828-1914

    2. Footstone - Sarah

    3. Footstone - Rachel

    4. Footstone - Charles

    5. Footstone - Hannah

LOT #10 -- 1 Stone - 1 Footstone

    1. John Bell 1838-1926
       Zilpha Bell 1835-1915

    2. Footstone - Mother

LOT #11 -- 1 Stone - 2 Markers - 1 Footstone

    1. Frederick F. Cook 1861-1906
       Emma P. Cook 1864-1938

    2. Charles A. Atkins 1864-1960
       Esther F. Atkins 1870-1949

    3. Hazel Y. Stone 1897-1956

    4. Footstone - Husband

LOT #12 -- 1 Stone

    1. Charles Baker 1873-1906
       Lizzie P. Baker 1865-1909

GIFFORD CEMETERY

LOT #12 (continued)
    Maud C. Baker -1898-
    Leroy C. Baker 1899-1900

LOT #13 -- No Stone

LOT #14 -- No Stone

LOT #15 -- 1 Stone - 4 Markers

1. Rear: John Darrow Adams Feb. 23, 1860 - Nov. 12, 1930
        Jennie Holmes Adams Mar. 3, 1862 - Aug. 12, 1896
        John Darrow Adams July 9, 1930 - May 5, 1948
        Adele Proctor Adams July 6, 1895 - Nov. 27, 1947

2. Babe

3. Babe

4. Harriet D. Adams 1892-1964

5. Darrow Adams 1894-1958

LOT #16 -- 1 Stone - 6 Footstones

1. Front: William Roberts 1830-1912
       His wife Elizabeth E. Pierce 1847-1923
       Edward Roberts 1854-1912
       His wife Emily K. Paine 1859-1933

   Rear: Alfred N. Brown 1846-1921
       His wife Annetta N. Pierce 1853-1929
       Ira W. Brown 1874-1925
       His wife Carrie L. Crooker 1875-(not cut)

2. Footstone - Annetta

3. Footstone - Alfred

4. Footstone - Elizabeth

5. Footstone - William

6. Footstone - Ira W.

7. Footstone - Emily

LOT #17 -- 1 Stone - 6 Footstones

1. Front: Capt. M. J. Cavanagh 1850-1921 (Michael J. Cavanagh)
       Mary J. Cavanagh 1854-1934
       Sara A. Cavanagh 1858-1938

   Rear: Walter E. Bucknam 1855-1937
       Celia T. Bucknam 1861-1937

2. Footstone - Walter

3. Footstone - Celia

4. Footstone - Celeste (no date)

GIFFORD CEMETERY

LOT #17 (continued)

    5. Footstone - Sara

    6. Footstone - Brother

    7. Footstone - Mary

LOT #18 -- 1 Stone

    1. Barachias F. Hartford 1803-1870
       Abigail N. Hartford 1809-1876
       Elvira H. Roop (maiden name Hartford) 1853-1877

LOT #19 -- 1 Stone - 4 Footstones

    1. Rear: Capt. Russell Knox Elliott 1817-1857
           His wife Olive Wadsworth Cook 1818-1907
           Russell Dunson Elliott 1849-1933
           His wife Elizabeth Hannum Kenney 1852-1933
           Russell Dunson Elliott, Jr. 1879-1880

    2. Footstone - O. W. E.

    3. Footstone - R. D. E.

    4. Footstone - E. H. E.

    5. Footstone - R. D. E. Jr.

LOT #20 -- 2 Stones

    1. Enos N. Atkins 1835-1897

    2. Neadom Rodgers 1837-1897
       Honorah A. his wife 1849-1921
       Mary J. 1867-1917
       Elijah Rodgers 1878-1960
       Clara Rodgers 1879-19(not cut)

LOT #21 -- 1 Stone

    1. Front: Caleb Eugene Fisher 1860-1923
           Frances C. Fisher 1832-1899

       Right: Jerome A. Mayo 1851-1905
           Bessie G. Mayo 1851-1901
           Bessie F. Mayo 1876-1881

       Rear: Margaret A. Hutchings 1819-1906

       Left: Almera C. (Fisher) 1856-1857
          Almera C. (Fisher) 1848-1852

LOT #22 -- 1 Stone - 7 Footstones

    1. Front: Eliza W. Cook 1836-1920
           Fred W. Cook 1858-(not cut)
           Addie his wife 1862-1919
           Capt. Joseph R. Atkins 1826-1911
           Martha W. Atkins 1830-1903

GIFFORD CEMETERY

LOT #22 (continued)

    Rear: Zaccheus R. (Atkins) 1852-1937
               Martha J. (Atkins) 1869-1952
               Charles F. Cate 1849-1909
               Etta A. Cate 1857-1909

2. Footstone - Eliza

3. Footstone - Father

4. Footstone - Mother

5. Footstone - Charles

6. Footstone - Etta

7. Footstone - Martha

8. Footstone - Zaccheus

LOT #23 -- 1 Stone - 2 Footstones

1. Front: Almira B. Conwell 1848-1901
         Walter L. Conwell 1849-1917

   Left: W. L. Conwell (Walter L.) 1871-1946
         His wife Arrilla M. 1878-1934

2. Footstone - Father

3. Footstone - Mother

LOT #24 -- No Stone

LOT #25 -- No Stone

LOT #26 -- 2 Stones

1. George Chester Field Nov. 24, 1877 - Feb. 4, 1916

2. Charles U. Tuck 1856-1901

LOT #26A -- 1 Marker

1. In memory of the Healey Family: (no dates on marker, following from VR:

   Willis Healey died at Medfield, Mass. Feb. 23, 1898 aged
      41 yrs. 9 mos.
   Adelaide Jones (Masten) Healey Cook died at Bourne, Mass.
      Oct. 14, 1937 age 77
   Louisa Bangs Masten Nickerson died May 19, 1919 aged
      89 yrs. 7 mos.)

LOT #27 -- 1 Monument - 2 Footstones

1. H. J. Lancy (Henry J.) 1826-1903
   Wife of H. J. Lancy, Helen McBrien 1820-1896

2. Footstone - Wife

GIFFORD CEMETERY

LOT #27 (continued)

    3. Footstone - Husband

LOT #28 -- 5 Stones

    1. John Worth, lost at sea Nov. 19, 1873 aged 37 years
George L. infant son of John & Lydia A. Worth
(VR: died Oct. 10, 1863 ae 8 days)

    2. Lydia A. Maddock 1841-1911
Lawrence Maddock Feb. 17, 1831 - Feb. 13, 1895

    3. Martha J. daughter of Lawrence & Lydia A. Maddock died Aug. 24, 1880 ae 1 yr. 10 ms. 6 ds.

    4. Albert V. Worth Aug. 19, 1867 - June 5, 1900

    5. William G. Loring 1816-1895
Mary C. Loring 1818-1895
Eugene W. Loring 1855-1927

LOT #29 -- 1 Stone - 2 Footstones

    1. Malcom Ramsey Aug. 1, 1832 - June 16, 1913
Mary G. Ramsey June 5, 1837 - June 6, 1908

    2. Footstone - Father

    3. Footstone - Mother

LOT #30 -- 1 Monument

    1. Front: Daniel Small died Aug. 10, 1878 aged 83 ys. 7 ms. 7 ds.
Hannah G. wife of Daniel Small died July 19, 1883 aged 84 ys. 6 ms. 14 ds.

    Right: Sally daughter of Daniel & Hannah Small died Apl. 7, 1832 aged 1 yr.
Ann Simmons dau. of Daniel & Hannah Small died Feb. 14, 1836 aged 3 yrs.

LOT #31 -- 1 Stone

    1. Rear: Reuben F. Brown 1850-1929
Albina F. his wife 1858-1937
Newell C. Brooks 1833-1907
Abby C. his wife 1838-1888
Their Children (Brooks)
Maria 1861-1883
Newell C. 2nd 1865-1866
Newell C. 3rd 1867-1868
Lillian N 1869-1929

LOT #32 -- 3 Stones - 2 Footstones

    1. Front: Dedie

    Rear: Adelia T. Ellis dau. of George W. & Abbie H. Tuttle

GIFFORD CEMETERY

LOT #32 (continued)

       died Dec. 28, 1880 ae 18 yrs. 3 ms. 5 dys. (wife of Benjamin Ellis)

2. Howard W. son of Frank R. & Ida K. Foss died Dec. 15, 1893 aged 1 year 4 mos. 18 das.

3. Leonard R. Foss 1882-1929
   Katie B. Foss 1885-(not cut)

4. Footstone - Father

5. Footstone - Mother

LOT #33 -- 1 Monument - 4 Footstones

1. Monument Front: Francis P. Smith 1835-1918
                   Fidelia P. Smith 1849-1934

   Monument Left: Francis P. Jr. 1885-1939

2. Footstone - Francis

3. Footstone - Father

4. Footstone - Mother

5. Footstone - Baby

LOT #34 -- 3 Stones - 3 Footstones - 1 Marker

1. Jesse I. Kendall Oct. 31, 1822 - Apr. 1, 1900
   Harriet wife of Jesse I. Kendall Mar. 12, 1820 - Sept. 9, 1894

2. Joshua A. Snow 1855-1921
   Nellie P. Kendall his wife 1861-1922

3. Clara N. Davis 1860-1907
   Frank A. Davis 1892-1910

4. Marker - Clifford Kendall 1857-1906

5. Footstone - Almon (Kendall) no date

6. Footstone - Jesse

7. Footstone - Maud (Kendall) (VR: died April 18, 1879)

LOT #35 -- 1 Stone - 5 Footstones

1. Front: Capt. Samuel T. Hatch 1851-1930
          His wife Abbie D. Childs 1853-1927

   Right: Florence R. (Hatch) Sept. 27, 1882 - June 13, 1900
          Gertrude W. (Hatch) Mar. 31, 1874 - Feb. 1, 1875

   Rear: Alfred H. Lewis 1868-1949
        His wife Jennie C. Hatch 1878-1966

   Left: Capt. Benj. F. (Hatch) 1872-1927

2. Footstone - Fred

GIFFORD CEMETERY

LOT #35 (continued)

    3. Footstone - Jennie

    4. Footstone - Father

    5. Footstone - Baby

    6. Footstone - Flossie

LOT #36 -- No Stone

LOT #37 -- No Stone

LOT #38 -- 1 Stone

    1. Freeman S. Lurten Sept. 21, 1836 - April 7, 1905
       Deborah M. wife of Freeman S. Lurten Sept. 20, 1842 - May 1, 1895

LOT #39 -- 3 Stones

    1. Theodore Winthrop Swift June 24, 1861 - Jan. 22, 1936
       His wife Mattie Hanson Gross Oct. 7, 1869 - Mar. 31, 1950

    2. George Thomas Gross August 30, 1836 - February 18, 1895
       Julia Frances Critchett November 15, 1842 - December 4, 1918

    3. Edward Blake son of George T. & Julia F. Gross February 21, 1872 - July 16, 1907

LOT #40 -- 1 Monument - 1 Stone - 5 Footstones

    1. Monument Front: Simeon S. Gifford 1819-Passed to Spirit Life-1894
                       Marinda A. Gifford 1822-Passed to Spirit Life-1906
       Monument Right: Romenia Gifford Lowell 1870-1906
                        Mary E. wife of B. D. Gifford 1840-1901
       Monument Left: Frederick A. H. Gifford 1847-1900
                       Laura his wife 1856-1942

    2. Front: Sister-Amelia Jennie Dods 1827-1886

       Rear: Willie (Dods) 1846-1849

    3. Footstone - Mother

    4. Footstone - Father

    5. Footstone - Mama

    6. Footstone - Romenia

    7. Footstone - Fred-Papa

LOT #41 - 1 Monument

    1. Monument Front: John Walton Davis 1817-1880
                       Laura Talmadge Davis 1820-1880

GIFFORD CEMETERY

LOT #41 (continued)

        Monument Right: Robert L. Harding 1842-1911
                        Elizabeth O. Harding 1843-1935
                        Lou Harding Cole (no date)
        Monument Rear: John Winthrop Davis 1861-1940
                        Ida Bell Burch his wife 1869-1948
        Monument Left: Frederick Walton Davis 1800-1885

LOT #42 -- 3 Stones - 1 Footstone

    1. James M. Holmes 1828-1865
       Salome C. Holmes 1831-1901

    2. James M. Burke 1865-1941
       Ada Holmes 1865-1948
       John (Burke) 1859-1934

    3. James P. Holmes 1852-1912
       Sarah C his wife 1863-1948
       Carrie L. 1886-1886
       Flo M. 1887-1898

    4. Footstone - Flo - Carrie

LOT #43 -- 1 Monument - 4 Footstones

    1. Monument Front: Rev. Josiah Higgins died in Fremont, N. H., Feb. 22, 1884 aged 80 yrs.
                         Sarah Hinks wife of Rev. J. Higgins died Dec. 9, 1870 aged 63 yr.

       Monument Right: Charles W. Higgins died May 7, 1867 aged 22 yrs.
                        Susan B. Higgins First Missionary to Yokohama of the W. F. M. Society of the M. E. Church, died in Tokio, Japan, July 3, 1879 aged 36 yrs.

       Monument Rear: Mary Abbie daughter of J. P. & L. A. Higgins died Aug. 12, 1869 aged 11 ms. 24 ds.
                       Vine Adams daughter of J. P. & L. A. Higgins died Sept. 27, 1871 aged 6 mos.

       Monument Left: Lavina Adams wife of J. P. Higgins Aug. 5, 1871 aged 28 yrs.

    2. Footstone - Mother

    3. Footstone - Charlie

    4. Footstone - May Abbie

    5. Footstone - Little Vine

LOT #44 -- 3 Stones - 2 Markers

    1. Capt. Reuben Atkins died Sept. 24, 1883 aged 74 yrs. 10 ms.

GIFFORD CEMETERY

LOT #44 (continued)

    2. Our Mother - Roxana Atkins died Sept. 20, 1888 aged 79 yrs. 9 ms. 8 ds.

    3. Richard Baxter 1826-1908
       Eliza C. Baxter 1831-1909

    4. Marker - Reinhold Waldin 1861-1897 buried in Quincy, Ill.
             His wife Florence M. Baxter 1858-1962

    5. Marker - Leslie Baumgartner 1893-1959
             His wife F. Louise Waldin 1896-1978

LOT #45 -- 5 Markers

    1. Willis F. Leonard, Massachusetts BMC, U. S. Coast Guard, World War II Dec. 13, 1911 - April 12, 1960

    2. William J. Leonard 1886-1942
       Josephine W. Leonard 1889-1957

    3. Leonard S. Batt -1940-

    4. Stanley Batt, Massachusetts, B. M. L. C. U. S. Coast Guard, World War II, Korea, Sept. 19, 1912 - April 3, 1971

    5. Antone P. Merrill 1895-1963
       Florence M. Merrill 1893-1976

LOT #46 -- 1 Monument - 1 Stone - 5 Footstones

    1. Monument Front: Nathaniel E. Atwood died Nov. 7, 1886 aged 79 yrs. 1 mo. 25 dys.

       Monument Right: Louisa M. Atwood died Feb. 28, 1873 aged 48 yrs. 3 ms. 4 dys.
                      Charlie S. died Mar. 10, 1858 aged 3 mos. 4 dys.
                      Lizzie S. died Ap. 27, 1858 aged 4 mos. 21 dys.

       Monument Left: Maria Atwood died July 31, 1849 aged 36 yrs. 9 mos. 8 dys.
                    John E. Atwood died July 30, 1849 aged 11 yrs. 8 mos. 5 dys.

    2. Myrick C. Atwood Aug. 16, 1852 - Apl. 12, 1929
       Elizabeth P. Atwood Sept. 26, 1853 - Jan. 31, 1925

    3. Footstone - Father

    4. Footstone - Louisa M.

    5. Footstone - Maria

    6. Footstone - John E.

    7. Footstone - Charles S. & Lizzie S.

GIFFORD CEMETERY

LOT #47 -- 1 Stone - 2 Footstones

    1. Robert Mulready 1899-1947
       Violette Mulready 1900-1977
       Minerva B. Kelley July 26, 1856 - Feb. 18, 1900
       Alice Kelley Hinman 1877-1913

    2. Footstone - Alice

    3. Footstone - Minnie

LOT #48 -- No Stone

LOT #49 -- No Stone

LOT #50 -- 1 Stone - 10 Footstones

    1. Front: Capt. Daniel Allen 1827-1909
            Flora Allen 1831-1897
            William T. Harvender 1851-1917
            Bessie A. Harvender 1855-1887

       Right: Donald M. (Allen) 1861-1887
            Jessie M. wife of D. K. Reynolds 1863-1931

       Left: Daniel R. (Harvender) 1883-1885
           Edwin A. (Harvender) 1876-1894
           Maude B. (Harvender) 1886-1905
           Dwight H. (Harvender) 1890-1941
           Florence W. (Harvender) 1881-1949

    2. Footstone - Wife

    3. Footstone - Husband

    4. Footstone - Dwight

    5. Footstone - Father

    6. Footstone - Mother

    7. Footstone - Baby

    8. Footstone - Maude

    9. Footstone - Eva

    10. Footstone - Jessie

    11. Footstone - Florence

LOT #51 -- 2 Stones - 1 Marker

    1. Father - Frederick T. Daggett Mar. 15, 1827 - Nov. 5, 1893
       Mother - Helen F. Daggett Dec. 11, 1836 - Oct. 29, 1897

    2. Howard R. Hopkins 1864-1940
       Cora M. Daggett 1873-1907

    3. Marker - John L. son of Frederick T. and Ellen F. Daggett
       died June 10, 1860 aged 2 yrs. 4 ms.

GIFFORD CEMETERY

LOT #52 -- 2 Stones - 2 Markers - 2 Footstones

   1. Thomas C. Newcomb 1845-1935
      Melissa 1852-1921
      Mabel 1873-1953
      Warren T. 1880-1927
      Sarah 1815-1876

   2. Samuel F. Newcomb 1849-1919
      Almena F. Newcomb 1851-1920
      Charles F. 1875-1896

   3. Marker - Husband - Jonah Newcomb

   4. Marker - Wife - Ella F. Newcomb

   5. Footstone - Ann (VR: Annie Almena born Nov. 15, 1884 dtr. of Thomas C. & Melissa Newcomb)

   6. Footstone - Warren

LOT #53 -- 1 Stone

   1. Front: Josiah A. Chase Dec. 17, 1849, died at Monrovia, West Africa, Apr. 14, 1898
          Amelia A. his wife Nov. 12, 1855 - June 8, 1942

      Right: Bessie Aldwell July 4, 1878 drowned at Isles of Shoals July 17, 1902. "Beloved" (surname Chase)

LOT #54 -- 1 Monument - 7 Footstones - 1 Base of footstone - 1 Stone

   1. Monument Front: Capt. William Cook died July 5, 1868 aged 60 yrs. 9 ms.

      Monument Right: Rebecca wife of Capt. William Cook died May 26, 1840 aged 29 yrs. 10 ms. 15 ds.

      Monument Rear: Horace W. Cook 1851-1896

      Monument Left: Joanna R. Cook wife of Capt. William Cook 1816-1893
                  Caroline F. Cook 1844-1924

   2. Levi Higgins died Nov. 22, 1838 aged 27 yrs.

   3. Footstone - Mother

   4. Footstone - Father

   5. Footstone - Mother

   6. Footstone - Eddie (no date)

   7. Footstone - Rubie (VR: died June 7, 1840 ae 1 mo.)

   8. Footstone - Johnnie (no date)

   9. Footstone - Carrie

   10. Footstone - Base only

GIFFORD CEMETERY

LOT #55 -- 2 Stones

    1. Robert Newcomb 1849-1937
       Sarah Newcomb 1851-1944

    2. Manuel Patrick 1875-1948
       Sadie M. Patrick 1886-1979

LOT #56 -- 1 Monument - 4 Markers - 2 Footstones - 3 Stones - 1 Base-no stone

    1. Monument Front: Capt. Wm. F. Remington Aug. 14, 1841 - Apr. 9, 1885
                      Orie M. wife of Wm. F. Remington 1845-1905

       Monument Right: Willie S. Remington Oct. 13, 1874 - July 27, 1875

       Monument Left: Orie P. Remington Dec. 23, 1876 - June 4, 1886

    2. Capt. Arnold Small 1818-1895
       Esther D. wife of Capt. Arnold Small 1818-1892

    3. Esther F. dau. of A. O. & L. S. Small 1871-1876

    4. Mother - Lydia S. wife of Capt. A. O. Small 1845-1891

    5. Capt. Arnold O. Small 1843-1921

    6. Josephine T. wife of Capt. Arnold O. Small 1852-1926

    7. Beatrice H. Proctor 1882-1909

    8. Willie S. son of Wm. & Orie M. Remington died July 27, 1875 ae 9 mos. 14 ds.

    9. Footstone - Baby

    10. Footstone - Orie

    11. Base - no stone

LOT #57 -- 2 Stones

    1. Front: Isaac H. Higgins 1838-1909
           His wife Harriet N. Higgins 1836-1894

       Rear: Infant Children
             Rotie Nye (Higgins) -1861-
             Clara E. (Higgins) -1868-
             Myra W. -1870-
             Hattie L. -1873-
             Stephen W. -1875-

    2. C. Lothrop Higgins 1863-1926
       Elmer A. Higgins 1879-1947
       Myra Goss 1882-(repaired)

LOT #58 -- 1 Stone - 3 Footstones

    1. Front: Thaddeus P. Dickson 1834-1914

GIFFORD CEMETERY

LOT #58 (continued)

    His wife Hannah W. Dickson 1836-1887

  Rear: Infant son of T. E. & O. E. Ross -1903-

 2. Footstone - Mother

 3. Footstone - Father

 4. Footstone - Baby

LOT #59 -- 1 Monument - 1 Stone - 3 Footstones

 1. Monument Front: Ephraim Cook died Feb. 22, 1891
    aged 84 yrs. 3ms. 18 ds.
    Rebecca E. Cook died Dec. 27, 1850
    aged 34 yrs. 4 ms. 24 ds.
    Betsey L. Cook died Sept. 5, 1891
    aged 75 yrs. 2 ms. 13 ds.

  Monument Rear: Cornelius Cook died Feb. 5, 1851 aged 2 ms.

 2. Sadie H. daughter of E. P. & A. H. Cook aged 10 mos. 25 ds. (died c1852)

 3. Footstone - Father

 4. Footstone - Mother

 5. Footstone - Mother

LOT #60 -- No Stone

LOT #61 -- 4 Stones

 1. Olive N. Paine wife of C. A. Hannum 1820-1894

 2. Chas. A. Hannum 1817-1889

 3. J. Ella Farwell wife of A. P. Hannum 1848-1893

 4. William Porter Hannum, Massachusetts Cox. USNRF World War I June 12, 1889 - May 26, 1946

LOT #62 -- 1 Monument

 1. Monument Rear: Alexander Hamlin 1815-1892
    Sarah A. Hamlin 1816-1851
    Mary E. Hamlin 1833-1912
    Minnie E. Hamlin 1862-1891
    Nathan Freeman 1793-1857
    Abigail Freeman 1797-1877
    Lucius A. Black (no date)
    Sara A. Hamlin 1849-1934

LOT #63 -- 1 Monument - 4 Footstones

 1. Monument Front: Capt. Benj. Freeman died at East Indies
    Nov. 8, 1871 aged 49 yrs.
    Betsey his wife died Dec. 25, 1896 aged
    72 yrs

GIFFORD CEMETERY

LOT #63 (continued)

    Monument Left: Emily B. (Freeman) 1862-1914
                          Betsey D. 1845-1928
                          Benjamin Jr. 1850-Lost at sea

  2. Footstone - Emma

  3. Footstone - Bessie

  4. Footstone - Mother

  5. Footstone - Father

LOT #64 -- 1 Monument - 5 Stones - 5 Footstones

  1. Monument Front: John W. Atwood 1842-1913
                        Abbie T. wife of John W. Atwood Feb. 6,
                            1845 - Dec. 5, 1874

     Monument Right: Mary F. Fuller 1859-1936 (maiden name
                        Sparks)

     Monument Rear: In memory of 6 infants (see stones #2 thru
                        #6)

     Monument Left: Capt. John Atwood, Dec. 26, 1811 - Oct. 10,
                        1896
                        Rebecca M. wife of John Atwood died May 1,
                        1888 aged 68 yrs. 8 ms. 12 ds.

  2. Alonzo F. son of John & Rebecca Atwood born May 8, 1846 died Sept. 18, 1847

  3. Edwin C. died Sept. 19, 1850 aged 3 mos. 9 ds.
An infant daughter born & died March 29, 1849
Children of John & Rebecca Atwood

  4. Ida Chester daughter of John & Rebecca M. Atwood born March 7 died July 15, 1854

  5. Willie Lester son of John & Rebecca M. Atwood born June 20, 1855 died Oct. 21, 1856

  6. George W. son of John & Rebecca M. Atwood born May 22 died Aug. 23, 1856

  7. Footstone - J. W. A.

  8. Footstone - Wife - A. T. A.

  9. Footstone - M. F. F.

 10. Footstone - Mother

 11. Footstone - Father

LOT #65 -- 2 Stones - 1 Marker - 2 Footstones

  1. Capt. James S. Dyer Sept. 25, 1877 aged 50 yrs. 3 ms.
Sarah S. Dyer Feb. 14, 1832 - May 6, 1904

  2. Little Alley (on Dyer side of lot)

GIFFORD CEMETERY

LOT #65 (continued)

    3. Capt. Robert M. Lavender born at Liverpool, N. S.
       1847-1928
      Louise J. his wife born at Yarmouth, N.S. 1847-1920
      Katie A. 1870-1871

    4. Katie Allen daughter of Robert M. & Louise J. Lavender died Mar. 10, 1871 aet 4 mos. & 17 das.

    5. Marker - Elbridge Lavender 1875-1944
              Albertina Lavender 1876-1944

LOT #66 -- 1 Stone - 3 Footstones

    1. Front: Capt. John MacMillan Sept. 15, 1835 - Sept. 21, 1895
             Mary H. MacMillan Jan. 31, 1854 - Jan. 10, 1906

      Right: Lorena D. MacDonald Dec. 24, 1876 - Mar. 10, 1892

      Rear: Capt. Murdock MacDonald June 15, 1842 - Feb. 18, 1890

    2. Footstone - Mother

    3. Footstone - Husband

    4. Footstone - Nena

LOT #67 -- 1 Stone - 1 Double Marker

    1. Harvey O. Sparrow 1831-1919
      Orianna C. Sparrow 1836-1921
      Harvey O. Sparrow Jr. 1866-1915
      Sylvanus Gross 1808-1897
      Clarissa P. Gross 1810-1868

    2. Double marker on one base:
      Clara C. died Feb. 2, 1869 ae 2 ms. 16 ds.
      Herbert C. died Sept. 27, 1872 ae 1 yr. 2 ms. 16 ds.
      Children of Harvey O. & Orrie C. Sparrow

LOT #68 -- 1 Monument - 5 Stones - 3 Footstones

    1. Monument Front: Capt. Xenophon S. Rich died June 24, 1890
                     ae 56 yrs. 10 ms. "Though lost to sight
                     to memory dear"
                Mary E. his wife 1836-1920
      Monument Right: Manie Steele dau. of Xenophon S. and Mary
                     E. Rich died Mch. 8, 1874 ae 9 ms.
                Asaph S. son of Asaph S. and Marion Atkins
                     1879-1901
      Monument Rear: Capt. Asaph S. Atkins died in Carriacoll, W.
                  I. Apl. 6, 1880 36 ys. 14 ds.
                Marion Atkins 1846-1917
      Monument Left: Benj. E. Atkins 1810-1846
               Lydia Atkins 1814-1884
               Capt. Nicholas White 1827-1879
               Harriet S. his wife 1833-1915

GIFFORD CEMETERY

LOT #68 (continued)

2. Benjamin E. Atkins died Aug. 25, 1846 aged 36 yrs. 17 dys. Lydia S. Atkins died May 31, 1884 aged 69 yrs. 6 mos. 10 ds.

3. Manie Steele dau. of Xenophen (sic) S. & Mary E. Rich died Mar. 3, 1874 aet 9 months

4. Asaph S. Atkins 1879-1901

5. Willie Lawson Atkins 1874-1901

6. Ira Bidwell son of Nicholas & Harriet S. White Aug. 26, 1853 - July 30, 1858

7. Footstone - H. S. White

8. Footstone - X. S. R.

9. Footstone M. E. R.

LOT #69 -- 2 Stones - 2 Footstones

1. Stone is 35½" high and 22¼" wide with 3/4" letters.
   Front: "Mehitable Cook Ghen - Born in Provincetown Sept. 15, 1812 died in Provincetown May 2, 1875. She was the eldest child of Thomas Ghen, a son of Samuel who came to Provincetown from Greensboro, Md. about 1780. Thomas, his father, went from Northumberland County, Va. to Greensboro about 1751." J. T. S.

   Back: "She married first John Smyth who was born in Provincetown, Mch. 6, 1809 and died in Clinton, Me. Feb. 28, 1837. He was a son of Edmund. Born in Chatham Jan. 26, 1765."

   Children of John and Mehitable:
   Edmund born in Provincetown Jan. 26, 1832 and died in Provincetown Apl. 25, 1879
   Alonzo born in Provincetown June 26, 1833 and died in Cohasset, Mass. Sept. 11, 1885
   John Thomas born in Clinton, Me. July 13, 1837 died in Boston, Mass. Feb. 5, 1901
   She married second, in Provincetown, Mch. 13, 1846, Samuel Parker, who died Apl. 21, 1850 ae 64 yrs. 5 ms. J. T. S. 1889

2. Edmund Smith died Apl. 25, 1879 aged 47 yrs. 3 ms.

3. Footstone - Mother

4. Footstone - John

LOT #70 -- 6 Stones - 1 Marker

1. Benjamin Brown 1825-1907
   His wife Adeline C. Hilliard 1831-1870

2. Mary B. Cook died Mch. 29, 1874 aged 46 yrs. 4 ms. 26 das.

3. Daniel C. Cook died Dec. 18, 1888 ae 66 yrs. 10 ms. 17 ds.

GIFFORD CEMETERY

LOT #70 (continued)

    4. Cornelius Cook died Nov. 16, 1849 ae 20 yrs.

    5. Father - George R. Whitney May 27, 1829 - May 7, 1905

    6. Mother - Pauline Hilliard wife of George R. Whitney Feb. 28, 1833 - April 27, 1897

    7. Marker - Abbie Hilliard 1858-1943 dau. of B. & A. H. Brown

LOT #71 -- No Stone (Lot listed in the name of John T. Freeman)

LOT #72 -- 1 Monument (of a dog) - 4 Footstones

    1. G. B. Smith - 1874 (Ed. note: Possibly 1874 is the date the monument was erected. Gamaliel B. Smith died at East Boston, Mass., Aug. 23, 1888 ae 76 yrs. His wife, Sarah (LeCount) died at East Boston, Jan. 13, 1888 ae 68 yrs. 5 mos.)

    2. Footstone - Wife

    3. Footstone - Husband

    4. Footstone - Mother - 1871

    5. Footstone - Father

LOT #73 -- 1 Monument - 2 Stones - 2 Footstones

    1. Monument Front: Simeon N. Freeman died at Fernandina, Florida, April 12, 1870 aet 37 yrs.

    Monument Right: Capt. Elisha Tillson died Oct. 10th, 1879 aged 75 yrs. 11 mos. 15 ds.
Tamsin wife of Elisha Tillson died Aug. 13, 1882 aged 72 yrs. 1 mo. 22 ds.

    2. John A. son of Elisha & Tamsin Tillson born January 4, 1843 died Sept. 26, 1843

    3. Mary L. daughter of Elisha & Tamsin Tillson died Mar. 14, 1843 ae 2 ys. 9 ms. 14 ds.

    4. Footstone - Mother

    5. Footstone - Father

LOT #74 -- 1 Stone - 1 Footstone

    1. Capt. Elisha Freeman died Nov. 6, 1855 ae 64 years

    2. Footstone - "Free"

LOT #75 -- 1 Stone - 3 Footstones

    1. Front: Capt. Allen W. Rich 1840-1912
Eunice S. Rich 1846-1919

    Rear: Allen O. (Rich) 1872-1873
Chester A. (Rich) 1884-1967

GIFFORD CEMETERY

LOT #75 (continued)

    2. Footstone - Father

    3. Footstone - Mother

    4. Footstone - Chester A.

LOT #76 -- 2 Stones

    1. Simeon L. West 1836-1919
       Eliza West 1842-1930
       Hattie M. West 1863-1871

    2. James Young 1823-1885
       Mary A. Young his wife 1826-1908

LOT #77 -- 4 Stones - 1 Marker

    1. William H. Law 1828-1886
       Mehitable Law 1831-1919

    2. Willie B. son of W. H. & Mehitable Law died Aug. 12, 1860 ae 1 yr. 2 ms. 8 ds.

    3. Louis A. Law 1871-1956
       Nellie N. Law 1872-1931

    4. Ida S. died Sept. 14, 1878 ae 23 yrs. 14 days
       Clarence B. died Mar. 7, 1878 ae 4 ms. 10 ds.
       Wife & son of John E. Jordan

    5. Wm. M. Law 1864-1934

LOT #78 -- 1 Monument - 10 Footstones

    1. Monument Front: Capt. Benjamin Ryder died Oct. 21, 1870 aged 73 yrs. 10 mos. 23 dys.
                      Anna wife of Capt. Benjamin Ryder died Oct. 8, 1869 aged 69 yrs. 6 mos. 22 ds.

       Monument Right: Jos. S. Atwood died Aug. 8, 1909 ae 76 yrs. 7 mos. 10 ds.
                      Betsey N. wife of Jos. S. Atwood died May 15, 1888 ae 54 yrs. 7 mos. 19 ds.

       Monument Rear: Fred S. son of J. S. & B. N. Atwood Mar. 10, 1875 ae 7 yrs. 10 mos.
                      Benj. R. Atwood 1864-1938
                      Lois N. Atwood 1865-1936
                      Doris Atwood 1897-1920

       Monument Left: Benjamin died May 6, 1832 aged 1 yr. 4 mos. 16 dys.
                      Ephraim Henry drowned June 7, 1838 aged 9 yrs. 9 mos. & 28 dys.
                      Lucy A. died Sept. 19, 1838 aged 1 year & 3 dys.
                      Children of Capt. Benjamin & Anna Ryder

GIFFORD CEMETERY

LOT #78 (continued)

    2. Footstone - Betsey

    3. Footstone - Joseph

    4. Footstone - Father

    5. Footstone - Mother

    6. Footstone - Fred

    7. Footstone - Doris

    8. Footstone - Janet (no date)

    9. Footstone - Ephraim E.

    10. Footstone - Lucy A.

    11. Footstone - Benjamin

LOT #79 -- 1 Monument - 2 Markers

    1. Monument Front: Daniel F. Lewis 1835-1920

        Monument Right: Hetty F. wife of Daniel F. Lewis died May 17, 1869 ae 38 ys. 6 mos.
Mercy M. wife of Daniel F. Lewis died Nov. 19, 1876 ae 38 yrs. 2 mos. 29 ds.

    2. Marker - Mertie J. Law 1871-1962

    3. Marker - Edward M. Law 1870-1944

LOT #80 -- 3 Stones

    1. Jesse Cook Jr. died Nov. 2, 1876 ae 62 yrs. 16 ds.

    2. Mrs. Adeline wife of Jesse Cook Jr. died Sept. 5, 1843 ae 25 yrs.

    3. John A. son of Jesse & Adeline Cook died June 13, 1864 aet 23 yrs. 3 ms. 28 days

LOT #81 -- 1 Monument - 6 Footstones - 1 Marker

    1. Monument Front: Stephen Nickerson died Nov. 4, 1879 ae 85 yrs. 11 mos. 17 ds.
Rebecca R. wife of Stephen Nickerson Dec. 19, 1804 - Mar. 18, 1896

        Monument Rear: Stephen T. Nickerson died Apr. 5, 1893 ae 68 yrs. 6 mos. 29 ds.
Ruth S. Covell wife of S. T. Nickerson died Dec. 5, 1908 ae 80 yrs. 3 ms. 6 ds.

        Monument Left: Mary R. daughter of Stephen & Rebecca R. Nickerson Feb. 19, 1832 - Oct. 25, 1840
Rebecca R. daughter of Stephen & Rebecca R. Nickerson Oct. 1, 1834 - Sept. 25, 1892

    2. Seth Nickerson died Nov. 11, 1860 ae 73 years

GIFFORD CEMETERY

LOT #81 (continued)

    3. Footstone - Father

    4. Footstone - Mother

    5. Footstone Rebecca R. Nickerson 1834-1892

    6. Footstone - Mary R.

    7. Footstone - Husband - Stephen T. Nickerson Sept. 6, 1824 - April 5, 1893

    8. Footstone - Wife - Ruth S. Nickerson Aug. 29, 1828 - Dec. 5, 1908

LOT #82 -- 1 Monument - 2 Markers

    1. Monument Front: Luther Nickerson 1829-1903
                        Elizabeth S. Nickerson 1829-1887

       Monument Left: Jacob Rood 1844-1914
                       R. Dora Rood 1853-1911

    2. Marker - Luther Colby Rood 1876-1930

    3. Marker - Elizabeth N. Rood 1880-1943

LOT #83 -- 1 Monument - 2 Markers - 4 Footstones

    1. Monument Front: Atkins Nickerson 1818-1899
                        Hannah J. Nickerson 1820-1895

       Monument Right: Walter I. 1845-1850
                        Herbert M. 1848-1849

       Monument Rear: Walter I. Nickerson 1850-1910

    2. Phebe Freeman (VR: died Feb. 23, 1851 ae 39 yrs. wife of Elisha L. Freeman)

    3. Footstone - Father

    4. Footstone - Mother

    5. Footstone - W. I. N. & H. M. N.

    6. A. N. - 1913

    7. Footstone - W. I. N. - 1910

LOT #84 & #85 -- 1 Monument - 5 Stones - 3 Footstones

    1. Monument Front: Isaiah Gifford died Mch. 17, 1888 aged 75 ys. 5 ms. 19 ds.
                       Nabby Y. wife of Isaiah Gifford and daughter of Nathaniel & Linda Nickerson died Aug. 16, 1884 aged 71 yrs. 6 ms. 29 ds.

       Monument Rear: Lemuel Gifford died Dec. 27, 1880 ae 86 yrs. 5 mos. 3 dys.

GIFFORD CEMETERY

LOT #84 & # 85 (continued)

    Monument Left: Nathaniel N. son of Isaiah and Nabby Y.
                        Gifford died June 25, 1834 aged 2 ys.
                        4 ms.

                        Rebekah A. wife of Charles H. Holway &
                        dau'ter of Isaiah & Nabby Y. Gifford
                        died July 6, 1867 aged 27 ys. 11 ms.
                        17 ds.

2. Nabby widow of Benjamin Gifford died Sept. 6, 1859 ae 71 ys.
   1 mo. 10 ds.

3. Benjamin Gifford died Sept. 16, 1828 ae 42 ys. 3 ms. 24 ds.
   Salome his wife died June 5, 1818 ae 32 ys. 2 ms. 10 ds.

4. Salome A. daughter of Benjamin & Nabby Gifford died
   Mar. 1, 1827 ae 2 ys. 11 ms. 10 ds.

5. Nathaniel N. son of Isaiah & Nabby Y. Gifford died June 25,
   1834 ae 2 ys. 4 ms.

6. Agnes Gifford 1865-1904
   James Gifford 1904-1904
   Isaiah Gifford 1844-1923

7. Footstone - Husband

8. Footstone - Mother

9. Footstone - Rebekah

LOT #85 -- see above

LOT #86 -- 2 Stones

   1. Rear: James Gifford 1821-1913
          Rebecca A. Gifford 1824-1915
          Annie G. Hopkins 1863-1940 (maiden name Gifford)

      Right: Moses N. Gifford 1848-1918
            Harriet C. 1843-1918
            Frances C. 1875-1965

      Left: Thomas Gifford 1853-1853
          James Gifford Jr. 1850-1874
          Stephen A. P. Gifford 1858-1866

   2. Rear: William A. Elder 1835-1911
          Salome A. G. Elder 1845-1937 (maiden name Gifford)

LOT #87 -- 1 Stone

   1. Rear: Thomas Nickerson 1791-1852
          Polly Nickerson 1793-1849
          Alfred Nickerson 1816-1897
          Mary H. Nickerson 1815-1893
          Caroline F. Dearborn 1844-1891 (maiden name Nickerson)

GIFFORD CEMETERY

LOT #87 (continued)

    Left: Children of Thomas & Polly Nickerson
        Moses P. Nickerson 1823-1842
        Thomas Nickerson 1830-1848
        Caroline F. Nickerson -1843-

LOT #88 -- 1 Stone

1. James Emery 1810-1891
Mary P. Emery 1820-1886
Their Children:
Willis N. 1852-1876
Priscilla 1856-1886
Horace A. Freeman 1847-1910
Mary E. Freeman 1849-1929 (maiden name Emery)

LOT #89 -- 1 Stone

1. Joseph H. Emery 1835-1912
Mary A. Emery 1839-1922
Sadie G. Dyer 1860-1879 (maiden name Emery)

LOT #90 -- 7 Stones

1. Father - Jonathan Hill Jr. died Dec. 9, 1870 ae 62 yrs.
Mother - Susan K. wife of Jonathan Hill Jr. died Dec. 29, 1886 aged 80 yrs.

2. Jonathan E. Hill Apr. 29, 1856 - June 9, 1886

3. Clarence H. Hill died Feb. 12, 1889 ae 29 yrs. 8 mos. 4 ds.

4. George C. Hill Mar. 9, 1832 - Jan. 10, 1903
Almira B. Hill Jan. 17, 1831 - Aug. 1, 1904

5. George C. Hill Jr. died Feb. 26, 1898 aged 31 yrs. 7 mos. 21 dys.

6. William G. Hill died Dec. 1, 1896 ae 33 ys. 1 mo. 6 dys.

7. Rebecca H. H. dau. of George C. & Almira B. Hill died June 29, 1878 ae 4 yrs. 14 dys.

LOT #91 -- 5 Stones

1. Joseph B. Baxter May 10, 1837 - April 17, 1872
Susan E. Baxter Copeland Oct. 5, 1847 - Feb. 7, 1908
(maiden name Morris)

2. Capt. Ira B. Atkins Aug. 16, 1839 - Mar. 20, 1904

3. Elry F. wife of Ira B. Atkins Oct. 12, 1837 - May 19, 1899
(maiden name Baxter)

4. Mother - Asenath Morris Knowles 1811-1886 (maiden name Kilburn)

5. Charles Morris died July 28, 1855 ae 47 yrs. 3 mos. 19 ds.

GIFFORD CEMETERY

LOT #92 -- 3 Stones - 3 Footstones

1. Capt. James Atkins 1833-1903
   His wife Hannah S. Higgins 1838-1926
   Daughter Lizzie Ainsworth (Atkins) 1859-1875

2. Maggie A. wife of Cullen A. Hughes 1855-1900

3. Donald J. Matheson died Aug. 3, 1874 aet 32 yrs. 8 days

4. Footstone - Husband

5. Footstone - Wife

6. Footstone - Lizzie

LOT #93 -- 8 Stones

1. Reuben Swift died July 2, 1889 aged 78 yrs. 5 ms. 1 dy.

2. Mrs. Sally M. wife of Mr. Reuben Swift & daughter of Richard & Phebe Smith of Eastham, died Feb. 4, 1839 in the 22 year of her age

3. Rebecca P. wife of Reuben Swift departed this life July 1, 1876 ae 70 ys.

4. Maria Francis daughter of Reuben & Sally M. Swift died April 19, 1838 age 3 weeks

5. Sally M. daughter of Reuben & Rebecca Swift died May 15th, 1843 age 2 yrs. 22 days

6. Mary E. daughter of Reuben & Rebecca Swift died Aug. 21, 1849 aged 1 yr. 10 ms. 22 days

7. Reuben W. Swift 1844-1889
   Mary E. Swift 1844-1919

8. Helen May dau. of R. W. and Mary Swift born July 24, 1882 died Sept. 26, 1882

LOT #94 -- 5 Stones

1. Isaac Small 3rd 1811-1892
   Winnifred S. Small his wife 1809-1890

2. Lot Small died Feby. 17, 1889 - 71 yrs. 8 mos. 3 days

3. Hannah Small died Sept. 26, 1900 - 76 ys. 1 mo. 4 days

4. Sarah C. Smith 1843-1925
   Joseph H. Smith 1867-(not cut)

5. Bertha F. dau. of Heman T. and Olive F. Small died Oct. 16, 1888 ae 18 ys. 1 mo. 16 ds.

LOT #95 -- 2 Stones - 4 Footstones

1. Basil E. son of Nathan K. & Nellie F. Rich died Sept. 5, 1891 ae 1 yr. 2 mos. 16 das.

2. J. Emerson son of Joseph S. & Mary R. Pine Nov. 28, 1894 - Sept. 14, 1900

GIFFORD CEMETERY

LOT #95 (continued)

    3. Joseph S. Pine 1847-1923
       His wife Mary R. 1858-1946
       J. Emerson (Pine) 1894-1900
       Grace I. (Pine) 1897-1979

    4. Footstone - Mother

    5. Footstone - Father

    6. Footstone - Mother

LOT #96 -- 4 Stones

    1. Melissa C. Patton 1833-1917
       Sarah C. (Patton) Dodge 1857-1902

    2. Minnie-Mary S. died Aug. 26, 1861 ae 18 ms. 28 ds.
       Bertie-H. Egbert died Feb. 25, 1864 ae 16 ms. 26 ds.
       Children of R. H. & M. C. Patton

    3. Robert H. son of R. H. and M. C. Patton born Dec. 26, 1867 died Dec. 30, 1890

    4. Capt. Elisha Cook 1819-1907
       Sarah H. Cook 1829-1905

LOT #97 -- 2 Stones - 1 Footstone

    1. James T. Sparks 1825-1889
       Sarah A. Sparks 1832-1910

    2. Footstone - Mattie (surname unknown - nearest Sparks stone)

    3. Mother - Bethia N. wife of Oliver B. Conant died July 15, 1889 aged 62 years 11 mos. 20 ds.
       Father - Oliver B. Conant died July 21, 1878 aged 58 years 6 mos. 21 ds.

LOT #98 -- 1 Monument - 2 Footstones

    1. Monument Front: Capt. Daniel W. Dowling April 15, 1835 - December 29, 1888
                       His wife Margaret Kemp July 1, 1845 - November 2, 1927

       Monument Rear: Daniel W. Dowling August 9, 1872 - March 3, 1898
                      Albert H. 1875-1969
                      His wife Blanche I. 1884-1946

    2. Footstone - Father

    3. Footstone - Daniel

LOT #99 -- 1 Monument - 6 Footstones

    1. Monument Front: Jesse Nickerson died Oct. 31, 1862 aged 70 Ye.

LOT #99 (continued)

       Mary, wife, died May 14, 1870 aged 73 Ye. 6 Ms.

  Monument Right: Nellie D. wife of Hosea Huckins died Nov. 2, 1867 aged 30 Ye.

  Monument Left: Addison Nickerson June 19, 1819 - Feb. 7, 1907
       Mary Lombard wife of Addison Nickerson September 8, 1825 - December 12, 1894 (Maiden name also Nickerson)
       Malvina J. N. Sweetser 1845-1918 (Maiden name Nickerson)

 2. Footstone - Papa - A. N.

 3. Footstone - Mamma - M. L. N.

 4. Footstone - Mother

 5. Footstone - Father

 6. Footstone - Sister

 7. Footstone - Tina

LOT #100 -- 1 Monument - 2 Footstones - marble replica of open Bible

 1. Monument Front: James Gaudin died May 12, 1884 ae 50 yrs.
       Malvina C. wife of Capt. James Gaudin died July 25, 1880 ae 43 yrs.

  Monument Right: Rebecca A. wife of Capt. Heman S. Rich died Sept. 22, 1862 ae 30 yrs.
       Lizzie J. Aspley died May 12, 1879 ae 25 yrs. 9 ms.

  Monument Rear: Malvina C. Higgins died July 7, 1836
       Chas. Aspley died Aug. 20, 1848

  Monument Left: Our father - Capt. Ebenezer Higgins died June 8, 1846 ae 38 yrs. 9 ms.
       Our mother - Martha wife of Capt. Chas. Aspley died April 4, 1860 ae 47 yrs. 10 ms.

 2. Footstone - James

 3. Footstone - Lizzie

 4. Replica of open Bible set in ground in front of monument

LOT #101 -- 1 Monument - 8 Footstones

 1. Monument Front: Abraham Small died Sept. 11, 1866 ae 71 ys. 11 ms. 27 ds.
       Jane C. wife of Abraham Small died Feb. 14, 1872 ae 72 ys. 6 ms. 23 ds.

  Monument Right: Norman S. K. Small died July 2, 1844 ae

GIFFORD CEMETERY

LOT #101 (continued)

       23 ys. 9 ms. 28 ds.
       Abraham Small died Apr. 11, 1875 ae 41 ys.
       8 ms. 13 ds.

  Monument Rear: Mary E. Small died June 12, 1832 ae 2 ys.
       9 ms. 25 ds.
       Abraham Small died June 12, 1832 ae 9 ms.
       18 ds.

  Monument Left: Jonathan Crosby died Jan. 25, 1848 ae 27 ys.
       1 mo.
       Jane C. wife of Jonathan Crosby died June
       15, 1854 ae 27 ys. 6 ms.
       Norman S. K. Crosby died Apr. 3, 1874
       ae 27 ys. 18 ds.

 2. Footstone - Mother

 3. Footstone - Father

 4. Footstone - Jonathan

 5. Footstone - Jane C.

 6. Footstone - Abraham

 7. Footstone - Norman

 8. Footstone - Mary E. & Abraham

 9. Footstone - Norman

LOT #102 -- 2 Stones - 5 Footstones

 1. Samuel A. Bennett 1847-1921
   Wife Irene F. 1854-1903
   Louis A. 1885-1910

 2. Melissa F. Bennett born May 19, 1853 died Sep. 17, 1873

 3. Footstone - Mother

 4. Footstone - Father

 5. Footstone - Brother

 6. Footstone - Father - S. A. B.

 7. Footstone - Mother - I. F. B.

LOT #103 -- 1 Monument - 2 Stones - 3 Footstones

 1. Monument Front: Charles D. Cook died Feb. 13, 1888 aged
       74 years 8 mos. 1 day
       Ellen B. wife of Charles D. Cook died May
       22, 1873 aged 53 yrs. 13 ds.

  Monument Left: Charles E. son of Charles D. & Ellen B.
       Cook died Aug. 25, 1847 ae 9 mos. 12 ds.

 2. Mother

GIFFORD CEMETERY

LOT #103 (continued)

    3. Chas. D. Cook died Feb. 13, 1888 aged 74 years 8 mos. 1 da.

    4. Charlie

    5. Mrs. Rebekah Cook died Sept. 27, 1849 ae 59 yrs. 2 ms.
       Capt. Lemuel Cook died at St. Gago De Cuba Jan. 25, 1828
          ae 41 ys. 5 ms.

    6. Sally Cook daughter of Lemuel & Rebekah Cook died July 29,
       1825 aged 5 mos. & 25 days

LOT #104 -- 1 Monument

    1. Wm. J. Stid died Aug. 12, 1870 ae 35 yrs.
       Mary Stid died Mch. 13, 1877 ae 40 yrs.

LOT #105 -- 1 Monument - 7 Footstones

    1. Monument Front: George Allen, Sergt. Co. I 3rd Mass.
                       Cavalry Vol 1845-1922
                       Eunice T. Allen 1849-1926

       Monument Right: Georgie B. Allen Dec. 28, 1873 - Sept. 21,
                       1874

       Monument Rear: Gideon Allen Dec. 5, 1809 - Dec. 22, 1891
                      Polly Allen Oct. 9, 1819 - Oct. 9, 1846
                      Tabitha Allen 1821-1897

       Monument Left: George M. Allen 1875-1957
                      Helen S. Allen 1881-1964
                      Hattie P. Doane Apl. 27, 1870 - Nov. 23,
                         1894 (Maiden name Allen)

    2. Footstone - Mother

    3. Footstone - Father

    4. Footstone - Mother

    5. Footstone - Georgie

    6. Footstone - Hattie

    7. Footstone - Husband

    8. Footstone - Wife

LOT #106 -- 1 Monument - 3 Stones - 1 Footstone

    1. Monument Front: John B. Rich 1837-1921
                       Cordelia E. Cordes 1839-1907

       Monument Right: Julia F. Rich 1859-1942

    2. Capt. Uriah Small 1833-1885
       Eliza S. Small 1837-1915

    3. Ira K. Small 1864-1907

    4. Our Babes: Ira Kilburn (Small) died Apl. 18, 1863 ae 3 yrs.

GIFFORD CEMETERY

LOT #106 (continued)

 5ms. 23 dys., Also an infant son (VR: died Oct. 23, 1857 ae 1 day)

 5. Footstone - Aunt Julie

LOT #107 -- 1 Monument - 7 Footstones

 1. Monument Front: Obadiah Snow died Apl. 24, 1906 ae 81 ys. 10 dys.
   Sarah M. wife of Obadiah Snow died Oct. 1, 1885 ae 56 yrs. 4 mos. 16 dys.

 Monument Right: Elijah O. Snow Apl. 24, 1851 - Sept. 30, 1909
   Mary E. Snow 1852-1924
   Hannah J. Morris 1823-1902

 Monument Left: Louis M. Snow 1872-1963
   Mabel F. Snow 1878-1924

 2. Footstone - Father - Obadiah Snow

 3. Footstone - Sarah M. Snow aged 56 yrs. 4 mos. 16 dys.

 4. Footstone - Husband - E. Olin Snow

 5. Footstone - Wife - Mary E. Snow

 6. Footstone - Mother - Hannah J. Morris 1823-1902

 7. Footstone - Husband - Louis M. Snow

 8. Footstone - Wife - Mabel F. Snow

LOT #108 -- 1 Monument - 6 Footstones

 1. Monument Front: Joseph Whitcomb 1841-1897
   Susie E. Whitcomb his wife 1846-1876
   Levenia C. Whitcomb his wife 1858-1944

 Monument Rear: Florence M. Whitcomb wife of Arthur O. Messer 1872-1904
   Josephine W. (Messer) - no date
   Infant (Messer) - no date
   Susie E. W. Lewis 1876-1934

 Monument Left: Emma J. infant daughter (VR: died Oct. 25, 1870, dau. of Joseph & Susie Whitcomb)

 2. Footstone - Mother

 3. Footstone - Father

 4. Footstone - Mother

 5. Footstone - Susie

 6. Footstone - Emma

 7. Footstone - Flossie & Josephine

GIFFORD CEMETERY

LOT #109 -- 1 Monument - 2 Stones - 4 Footstones

1. Monument Front: Capt. Norman MacKenzie born Sept. 12, 1845
      lost at sea Aug. 31, 1898
      Sarah MacKenzie born Apr. 20, 1842 died Apr. 1, 1925

   Monument Right: Maggie A. Sept. 7, 1876 - June 21, 1886

   Monument Rear: Harry B. Crawford 1871-1931
      Sadie M. Crawford 1877-1967

   Monument Left: Lawrence MacKenzie 1879-1955

2. Footstone - Mother

3. Footstone - Lawrence

4. Footstone - Harry

5. Footstone - Maggie

6. Edwin Sears 1840-1887
   His wife Elizabeth Sears 1845-1922

7. Frank I. Sears 1867-1940
   His wife Mary E. 1870-1931

LOT #110 -- 1 Stone - 8 Footstones

1. Joseph F. Rogers 1824-1892
   His wife Hannah F. 1822-1914
   Frank M. Rogers 1864-1935
   His wife Lillian E. 1882-1911
   Emerson F. Rogers 1905-1915
   Hannah F. Rogers 1861-1886
   Frances E. Rogers 1869-1936
   Hannah Francis 1787-1861

2. Hannah F. dau. of Joseph F. & Hannah F. Rogers died April 2, 1886 ae 24 yrs. 5 mos. 2 dys.

3. Footstone - Father

4. Footstone - Mother

5. Footstone - Frances

6. Footstone - Frank

7. Footstone - Grandma

8. Footstone - Emerson

9. Footstone - Lillian

LOT #111 -- 5 Stones - 3 Footstones

1. Francis P. Cook 1836-1919
   Betsey F. Cook 1841-1918
   Isaiah W. Cook 1867-1888

2. Rebecca A. Cook died June 14, 1898 ae 59 yrs. 11 mos. 15 ds.

GIFFORD CEMETERY

LOT #111 (continued)

   3. Lemuel Cook 2nd died Nov. 30, 1885 ae 57 years 8 mos.

   4. Walter S. Cook 1852-1922
      Annie W. his wife 1867-(not cut)

   5. Warren H. son of Geo. & Sophia Whorf died Sept. 13, 1888 aged 24 yrs. 10 ms. 26 ds.

   6. Footstone - Isaiah

   7. Footstone - Husband

   8. Footstone - Wife

LOT #112 -- 1 Monument - 1 Stone

   1. Monument Front: Stephen H. Smith 1847-1885
                   Simeon C. Smith 1845-1921
                   Emily A. Smith 1849-1923
                   Simeon C. Smith Jr. 1874-1932
      Monument Right: Sadie J. Smith 1872-1872
                   Sadie W. Smith 1878-1879
      Monument Rear: Rebecca W. Atkins 1815-1878
                   Capt. Joshua Atkins 1809-1894
      Monument Left: John Smith 1804-1873
                   Sarah J. Smith 1819-1849

   2. Charles Loring Mar. 8, 1836 - Jan. 14, 1895
      Rebecca W. Loring June 5, 1838 - Aug. 20, 1897
      Infant daughter Mar. 2, 1873 - Mar. 9, 1873

LOT #113 -- 1 Monument - 3 Stones

   1. Monument Front: Archibald W. Dowling 1838-1889
                   Experience L. his wife 1849-1908
      Monument Rear: Sadie L. 1873-1877
                   Bessie F. 1876-1881

   2. John A. McRitchie died May 19, 1888 at Mobile, Ala. ae 38 yrs.

   3. Ann Eliza wife of Capt. Angus McRitchie died May 13, 1886 ae 39 yrs. 10 mos. 9 dys.

   4. Eddie Burt son of Angus & Ann Eliza McRitchie died Aug. 12, 1877 ae 5 yrs. 18 ds.

LOT #114 -- 3 Stones - 1 Footstone

   1. Front: John Freeman Oct. 17, 1821 - Dec. 20, 1904
          Mary H. Freeman Jan. 28, 1823 - Dec. 15, 1904

      Rear: J. Everett Freeman 1844-1925
           Annie E. Freeman 1854-(not cut)

   2. Hannah wife of John E. Freeman died Sept. 20, 1872 ae 28 yrs. 3 mos.

GIFFORD CEMETERY

LOT #114 (contonued)

    3. George Everett son of Everett & Hannah Freeman died July 15, 1868 aged 8 mos. 11 ds.

    4. Footstone - Hannah

LOT #115 -- 5 Stones - 1 Footstone

    1. Captain Newton P. West 1849-1939
       Elizabeth A. his wife 1850-1919
       May 1875-1875

    2. Mary W. wife of Charles Taylor died Apr. 25, 1906 ae 80 yrs. 8 mos.

    3. Father - Charles Taylor died May 27, 1890 ae 81 yrs. 4 mos. 5 ds.

    4. Mother - Hannah wife of Charles Taylor died May 27, 1877 ae 70 yrs. 1 mo. 25 ds.

    5. Little May daughter of N. P. & Lizzie A. West died Sept. 9, 1875 ae 7 mos. 9 dys.

    6. Footstone - May

LOT #116 -- 1 Stone

    1. Father Roderick Matheson Aug. 1, 1835 - Jan. 1, 1873
       Mother - Sarah his wife Nov. 25, 1847 - Aug. 21, 1896

LOT #116A -- 2 Stones

    1. John C. Heim 1842-1918
       Mary K. Heim 1838-1894

    2. George E. R. died Sept. 15, 1878 aged 5 wks. 1 dy.
       Infant daughter died Sept. 10, 1875
       Children of J. C. & M. K. Heim

LOT #117 -- 1 Monument - 2 Stones - 1 Marker - 4 Footstones

    1. Monument Front: Daniel Kemp 1839-1920
                       Katherine A. R. Kemp 1849-1927

       Monument Right: Jennie F. Kemp Feb. 2, 1881 - Aug. 5, 1904

       Monument Left: Annie R. Kemp Oct. 23, 1870 - Feb. 10, 1896

    2. Francis Kemp died May 16, 1883 aged 31 yrs. 1 mo. 10 ds.

    3. Jane M. Kemp died June 12, 1877 aged 33 yrs. 8 mos. 28 ds.

    4. Ella MacKenzie 1842-1905

    5. Footstone - Mother

    6. Footstone - Father

    7. Footstone - Jennie

    8. Footstone - Annie

GIFFORD CEMETERY

LOT #118 -- 3 Stones

1. Husband - Joseph W. Moore 1841-1909

2. Wife - Huldah C. wife of Joseph W. Moore died Jan. 11, 1887 aged 42 yrs. 2 mos.

3. Elizabeth H. Young 1869-1914
Two Infants
(Ed. note: no record of deaths of the infants)

LOT #119 -- 1 Stone - 2 Footstones

1. Josiah T. Sumner Dec. 15, 1833 - June 2, 1908
His wife Hannah M. Prince Sept. 28, 1840 - Apr. 27, 1908
Enoch N. Sumner 1831-1899
Sophronia A. Sumner 1836-1927

2. Footstone - S. A. S.

3. Footstone - E. N. S.

LOT #119A -- No stone - Lot in the name of Archibald Campbell

(VR: Archibald Campbell died at sea on Schooner C. H. Hodgden Sept. 10, 1887 ae 42 years, son of Malcolm & Florence Campbell)

LOT #120 - No Stone - Lot listed in the name of James H. Small

(VR: James H. Small died Feb. 2, 1913 ae 78 years 6 mos. 16 days, son of James and Betsey (Cook) Small)

LOT #121 -- 1 Stone - 4 Footstones

1. Elijah Bangs Sept. 4, 1838 - Oct. 25 1887
Hattie N. wife of Capt. Bangs July 31, 1842 - Nov. 14, 1899
Frank Sparks Bangs Dec. 26, 1865 - May 23, 1890
Anne Lyford Bangs Aug. 13, 1866 - Jan. 1, 1961
Charles Dana Bangs June 16, 1863 - Nov. 22, 1864
Elijah Dana Bangs Mar. 6, 1873 - Jan. 18, 1887

2. Footstone - Husband

3. Footstone - Wife

4. Footstone - Frank

5. Footstone - Dana

LOT #122 -- 4 Stones - 1 Marker

1. George H. Marshall 1868-1888

2. Reuben Freeman died Aug. 26, 1888 aged 69 yrs. 7 dys.
Elizabeth Freeman died July 28, 1893 aged 63 yrs. 11 mos. 28 dys.

3. Lewis M. son of Reuben & Elizabeth Freeman died Sept. 8, 1887 aged 26 yrs. 11 mos. 26 ds.

GIFFORD CEMETERY

LOT #122 (continued)

    4. Henry M. Walradt 1852-1923
       Elnora F. Walradt 1853-1925

    5. Reuben F. Freeman 1852-1920
       Reuben F. Freeman 1849-1852

LOT #123 -- 1 Monument

    1. Monument Front: James Whorf 1814-1886
                          Phebe M. his wife 1819-1898
                          Lucinda W. 1855-1920
                          Lucinda F. 1853-1854
                          Josiah F. 1851-1852

       Monument Rear: Andrew Kennedy 1846-1921
                           Nettie P. his wife 1849-1919
                           Lillian M. 1870-1887

LOT #124 -- 6 Stones

    1. Joshua A. Mayo died Jan. 5, 1864 ae 77 ys. 3 ms.

    2. Betsey widow of Joshua A. Mayo died Dec. 23, 1867 ae 77 ys. 2 ms.

    3. Joseph Mayo 1819-1885
       Susan Mayo 1819-1852
       Eliza L. Mayo 1832-1909
       George R. 1849-1859
       Joseph A. 1851-1852

    4. Joseph A. Mayo 1853-1916
       Lizzie his wife 1872-1906

    5. Adeline wife of Joseph A. Mayo died June 12, 1886 ae 20 yrs. 2 dys.

    6. Mary Franklin dau. of Joseph A. & Lizzie F. Mayo Aug. 14, 1902 - Feb. 17, 1903

LOT #125 -- 1 Monument - 1 Stone - 2 Footstones

    1. Monument Front: Capt. John W. Campbell lost at sea April 18, 1893 aged 37 yrs.
                          Three infants (VR: Hattie L. died Dec. 27, 1887 ae 20 days; Stillborn died June 16, 1892; third infant unidentified - children of John W. & Jessie Campbell)

       Monument Right: Capt. Daniel McKinnon lost at sea Sept. 1, 1884 aged 49 years
                         His wife Margaret died Aug. 27, 1884 aged 44 yrs.
                         Their dau. Sadie B. died June 21, 1885 aged 19 yrs.

    2. Front: Nathaniel Rich Sept. 22, 1833 - Jan. 15, 1876

GIFFORD CEMETERY

LOT #125 (continued)

          Sophronia B. Rich Sept. 6, 1838 - Feb. 28, 1915
          Austin W. Rich Feb. 22, 1871 - Mch. 9, 1887

  Rear: Mary E. Rich Sept. 11, 1863 - Aug. 7, 1924

3. Babie - infant dau. of John W. & Jessie Campbell died Dec. 27, 1887 ae 20 ds. (VR: infant listed as Hattie L. in death records)

4. Footstone - Austin

LOT #126 -- 2 Stones

1. Joshua Paschal died July 5, 1884 ae 78 yrs.
Rebecca Paschal died June 5, 1890 ae 80 yrs.
Carrie E. dau. of Joshua & Rebecca Paschal died Aug. 28, 1880 ae 39 yrs.
Carrie F. dau. of Carrie & Samuel Bangs died Apl. 29, 1876 ae 1 yr. 3 mos.

2. Ama S. died Feb. 4, 1834 aged 22 ys. 2 ms. 24 ds.
Sally died Mar. 21, 1876 aged 68 yrs. 7 mos.
Wives of Jason Taylor

LOT #127 -- 1 Monument - 5 Stones - 5 Footstones

1. Monument Front: To the memory of David H. Atkins born in Provincetown, Oct. 9, 1834 died Nov. 30, 1880 aged 46 yrs. 1 mo. 22 dys. Capt. Atkins was in charge of the U. S. Life Saving Station No. 7 and lost his life in the act of Rescuing the crew of the Sloop C. E. Trumbull. He was a devoted husband and father. A good citizen and sealed his fidelity to duty with his life.

  Monument Left: Ellen F. Atkins 1837-1913
                  Anna W. Atkins 1870-1920

  Monument Right: Albert W. Atkins 1856-1925

2. Joshua R. Atkins died July 31, 1878 aged 38 yrs. 10 ms.

3. Henry Atkins 1808-1887
Esther Atkins 1810-1868

4. Clara W. Dawes 1865-1875

5. Mary M. Atkins 1873-1915

6. Ida E. Atkins Feb 9, 1857 - May 1, 1909

7. Footstone - Mother

8. Footstone - Father

9. Footstone - Albert

10. Footstone - Mary Emma

11. Footstone - Anna

GIFFORD CEMETERY

LOT #128 -- 6 Stones

1. Angus McIntyre died Jan. 22, 1879 aged 39 yrs.

2. Annabella wife of Angus McIntyre died May 8, 1876 ae 34 yrs. 1 mo. 5 days
   Katie Bell dau. of Angus & Annabella McIntyre died Oct. 11, 1875 ae 6 mos. 8 days

3. Duncan A. McIntyre lost at sea on Schooner Joseph H. Chandler of Gloucester, Mass., Jan. 1875 ae 24 yrs. Erected by John & Angus McIntyre

4. William Stowell son of Raymond A. & Elizabeth K. Hopkins Apr. 30, 1902 - Aug. 5, 1902

5. Isabel M. dau. of Raymond A. & Elizabeth K. Hopkins Dec. 7, 1903 - Mar. 6, 1906

6. Mary A. dau. of Raymond A. & Elizabeth K. Hopkins Aug. 6, 1899 - Apr. 17, 1906

LOT #129 -- 5 Stones

1. John Swift died Nov. 5, 1896 ae 84 yrs. 8 ms. 27 dys.

2. Betsey C. wife of John Swift died May 5, 1888 ae 81 yrs. 7 mos. 2 dys.

3. Josiah Swift 1837-1914
   Delia Cook his wife 1841-1930

4. John N. Swift 1854-1919
   Sarah J. his wife 1865-1926

5. Elisha H. Cook 1838-1909
   Eliza S. Cook 1840-1905

LOT #130 -- 1 Monument - 10 Footstones

1. Monument Front: Franklin Atkins Oct. 2, 1806 - Mar. 5, 1885
   Mary T. his wife Oct. 27, 1809 - Apr. 28, 1847

   Monument Right: James T. 1831-1832
   James F. 1836-1836
   Maria E. 1845-1846

   Monument Rear: Ruhama H. Jan. 19, 1833 - Oct. 17, 1847
   Hannah W. Aug. 28, 1834 - Dec. 11, 1851
   Isaac F. Aug. 22, 1841 - June 1, 1867

   Monument Left: Mary L. wife of G. P. Johnson 1837-1906
   Carrie O. Atkins 1839-1919

2. Footstone - Mother

3. Footstone - Father

4. Footstone - James

5. Footstone - James

GIFFORD CEMETERY

LOT #130 (continued)

    6. Footstone - Maria

    7. Footstone - Ruhama

    8. Footstone - Hannah

    9. Footstone - Isaac

    10. Footstone - Mary

    11. Footstone - Carrie

LOT #131 -- 1 Monument - 9 Footstones

    1. Monument Front: Capt. Alexander Livingston 1842-1926
                           His wife Susan R. 1843-1924
                           Capt. Leslie A. Spinney 1869-1912
                           His wife Nellie B. 1870-1955

       Monument Rear: Christopher L. Frellick 1844-1871
                          George -1868-
                          Fred H. Dearborn 1876-1950
                          Addie A. Dearborn 1883-1960

       Monument Left: Bessie M. (Livingston) 1881-1888
                          Elizabeth I. (Livingston) 1878-1945

    2. Footstone - Mother

    3. Footstone - Father

    4. Footstone - Husband

    5. Footstone - Wife

    6. Footstone - Father - Brother

    7. Footstone - Bessie

    8. Footstone - Elizabeth

    9. Footstone - Fred

    10. Footstone - Addie

LOT #132 -- 4 Stones - 1 Marker

    1. Eli Mackay Aug. 11, 1852 - Feb. 8, 1906
       Mary W. Mackay May 20, 1860 - Nov. 24, 1891

    2. George W. Standish July 20, 1827 - Feb. 3, 1905
       Ann C. Standish July 13, 1830 - Feb. 17, 1916

    3. In memoriam: Capt. Charles D. Hodgdon 1832-1864
       Helena E. 1834-1924

    4. Helen C. MacPhee 1872-1902
       William K. MacPhee 1875-1904
       Donald F. MacPhee 1877-1914

    5. Dora B. Creighton 1832-1914

GIFFORD CEMETERY

LOT #133 -- 1 Stone - 4 Footstones

    1. Front: Zephaniah Rich 1827-1900
            Margery T. Rich 1830-1918
            Z. Thomas Rich (no date) Lost at sea

       Rear: Eleanor J. Kiley 1849-1928 (Maiden name Rich)
              Arthur L. Lombard 1867-1927

    2. Footstone - A. L. L.

    3. Footstone - E. J. K.

    4. Footstone - Z. R.

    5. Footstone - M. T. R.

LOT #134 -- 1 Monument - 5 Footstones

    1. Monument Front: James Smith 1803-1853
                       Rebecca Smith 1806-1891
                       James H. Smith 1836-1894
                       Mary M. Smith 1846-1899

       Monument Right: James E. Rich 1840-1919
                       Rebecca A. Rich 1840-1904

    2. Footstone - Father

    3. Footstone - Mother

    4. Footstone - Brother

    5. Footstone - Sister

    6. Footstone - Rebecca

LOT #135 -- 1 Monument - 2 Footstones

    1. Monument Front: Francis Nickerson 1815-1888
                       Malvina Nickerson 1817-1904

       Monument Left: Malvina 1839-1849

    2. Footstone - Father

    3. Footstone - Mother

LOT #136 -- 1 Monument - 1 Marker - 1 Footstone

    1. Capt. Murdock Kemp 1841-1908
       His wife Margaret M. 1846-1924

    2. Katherine MacLeod born Aug. 24, 1868 died June 14, 1952

    3. Footstone - M. K.

LOT #137 -- 4 Stones

    1. Daniel McIntosh died Dec. 19, 1870 aged 30 yrs. 6 ms.

    2. Isabella McIntosh May 15, 1839 - June 15, 1907
       Alexander McLean Oct. 10, 1836 - July 30, 1893

GIFFORD CEMETERY

LOT #137 (continued)

    3. Francis Godfrey died Sept. 10, 1876 aged 45 years

    4. John McIntosh 1838-1917
       Martha wife of John McIntosh died Feb. 15, 1887 ae 44 yrs. 3 mos. 15 dys.

LOT #138 -- 1 Monument - 7 Footstones

    1. Monument Front: William Curren Sept. 29, 1829 - Jan. 14, 1902
                     His wife Mary G. Curren Feb. 28, 1839 - Apl. 26, 1920

       Monument Right: Hugh Curren Aug. 12, 1787 - Sept. 16, 1862
                     His wife Hannah Curren May 4, 1797 - June 22, 1846

       Monument Left: Moses Sumner Feb. 6, 1799 - Jan. 5, 1855
                    His wife Hannah F. Sumner May 19, 1798 - July 22, 1881
                    Children:
                    Hannah J. Sumner Feb. 7, 1829 - Aug. 17, 1854
                    Hulda C. Sumner Jan. 11, 1842 - Jan. 11, 1845

    2. Footstone - Mother - Hannah F. Sumner

    3. Footstone - Father - Moses Sumner

    4. Footstone - Husband - William Curren

    5. Footstone - Wife - Mary G. Curren

    6. Footstone - Father - Hugh Curren

    7. Footstone - Sister - Hannah J. Sumner

    8. Footstone - Sister - Hulda C. Sumner

LOT #139, #140, #149 & #150 - Monument - Town of Provincetown

    1. Erected by the Town of Provincetown in 1867, in gratitude to the memory of the fallen, who sacrificed their lives to save their country during the Great Rebellion of 1861-1865

       Monument Right: *Army* - Thomas J. Gibbons
                           George Lockwood
                           Henry A. Smith
                           George E. Crocker
                           Jeremiah Bennett
                           Elkanah Smith
                           Taylor Small Jr.
                           John C. Lurten
                           John W. Hobbins
                           John R. Smith
                           Solomon R. Higgins
                           Joseph King

GIFFORD CEMETERY

LOT #139, #140, #149 & #150 (continued)

    Monument Left: <u>Navy</u> - Josiah C. Freeman
                        Samuel T. Paine
                        William E. Tupper
                        John W. Small
                        William H. Chipman
                        Asa A. Franzen

LOT #140 -- see LOT #139 - Civil War Memorial

LOT #141 -- 2 Stones

    1. Duncan McKenzie Nov. 14, 1827-Mar. 17, 1869
       Margret McKenzie Jan. 13, 1834 - Aug. 10, 1905

    2. Jannie wife of Murdoch McDonald died Dec. 23, 1870
         aet 23 yrs. 6 mos. 8 days
       Flora Jane daugh of Murdoch & Jane McDonald died July 16,
         1871 aet 7 mos. 6 days

LOT #142 -- 3 Stones

    1. Stephen D. Pierce died Dec. 23, 1863 aged 45 yrs.

    2. Mary Carrie dau. of Stephen D. and Louisa Pierce died
       Apr. 23, 1857 ae 7 yrs. 9 ms. 27 ds.

    3. Nathan Dunham 1819-1889
       Olive N. Dunham 1825-1893
       James B. 1844-1864 Lost at sea

LOT #143 -- 1 Monument - 6 Footstones

    1. Monument Front: Nancy H. wife of James Burch 1818-1892
                        John M. 1853-1917
                        Carrie T. 1855-1929

       Monument Right: Eben F. 1854-1902
                        Theodora A. 1890-1959

       Monument Left: Wallace A. 1857-1934
                     His wife Maria P. 1861-1933
                     Wallace F. 1898-1899

    2. Footstone - Husband

    3. Footstone - Wife

    4. Footstone - Husband

    5. Footstone - Mother

    6. Footstone - John & Carrie

    7. Footstone - Baby

LOT #144 -- 2 Stones - 1 Marker - 2 Footstones

    1. Herman L. Mayo 1857-1934
       Annie M. 1863-1922

GIFFORD CEMETERY

LOT #144 (continued)

    Nellie F. 1889-1891
    Bernice R. 1905-1967

2. Lillian McKenzie 1869-1963

3. Nellie Florence dau. of Herman L. & Annie M. Mayo died Dec. 30, 1891 ae 2 yrs. 20 mos. 4 ds.

4. Footstone - Father

LOT #145 -- 1 Monument - 1 Stone

1. James Bradford Cook May 14, 1840 - May 17, 1901
Almena Ellen wife of James B. Cook dau. of Nathaniel & Apphia L. Hopkins born in Truro June 18, 1848 died in Attleboro (Mass.) March 5, 1889
"To the memory of her who filled the home with sunshine and who has now passed into the light that knows no shadow"

2. Joshua Cook 1843-1920 U. S. N. 1863-1867
Effie L. his wife 1845-1914

LOT #146 -- 6 Stones

1. Atkins D. Snow 1828-1892
Hattie A. Snow 1836-1922

2. Olin B. Snow 1858-1905

3. Lucy E. Snow 1868-1909

4. Thomas K. Paine 1846-1902
Lizzie Paine 1841-1917

5. Charles Ellsworth Browne 1875-1908

6. Elsie Hadley Browne 1908-1912

LOT #147 -- 4 Stones

1. Thomas N. Paine December 19, 1833 - November 28, 1892
His wife Martha H. May 17, 1833 - October 21, 1910

2. Annie Putnam 1 yr. 10 mo. (VR: died April 23, 1863 dau. of Thomas N. & Martha H. Paine)
Eugene Willard son of Thomas N. and Martha H. Paine died Sept. 19, 1853 ae 2 ys. 1 mo. 21 ds.

3. Willard H. son of Thomas N. & Martha H. Paine August 4, 1856 - October 6, 1893

4. Front: Benjamin S. Henderson 1855-1920 U.S.L.S. Peaked Hill Bars, 1885 to 1909
His wife Mary J. Dears 1864-1904

   Rear: Addie Bell 1886-1892
          Grace May 1894-1946

GIFFORD CEMETERY

LOT #148 -- No Stone (Lot listed in the name of Collin Stevenson)
   (VR: Collin A. Stevenson, lost at sea in 1904, aged 57 years. He was captain of the Schooner Carrie D. Knowles which disappeared on a whaling voyage to the South Atlantic)

LOT #149 -- see LOT #139 - Civil War Memorial

LOT #150 -- see LOT #139 - Civil War Memorial

LOT #151 -- 1 Stone

   1. Obadiah Smith 1826-1902
      Maria D. Smith 1828-1914
      Charles K. 1849-1850
      Frankie C. 1856-1859
      Frankie C. 1859-1862

LOT #152 -- 4 Stones

   1. Father - Robert L. West lost at sea in gale Apl. 1889 ae 44 yrs. 3 mos.

   2. Mother - Phebe A. wife of Robert L. West died Oct. 5, 1880 ae 34 yrs. 3 mos. 1 day

   3. Capt. Hugh McFadyen Feb. 2, 1835 - May 21, 1898
      Susan West McFadyen Jan. 29, 1840 - Jan. 23, 1926

   4. Ebbie Leonard son of Hugh & Susie C. McFadyen died May 26, 1878 ae 11 yrs. 11 mos.

LOT #153 -- 6 Stones

   1. Father - Lathrop Doggett died Sept. 30, 1882 ae 80 ys. 11 mos. 25 ds.

   2. Mother - Janet Doggett born Apl. 10, 1806 died Apl. 4, 1893

   3. Husband - James Daggett born Oct. 10, 1832 died Sept. 26, 1891

   4. Wife - Mary S. Daggett died May 20, 1902 ae 68 yrs.

   5. Frankie F. son of James & Mary S. Doggett (sic) died Dec. 1, 1865 aged 3 mos.

   6. David F. Snow died Oct. 17, 1864 aged 33 years

LOT #154 -- 1 Monument - 4 Footstones

   1. Monument Front: Samuel S. Swift May 9, 1846 - Dec. 12, 1891
                      Ellen A. May 14, 1852 - Aug. 10, 1930
                      Leon S. Apr. 23, 1878 - Jan. 6, 1927
      Monument Left: Nellie Swift Swenson July 9, 1876 - Feb. 24, 1933

   2. Footstone - Father

   3. Footstone - Mother

GIFFORD CEMETERY

LOT #154 (continued)

    4. Footstone - Leon

    5. Footstone - Nellie

LOT #155 -- 1 Monument - 4 Footstones

    1. Monument Front: Capt. Harvey S. Cook Dec. 13, 1838 - Feb. 22, 1905
                        Charlotte A. Hooton Jan. 1, 1841 - June 26, 1912

    Monument Right: Harvey A. Jan. 10, 1857 - Mar. 4, 1892

    2. Footstone - H. S. C.

    3. Footstone - C. A. C.

    4. Footstone - H. A. C.

    5. Footstone - Bertha (no date)

LOT #156 -- No Stone - Lot in the name of Hatsuld Freeman

    (VR: Hatsuld Freeman died Feb. 2, 1892 ae 75 yrs. 4 mos. His wife, Apphia D. (Cook) Freeman died Jan. 3, 1892 ae 66 yrs. 4 mos. 19 days. A daughter, Flora M., died March 23, 1864 ae 2 yrs. 5 mos. 17 ds.)

LOT #157 -- 1 Monument - 1 Stone - 2 Footstones

    1. John C. Weeks 1816-1896
       Charlotte Mary 1821-1899
       John C. Weeks Jr. 1856-(not cut)
       Carrie A. Weeks 1870-1936

    2. Joseph H. Weeks 1844-1926
       Chas. J. Spear 1855-1940
       Harriet F. Spear 1851-1940

    3. Footstone - C. A. W. - Wife

    4. Footstone - J. C. W. Jr - Husband

LOT #158 -- 1 Monument - 2 Stones - 2 Footstones

    1. William Lurten died June 14, 1880 ae 72 ys. 8 m. 27 ds.
       Susan J. Lurten died Jan. 26, 1902 ae 89 ys. 8 m. 8 ds.

    2. Frankie (VR: Frank W. Lurten died Dec. 11, 1870 ae 18 days son of Jonathan and Susan K. Lurten)

    3. Jonathan C. Lurten 1843-1922
       Martha E. Lurten 1847-1921

    4. Susie K. wife of J. C. Lurten died Dec. 1, 1870 ae 33 yrs.

    5. Martha wife of George H. Dyer 1823-1898

GIFFORD CEMETERY

LOT #159 -- 1 Stone

1. Nancy A. wife of Silas R. Atkins died Mar. 9, 1889 ae 43 years (Ed. note: Also listed as owner of this lot is Benjamin Cook. There is no stone for a Cook, nor can we find a death of Benjamin Cook)

LOT #160 -- 7 Stones

1. Aaron Ryder died Nov. 26, 1874 ae 38 yrs. 7 mos. 21 dys.

2. David Rich Aug. 18, 1837 - Feb. 3, 1897

3. Mary R. Rich June 8, 1845 - Dec. 17, 1915

4. Priscilla K. wife of David Rich died Feb. 13, 1874 ae 35 yrs. 1 mon. & 23 ds.

5. Mother - Mrs. Lydia Mack died Apr. 12, 1885 ae 77 ys. 12 ds.

6. Elisha Rich Feb. 15, 1845 - Nov. 3, 1903
His wife Georgianna F. Aug. 4, 1842 - June 29, 1918

7. Elisha T. son of Elisha & G. F. Rich died Jan. 24, 1877 aet 1 yr. 5 mos. 18 dys.

LOT #161 -- 3 Stones - 3 Footstones

1. Front: Atwood Mott 1837-1906
Bertha Mott 1842-1870
Annie C. Mott 1835-1914

   Rear: George P. (Mott) 1874-1956
Phillis M. (Mott) 1894-1961

2. Stephen Mott Dec. 16, 1807 - Jan. 2, 1902

3. Eveline L. wife of Stephen Mott died Oct. 27, 1883 ae 69 yrs. 5 mos. 4 dys.

4. Footstone - Wife

5. Footstone - Husband

6. Footstone - Wife

LOT #162 -- 1 Monument - 2 Markers - 2 Footstones

1. Roderick McIntosh 1842-1897
Sarah McIntosh 1844-1885

2. Roderick Chisholm 1842-1916
Mary Matheson his wife 1846-1921

3. Duncan Chisholm 1834-1884

4. Footstone - Father

5. Footstone - Mother

LOT #163 -- 4 Stones - 1 Base with no stone

1. Francis Crocker died Mch. 19, 1875 ae 66 ys. 4 ms. 7 ds.

GIFFORD CEMETERY

LOT #163 (continued)

    2. Susanna Crocker July 12, 1808 - Mar. 25, 1895

    3. Josephine wife of George F. Crocker Sept. 8, 1839 - July 27, 1915

    4. John Myrick son of Francis and Susanna Crocker born Dec. 8, 1837 died June 14, 1843

    5. Base - no stone

LOT #164 -- 1 Monument - 6 Footstones

    1. Jerome S. Smith 1850-1922
       Abbie H. Smith 1853-1887
       Elizabeth B. Smith 1857-1925
       Katie N. 1877-1884
       Alma F. 1876-1907
       Ethel B. 1879-1907

    2. Footstone - Jerome

    3. Footstone - Elizabeth

    4. Footstone - Katie

    5. Footstone - Abbie

    6. Footstone - Alma

    7. Footstone - Ethel

LOT #165 -- 6 Stones

    1. Father - Samuel S. Smith June 4, 1821 - July 27, 1892

    2. Mother - Sarah A. Smith May 15, 1827 - July 25, 1896

    3. Samuel S. Smith 1864-1919
       Emily E. Smith 1862-1930

    4. Aunt Nellie - Ellen S. Gifford 1839-1917

    5. Mamma - Bertha Smith wife of J. Ellwood Crowell May 18, 1871 - Oct. 17, 1899
       Dorothy daughter of J. Ellwood & Bertha S. Crowell April 3, 1894 - May 25, 1900

    6. William A. Card May 5, 1851 - Oct. 17, 1908
       Sarah F. Card Sept. 5, 1857 - Dec. 13, 1937

LOT #166 -- 1 Stone - 7 Footstones

    1. Front: Jeremiah A. Rich 1844-1922
           Martha J. Rich 1850-1937
           Lombard Rich 1810-1892
           Lydia N. Rich 1813-1895

       Rear: Thomas Julian Lewis 1867-1955
           Mattie A. Lewis 1874-1955
           Janet W. Lewis 1895-1962

GIFFORD CEMETERY

LOT #166 (continued)

    2. Footstone - Husband

    3. Footstone - Wife

    4. Footstone - Father

    5. Footstone - Mother

    6. Footstone - T. J. L.

    7. Footstone - M. A. L.

    8. Footstone - J. W. L.

LOT #167 -- 1 Monument

    1. Monument Front: Capt. Francis Small died April 17, 1873 aged 65 yrs. 7 ms.
Lydia B. wife of Francis Small died Feb. 15, 1882 aged 70 ys. 4 ms. 22 ds.

    Monument Right: Capt. E. H. Tillson 1836-(not cut)
Martha A. his wife 1845-1909
Mary C. wife of Elisha H. Tillson died Mar. 15, 1891 aged 52 ys. 9 ms. 15 ds.

    Monument Left: Reuben C. Small died Sept. 15, 1911 aged 75 ys. 7 mos. 27 ds.
Catherine T. wife of Reuben C. Small born in Boston, Mass. June 7, 1837 died Mar. 24, 1881 aged 43 ys. 9 mos. 11 ds.

LOT #168 -- 1 Monument - 6 Footstones

    1. Monument Front: Caleb Nickerson died Sept. 5, 1877 ae 79
Sally his wife died June 30, 1827 ae 26
Bathsheba Freeman his wife died August 3, 1890 aged 82

    Monument Right: Caleb A. Nickerson died Nov. 14, 1876 ae 49 ys. 5 ms.
Mary S. his wife died Sept. 6, 1904 ae 78 ys. 5 ms.
Son & Dau. of Caleb A. & Mary S. Nickerson died Aug. 20, 1864

    Monument Rear: Henry P. Nickerson June 22, 1866 - Jan. 23, 1960

    Monument Left: Charles H. Nickerson 1858-1931
Anna S. his wife 1862-1935

    2. Footstone - Father

    3. Footstone - Mother

    4. Footstone - Mary S.

    5. Footstone - Caleb A.

    6. Footstone - Charles

GIFFORD CEMETERY

LOT #168 (continued)

    7. Footstone - Anna

LOT #169 -- 3 Stones

    1. B. F. Hutchinson (Benjamin) 1821-1882
       A. J. Hutchinson (Anna) 1823-1898
       Anna Edith Hutchinson 1861-1863
       Frances Sturgis Hutchinson 1866-1867

    2. Front: Elijah Smith 1816-1867
       Rear: Lydia daughter of Elijah & Amanda M. Smith 1845-1870

    3. Amanda M. Smith 1821-1889

LOT #170 -- 2 Stones - 2 Footstones

    1. Front: Charles E. Johnson 1858-1938
           His wife Clara C. 1859-1954

       Rear: Children of Charles E. & Clara C. Johnson:
              Alice A. July 7, 1885 - Aug. 28, 1886
              Lina B. Jan. 4, 1890 - Apr. 10, 1890

    2. Footstone - Lina

    3. Footstone - Alice

    4. Izetta F. wife of Richard S. Rich died Dec. 22, 1873
       aet 19 yrs. 1 day, daughter of Isaac F. Mayo

LOT #171 -- 3 Stones

    1. John McFadden 1836-1918
       Ann McFadden 1840-1910

    2. Dan McFadden Feb. 10, 1867 - July 3, 1898

    3. John McFayden Aug. 14, 1869 - Aug. 10, 1959

LOT #172 -- 1 Monument - 3 Markers

    1. Monument: "Gordon"

    2. Abbie H. wife of Wm. Gordon 1849-1877

    3. Willie T. Gordon 1871-1895

    4. Lizzie B. wife of A. R. Young 1868-1901
       Stanley M. (Young) 1895-1896

LOT #173 -- 5 Stones

    1. Richard P. Bush Sept. 20, 1828 - Aug. 30, 1903

    2. Mary W. Bush June 11, 1833 - Jan. 21, 1913

    3. Richard Perry Bush 1855-1926
       His wife Emma Linwood Bush 1860-1947
       Edith Linwood Bush 1882-1977

    4. Edwin Willis Bush born Jan. 15, 1860 died Aug. 8, 1884

GIFFORD CEMETERY

LOT #173 (continued)

    5. Lysander N. Paine 1831-1918
       Rebecca S. Paine 1836-1887
       Joshua S. (Paine) 1861-1862

LOT #174 -- 1 Monument - 10 Footstones

    1. Monument Front: Andrew Williams lost at sea on board Schooner James Porter on his passage home from the Grand Banks in Oct. 1858 ae 63 ys.

                        Sarah his wife died Sept. 8, 1871 ae 71 ys. 8 mos.

       Monument Right: William C. Sparrow Dec. 3, 1858 - Feb. 20, 1932
                        Mary E. W. Sparrow Oct. 8, 1862 - Oct. 7, 1961
                        Nina Soper Williams 1879-1969

       Monument Rear: Andrew T. Williams Mar. 18, 1836 - Jan. 29, 1920
                       Eveline N. Williams Feb. 28, 1838 - Dec. 19, 1930

       Monument Left: Eliza Ann died Sept. 13, 1842 ae 14 yrs. 6 mos.
                      Louvisa died Feb. 1, 1824
                      Sarah Eldridge died Mar. 24, 1831
                      Children of Andrew & Sarah Williams

    2. Footstone - Father

    3. Footstone - Mother

    4. Footstone - Andrew T. Williams

    5. Footstone - Eveline N. Williams

    6. Footstone - Louvisa

    7. Footstone - Eliza

    8. Footstone - Sarah

    9. Footstone - Capt. William Chester Sparrow 1858-1932

   10. Footstone - Mary E. W. Sparrow 1862-1961

   11. Footstone - N. S. W.

LOT #175 -- 3 Stones - 1 Marker

    1. H. Merril (sic) Smith Nov. 8, 1827 - Nov. 27, 1896
       Catherine Smith Dec. 14, 1827 - July 18, 1902

    2. Eva M. dau. of H. Merrill & Katie Smith died Dec. 8, 1881 ae 21 yrs.

    3. Franklin N. Smith 1854-1913
       His wife Emma M. Holmes 1854-1949

GIFFORD CEMETERY

LOT #175 (continued)

    4. Emma F. Bent 1878-1933

LOT #176 -- 4 Stones - 1 Marker

    1. Horace H. Watson died May 13, 1890 ae 73 yrs. 4 mos.

    2. Our mother - Rebecca T. wife of H. H. Watson died Feb. 27, 1884 ae 62 yrs. 6 mos. 15 dys.

    3. Effie Y. wife of Eugene W. Watson died July 24, 1886 ae 19 yrs. 9 mos. 19 dys.

    4. Eugene W. Watson 1850-1933
       Clara Smith Watson 1863-1951
       Horace S. Watson 1891-1968
       Louise Watson Peale 1905-(not cut)

    5. Eldridge Rich Watson Apr. 30, 1920 - Apr. 12, 1921
       Eleanor Louise (Watson) Dec. 15, 1918 - (not cut)

LOT #177 -- 1 Monument - 3 Footstones

    1. Monument Front: Nathan Young Oct. 9, 1824 - July 1, 1898
                     Mrs. Abbie Young May 5, 1824 - Feb. 19, 1899

       Monument Right: Millie W. Young June 14, 1865 - Jan. 25, 1900

    2. Footstone - Father

    3. Footstone - Mother

    4. Footstone - Millie

LOT #178 -- 6 Stones

    1. John L. Rich Aug. 11, 1844 - Nov. 26, 1922

    2. Amelia O. Gross wife of John L. Rich Mar. 30, 1846 - Nov. 10, 1906

    3. Bartholomew O. Gross March 15, 1814 - May 17, 1898

    4. Susan B. Hopkins wife of Bartholomew O. Gross Feb. 22, 1817 - Sept. 4, 1841

    5. Bertha G. Atwood wife of Bartholomew O. Gross Nov. 2, 1820 - Sept. 20, 1891

    6. Melville A. died Sept. 2, 1859 ae 8 mos. son of B. O. & B. A. Gross

LOT #179 -- 1 Monument - 5 Footstones

    1. Monument Front: Henry T. Chipman 1849-1910
                     His wife Fannie H. 1865-1954
                     Gladys (Chipman) -1891-

       Monument Rear: Stephen F. Atwood 1840-1920

GIFFORD CEMETERY

LOT #179 (continued)

                    Adelia C. Atwood 1844-1936

2. Footstone - Mother

3. Footstone - Father

4. Footstone - Husband

5. Footstone - Wife

6. Footstone - Gladys

LOT #180 -- 1 Monument - 4 Footstones

1. Monument Front: William H. Hedge died Mar. 22, 1900
               ae 70 yrs. 8 mos.
             Margaret W. Covell wife of Wm. H. Hedge
             died Sept. 19, 1891 ae 60 yrs. 5 mos.

   Monument Right: R. Eugene Conwell died July 22, 1909
              ae 55 yrs. 1 mo.
             Ruth S. Hedge wife of R. E. Conwell died
             May 8, 1932 ae 79 yrs. 1 mo. 24 dys.

2. Footstone - Husband

3. Footstone - Wife

4. Footstone - Mother

5. Footstone - Father

LOT #181 -- 6 Stones - 1 Footstone

1. Capt. Henry N. West born Sept. 5, 1838 died Sept. 1, 1876

2. Rebecca P. West died Feb. 16, 1879 ae 34 years 3 mos.

3. John T. Dunham died Oct. 25, 1882 ae 67 yrs. 2 mos.
Edwin W. lost at sea Jan. 25, 1867 ae 17 yrs. 2 mos. 25 ds.
Austin R. lost at sea June 16, 1883 ae 25 yrs. 9 mos.
   23 dys.
Sons of John T. & Abbie Dunham

4. Mrs. Abbie Dunham died Jan. 4, 1891 ae 65 yrs. 8 ms. 3 das.

5. Abbie F. daughter of John T. & Abbie Dunham died June 28, 1881 ae 27 yrs. 8 ms. 28 ds.

6. Capt. John A. Dunham 1847-1912
Margaret A. his wife 1856-1945
John T. (Dunham) 1874-1894
George L. (Dunham) 1877-1919 lost at sea

7. Footstone - Johnnie
(Ed. note: Also buried in this lot - Edith Dunham Christopher, daughter of John T. & Abigail Dunham, born 1875, died 1959, no stone)

GIFFORD CEMETERY

LOT #182 -- 1 Monument

    1. Monument Front: Ambrose D. Knowles 1805-1877
                         Rebecca Knowles 1808-1890

        Monument Rear: Ruth G. Knowles 1828-1830
                         Josiah F. (Knowles) 1830-1831
                         Rebecca D. (Knowles) 1834-1841
                         Rebecca D. (Knowles) 1842-1859
                         Adelia G. (Knowles) 1851-1851

LOT #183 -- 4 Stones - 1 Marker

    1. Benjamin Kelley 1854-1944
        Susan C. his wife 1863-1924
        Sherborn S. 1886-1890
        Mertie C. 1882-1948

    2. George M. Whelden 1851-1920
        Adelaide H. (no date)
        George M. Jr. 1882-1912
        Elmer G. 1893-1895

    3. Mother - Mercie F. Whelden died July 4, 1891 aged 56 yrs. 3 ms.

    4. Father - John G. Whelden died June 20, 1895 aged 64 yrs. 3 ms.

    5. Hernaldo H. Kelley, Massachusetts CBM Coast Guard World War I, July 7, 1884 - Sept. 28, 1951

LOT #184 -- 1 Monument - 5 Footstones

    1. Monument Front: Capt. John A. Cook 1857-(uncut)
                            (Ed. note: buired in Coral Gables,
                              Florida, July 1938)
                          Viola D. Fish 1855-1922

        Monument Right: James Cook 1820-1889
                          Emily A. Cook 1827-1906

        Monument Rear: Frank K. Atkins 1877-1940
                         Emma W. Cook 1879-1945
                         Viola F. (Atkins) (Miller) 1904-(not cut)
                            (VR: died 1972)
                         Samuel K. (Atkins) 1905-(not cut)

        Monument Left: Emma F. Howes 1853-1912

    2. Footstone - Emma - E. F. H.

    3. Footstone - Viola - V. D. C.

    4. Footstone - Viola F.

    5 Footstone - Mother - Emily A. Cook

    6. Footstone - Father - James Cook

GIFFORD CEMETERY

LOT #185 -- 1 Monument - 1 Marker - 6 Footstones

   1. Monument Front: J. Emmons Dyer 1850-1917
                          Emily M. wife of J. Emmons Dyer died
                              Nov. 30, 1884 ae 25 yrs. 2 mos. 24 dys.

       Monument Right: Thomas Mayo died June 21, 1890 ae 75 yrs.
                          1 mo. 1 d.
                          Phebe Dyer 1820-1908
                          Emily J. Mayo died in Virginia Jan. 11,
                          1857 ae 15 yrs. 4 mos. 7 dys.

       Monument Left: Ezra D. Ewell born 1830 died 1893
                         Melintha D. his wife 1835-1917
                         Florence M. wife of Warren F. Freeman died
                            Feb. 1, 1921
                         Josephine Ewell born 1861 died 1888

   2. Marker - Georgie M. Connell 1862-1936

   3. Footstone - Father

   4. Footstone - Mother

   5. Footstone - Florence

   6. Footstone - Emmons

   7. Footstone - Emily

   8. Footstone - Josie

LOT #186 -- 1 Monument

   1. Monument Front: Small - Crocker

       Monument Rear: D. Francis Small 1848-1925
                          Leonora S. Small 1852-1932
                          Daniel F. Small 1824-1853
                          Maria C. Small 1829-1878
                          Waterman C. (Small) 1850-1853
                          George (Small) 1852-1853
                          George W. (Small) 1854-1854
                          Waterman Crocker 1804-1866
                          Louisa W. Crocker 1808-1871

LOT #187 -- 3 Stones

    1. Father - Allen Lavender died Oct. 10, 1860 aged 56 yrs.
          6 mos. 15 dys.
       Mother - Katie wife of Allen Lavender died May 11, 1884
              aged 75 yrs. 7 mos. 25 days

    2. Stephen S. Lavender 1852-1910
       Maria Y. Lavender 1854-1935
       Mabel A. Lavender 1875-1881
       Stephen A. Lavender 1885-1918

    3. Father - Capt. John Smith Aug. 23, 1829 - June 3, 1900
       Mother - Mary E. Smith Nov. 7, 1838 - April 7, 1900

GIFFORD CEMETERY

LOT #188 -- 3 Stones

1. Husband - Nicholas B. Witham September 30, 1835 - December 21, 1889

2. Henrietta A. Lavender wife of Peleg S. Burgess 1850-1928

3. Joseph E. Weeks 1840-1917
   Isadore L. Weeks 1853-1932
   Harold Stillman Weeks 1888-1916

LOT #189 -- No Stone (Cemetery records listed in the name of Joseph H. Hopkins)

LOT #190 -- No Stone

LOT #191 -- No Stone

LOT #192 -- 1 Stone - 3 Footstones

1. Josiah L. Young Aug. 22, 1861 - Apr. 6, 1950
   Susan M. Young May 2, 1862 - Sept. 19, 1939
   Lucena M. Young Dec. 17, 1880 - Mar. 9, 1904

2. Footstone - Louie

3. Footstone - Mother

4. Footstone - Father

LOT #193 -- 3 Stones - 1 Footstone

1. Father - Isaiah Young Aug. 17, 1835 - Aug. 20, 1925

2. Wife - Betsey A. Young died Jan. 1, 1891 ae 53 ys. 3 ms. 11 ds.

3. Our Baby (surname Young - no date)

4. Brother - Willie F. Young died June 21, 1890 aged 31 ys. 3 ms. 18 ds.

LOT #194 -- 1 Stone

1. Capt. Samuel Fisher 1827-1890
   L. Jane Talbot (Fisher) 1837-1906
   Capt. Sam'l O. Fisher 1861-1919
   Elmira N. Marston 1861-1933 (Maiden name Pierce, married (1) Samuel Fisher, (2) ____ Marston)

LOT #195 -- 1 Stone - 2 Footstones

1. Sadie S. Bradshaw wife of Clarence M. Ghen 1868-1895
   An infant (Ghen) no date

2. Footstone - Father - W. M. B.
   (VR: William M. Bradshaw died April 5, 1919 ae 75 yrs. 3 mos. 28 days)

3. Footstone - Mother - J. K. B.

GIFFORD CEMETERY

LOT #195 (continued)

                (VR: Jerusha K. Bradshaw died Oct. 13, 1925 ae 79 yrs. 9 mos. 23 days)

LOT #196 -- 4 Stones

1. Husband - William T. Atkins 48 yrs. 8 mos. 26 dys. (no date) (VR: born June 20, 1853 died circa 1902)

2. Lillie L. wife of W. T. Atkins died Apr. 11, 1885 ae 28 yrs. 8 ms. 26 ds.

3. Lillian Russell dau. of W. T. & B. E. Atkins Apr. 14, 1894- Aug. 31, 1898

4. Andrew T. Powe 1867-1930 (married Middleboro, Mass. in 1910)
   His wife Bessie E. formerly wife of W. T. Atkins 1858-1931

LOT #197 -- No Stone

LOT #198 -- No Stone

LOT #199 -- No Stone

LOT #200 -- No Stone

LOT #201 -- No Stone

LOT #202 -- No Stone

LOT #203 -- No Stone

LOT #204 - 1 Monument - 1 Stone - 5 Footstones

1. Monument Front: Charles Carroll Atkins 1835-1907
                     His wife Christie Kemp 1836-1923

   Monument Rear: Mary Pauline Atkins 1870-1871
                   Pauline Jennie Carroll (Atkins) Hasting 1872-1950 (VR: wife of Walter G. Hasting of Bridgewater)
                   Bertha Evelyn Atkins 1882-1907

2. Capt. Benjamin H. Atkins 1836-1896
   Eliza L. Atkins 1842-1902

3. Footstone - Father

4. Footstone - Mother

5. Footstone - Baby

6. Footstone - Bertha

7. Footstone - Pauline

GIFFORD CEMETERY

LOT #205 -- 1 Monument - 1 Stone - 2 Markers - 3 Footstones

   1. Monument: Capt. Chas. A. Foster 1863-1920
                 Lizzie B. his wife 1870-1956
                 Anna F. Weldon (Maiden name Foster) 1884-1914

   2. Emanuel Williams 1823-1906
      Joan Williams 1834-1910

   3. Louis F. Bennett, Massachusetts Pvt. Sig. Corps., May 20, 1906 - Dec. 14, 1944

   4. Footstone - Husband

   5. Footstone - Wife

   6. Footstone - Anna F. Our loved one (VR: died Lansing, Michigan Dec. 27, 1914)

   7. Mary W. Davis 1857-1927

LOT #206 -- 1 Stone

   1. Annie Q. Hooton Feb. 12, 1847 - Nov. 24, 1903
      Joseph H. Hooton Nov. 19, 1845 - June 28, 1902

LOT #207 -- 1 Monument - 3 Stones

   1. Monument Front: Everett B. Davis 1867-(not cut)
                       Cora A. Davis 1870-1939

      Monument Right: Joseph L. Chase Aug. 26, 1857 - June 28, 1899
                       Mariner H. Chase Dec. 6, 1895 - Mar. 24, 1900
                       (Ed. note: This inscription is identical to the one on the rear of the monument. It is our opinion that the monument was recut in error)

      Monument Rear: Mariner H. Chase Dec. 6, 1895 - Mar. 24, 1900

   2. Capt. Joseph M. Caton born Nov. 24, 1823 died Jan. 20, 1894

   3. Abbie B. Caton born Dec. 4, 1830 died Oct. 1, 1899

   4. Matilda A. Caton died Aug. 29, 1882 ae 45 yrs. 11 ms. 9 ds.
      Emanuel Caton died Feb. 21, 1865 ae 30 yrs. 9 ms. 25 ds.

LOT #208 -- 1 Monument - 8 Footstones

   1. Monument Front: Capt. William H. Matheson 1860-1906
                       Lost at sea
                       Addie J. his wife 1861-1890
                       Maude J. 1888-1905

      Monument Left: Osborne M. Sparrow 1892-1929

      Monument Rear: Capt. Duncan Matheson 1829-1913
                      Ellen Matheson 1836-1909

GIFFORD CEMETERY

LOT #208 (continued)

    2. Footstone - Anabel (Matheson) no date

    3. Footstone - Catherine (Matheson) no date

    4. Footstone - Mother

    5. Footstone - Osborne

    6. Footstone - Mother

    7. Footstone - Maude

    8. Footstone - Father - D. M.

    9. Footstone - Mother - E. M.

LOT #209 -- 2 Stones - 1 Marker - 2 Footstones

    1. Capt. William Newcomb Mar. 17, 1814 - June 5, 1902
       Susan S. Newcomb Sept. 21, 1820 - June 30, 1902

    2. Alfred J. Emery Oct. 3, 1843 - Aug. 30, 1898
       Eliza A. Emery 1846-1918

    3. Eva Emery 1871-1953
       Fred Emery 1867-1941

    4. Footstone - Irma (Newcomb) no date

    5. Footstone - Willie (Newcomb) no date

LOT #210 -- Monument missing - 6 Footstones - Lot listed in the name of Frederick A. Lewis (VR: Frederick A. and Minnie A. (Ellis) Lewis married in 1893)

    1. Footstone - Minnie A. (Lewis) no date

    2. Footstone - Mother

    3. Footstone - Ensley (Lewis) no date

    4. Footstone - Edna (Lewis) (VR: born & died in 1895)

    5. Footstone - Lloyd (Lewis) (VR: Lloyd born May 26, 1901 died April 17, 1902)

    6. Footstone - Marguerite (Lewis) no date

    (Ed. note: We could find no death dates for the parents above mentioned, Frederick A. & Minnie A. Lewis, nor dates for three of the children)

LOT #211 -- 1 Stone - 4 Footstones

    1. Nehemiah Y. Higgins 1828-1884
       Lucy J. his wife 1832-1913
       Charles A. Higgins 1862-1942
       Bessie L. his wife 1874-1958

    2. Footstone - Bessie L. wife of Charles A. Higgins
                June 3, 1958

GIFFORD CEMETERY

LOT #211 (continued)

    3. Footstone - Charles Alden Higgins, Massachusetts Surfman U. S. Coast Guard Jan. 30, 1942

    4. Footstone - Mother

    5. Footstone - Father

LOT #212 -- 2 Stones

    1. Phineas S. Cutter Jr. Apr. 30, 1836 - June 8, 1897

    2. Rebecca F. Cutter Oct. 20, 1862 - Dec. 6, 1884

LOT #213 -- No Stone

LOT #214 -- No Stone

LOT #215 -- 1 Monument - 5 Footstones

    1. Monument Front: Reuben Nickerson 1834-1913
                        His wife Abigail N. 1834-1918

       Monument Right: Ephm. Nickerson 1808-1855
                        Thomas Jacobs 1815-1874
                        Abigail Cook (Jacobs) 1814-1896

       Monument Rear: William Allen 1859-1887
                       His wife Carrie H. 1867-1915

       Monument Left: Wilfred C. Snow 1898-1975
                       His wife Eleanor C. 1906-(living 1979)
                       Their son William C. 1939-1957

    2. Footstone - Wilfred

    3. Footstone - Billy

    4. Footstone - C. H. S.

    5. Footstone - Father

    6. Footstone - Mother

LOT #216 -- 1 Monument - 8 Footstones

    1. Monument Front: William K. Nickerson 1855-1932
                        A. Loretta Nickerson 1853-1916

       Monument Right: Jesse Nickerson 1829-1898
                        His wife Mary A. 1825-1898
                        Nellie D. V. 1865-1869

       Monument Left: Nehemiah Nickerson 1818-1899
                       His wife Lavinia 1820-1899
                       Rawlins A. 1843-1844

    2. Footstone - Father

    3. Footstone - Mother

    4. Footstone - Husband

GIFFORD CEMETERY

LOT #216 (continued)

    5. Footstone - Wife

    6. Footstone - Aunt

    7. Footstone - Uncle

    8. Footstone - Nellie

    9. Footstone - Our baby

LOT #217 -- 3 Stones

    1. Joseph W. Snow July 3, 1831 - Mar. 30, 1895
       His wife Betsey D. Snow Feb. 19, 1832 - Mar. 30, 1907

    2. Louise R. Mackay 1864-1916

    3. Herman Holden Snow Oct. 11, 1875 - May 12, 1954

LOT #218 -- 1 Monument - 3 Footstones

    1. Monument Front: Henry Shortle Oct. 15, 1834 - Sept. 11, 1892
                     Mary N. Shortle Oct. 29, 1837 - Aug. 28, 1907

       Monument Left: C. G. Goodrich Sept. 19, 1869 - (not cut)
                       Annie Y. Shortle his wife Jan. 28, 1871 - June 18, 1914

    2. Footstone - Annie

    3. Footstone - Mother

    4. Footstone - Father

LOT #219 -- 1 Monument - 5 Footstones

    1. Monument Front: Henry Cook Nov. 29, 1813 - May 26, 1893
                     Abigail R. Cook Apr. 10, 1819 - Oct. 16, 1902

       Monument Rear: A daughter (surname Cook) died Sept. 12, 1838 aged 4 days

       Monument Left: A. Louis Putnam 1834-1925
                    Adelaide O. Putnam 1840-1928
                    Nellie F. Putnam 1863-1930
                    Abbie C. Putnam 1869-1956

    2. Footstone - Father

    3. Footstone - Mother

    4. Footstone - Louis

    5. Footstone - Addie

    6. Footstone - Nellie

GIFFORD CEMETERY

LOT #220 -- 2 Stones - 1 Footstone

    1. George W. King 1834-1915
       Hannah C. King 1834-1919

    2. Ouvra K. Smith 1853-1922
       Sarah K. his wife 1854-1929

    3. Footstone - Geo. W. King, Co. I 47 Mass. Inf.

LOT #221 -- 1 Monument - 8 Markers

    1. Monument: Matheson - Rouse

    2. Wm. K. Matheson April 3, 1855 - August 6, 1918

    3. Christie MacKay Matheson Sept. 25, 1855 - Feb. 25, 1933

    4. John W. K. son of Wm. K. & Christie Matheson died Nov. 5, 1887 aged 2 yrs. 11 ds.

    5. Ida Matheson Rouse July 1, 1888 - Feb. 11, 1971

    6. Edwin W. Rouse Jr. May 3, 1887 - Oct. 5, 1973

    7. Edwin Lyman Hotckiss (died) January 31, 1907

    8. Christine Rouse Hotckiss (died) July 13, 1912

    9. Isabelle MacKay 1825-1923

LOT #222 -- 1 Monument - 1 Footstone

    1. Monument Front: Lewis Nickerson Nov. 2, 1851 - April 20, 1895
                     Sarah E. Nickerson Dec. 25, 1851 - Jan. 27, 1939

       Monument Right: George Q. Sparks 1853-1904
                      His wife Serviah 1865-1955

    2. Footstone - Husband - G. Q. S.

LOT #223 -- 1 Monument - 1 Footstone

    1. Monument Front: Lewis Nickerson Jan. 21, 1807 - Aug. 30, 1854
                     Bethiah Nickerson Oct. 26, 1812 - Oct. 27, 1848
                     Delia A. Nickerson Dec. 5, 1814 - Oct. 3, 1895

       Monument Rear: Solomon D. Nickerson 1838-1926
                      Susan L. Nickerson 1843-1931

    2. Footstone - Husband

LOT #224 -- 3 Stones

    1. Benjamin D. Atkins 1832-1888
       Hannah Y. Atkins 1843-1926 (Maiden name Sparks)

    2. Charles A. Sparks 1853-1925

GIFFORD CEMETERY

LOT #224 (continued)

    His wife Ada M. (Mullins) 1857-1943
    (Ed. note: Stone not inscribed, Charles P. Sparks died Mar. 2, 1883 ae 9 days, son of Charles A. and Ada (Mullins) Sparks)

  3. Thomas W. Sparks Sept. 8, 1848 - Feb. 25, 1922
     Hannah C. wife of T. W. Sparks Feb. 2, 1852 - Mar. 23, 1895

LOT #225 -- 1 Monument - 2 Footstones

  1. Nathaniel N. Gifford 1836-1908
    Orra K. Gifford 1843-1935

  2. Footstone - N. N. G.

  3. Footstone - O. K. G.

LOT #226 -- 1 Stone

  1. Lt. Commander Frederick A. Sparks 1879-1919 (lost at sea) (son of Charles A. & Ada (Mullins) Sparks)

LOT #227 -- 2 Stones

  1. Arline M. Franzen 1883-1901

  2. William W. Bowly 1851-1908
    His wife Marcia N. Franzen 1865-1934

LOT #228 -- 2 Stones - 2 Footstones

  1. Osman D. Richardson born Aug. 1, 1842 died May 9, 1894
    Susan Emma born June 15, 1854 died Aug. 13, 1930
    Nettie C. daughter of Osman D. and Emma Richardson aged 4 mos. (no record of date of death)

  2. Footstone - Osman

  3. Footstone - Emma

  4. Freeman Cook 1826-1890
    Hannah K. Cook 1830-1918

LOT #229 -- 1 Monument - 1 Stone - 7 Footstones

  1. Monument Front: Andrew Crocker 1812-1899
                    Elizabeth S. Crocker 1817-1891

    Monument Right: Benjamin T. Crocker 1838-1916
                   Rebecca N. Crocker 1839-1912

    Monument Rear: Benjamin I. Crocker Jan'y 25, 1878 - Feb. 12, 1878
                 Lillian A. Crocker Oct. 18, 1879 - Nov. 4, 1879

    Monument Left: Joshua A. Crocker Aug. 20, 1841 - Sept. 4, 1842

GIFFORD CEMETERY

LOT #229 (continued)

    2. Capt. David Crocker died Sept. 5, 1863 aged 57
       Sarah wife of Capt. D. Crocker died Sept. 11, 1873 ae 65

    3. Footstone - Joshua A. son of Andrew & Elizabeth Crocker died Sept. 4, 1842 ae 1 yr. 14 ds.

    4. Footstone - E. S. C.

    5. Footstone - A. C.

    6. Footstone - R. N. C.

    7. Footstone - B. T. C.

    8. Footstone - B. I. C.

    9. Footstone - L. A. C.

LOT #230 -- 2 Stones - 1 Base with no stone

    1. Paul Atkins 1821-1908
       Margaret H. Atkins 1824-1902

    2. Charlie P. son of Paul & Margaret H. Atkins died June 20, 1871 ae 20 ys. 7 ms. 20 ds.

    3. Base only

LOT #231 -- 1 Stone

    1. Alonzo F. Atwood Feb. 29, 1848 - Dec. 12, 1895
       Harriet G. Atwood Oct. 12, 1850 - June 15, 1925

LOT #232 -- 2 Stones - 4 Footstones

    1. Front: Woodbridge C. Snow Mar. 6, 1840 - Nov. 11, 1911
            Joanna Snow Nov. 15, 1846 - Dec. 18, 1932

       Rear: William N. Snow Feb. 25, 1872 - Nov. 5, 1935
            Sadie A. Snow Jan. 19, 1871 - July 15, 1909

    2. Eugene C. son of Woodbridge C. & Joanna Snow 1874-1891

    3. Footstone - Father

    4. Footstone - Mother

    5. Footstone - Will

    6. Footstone - Sadie

LOT #233 -- 2 Stones - 1 Marker

    1. George W. Pettes 1831-1913
       Elsiaida B. his wife 1837-1931

    2. Augusta R. wife of Murray Williams 1839-1915

    3. Sam'l Pettis, Co. H 56 Mass. Inf. (VR: died Aug. 6, 1886 ae 44 yrs.)

GIFFORD CEMETERY

LOT #234 -- 4 Stones

1. Henry B. Ryder died Sept. 24, 1872 ae 26 yrs. 1 mo. 11 ds.
2. Abbie Ryder Atwood 1854-1947
3. Helen Ryder Nickerson 1869-1940
4. Eddie son of Reuben & Emma Ryder aged 1 year
  (VR: died Feb. 14, 1866)

LOT #235 -- 2 Stones

1. Robert Morrow Mar. 17, 1822 - Feb. 5, 1898
  Rebecca S. Morrow Apr. 22, 1824 - Jan. 26, 1900
2. Luella W. Putnam 1856-1907

LOT #236 -- 1 Stone

1. Asa F. Bowley Nov. 9, 1825 - Feb. 5, 1897

LOT #237 -- 1 Monument

1. Monument Front: Charles Cordes 1829-1911
  His wife Martha A. Paine 1832-1911

  Monument Right: John A. Cordes 1854-1942

  Monument Rear: William F. Baker 1862-1942
  His wife Ellie R. 1867-1951
  Charles F. Cordes 1869-1944

LOT #238 -- 5 Stones

1. Charles S. Hopkins 1856-1917
  Charlotte S. Hopkins 1866-1944
2. Joshua F. Hopkins died August 10, 1898 aged 77 ys. 3 ms. 9 ds.
3. Elizabeth G. Sumner wife of Joshua F. Hopkins died August 10, 1893 aged 69 ys. 4 ms. 15 ds.
4. Moses F. son of Joshua F. & Elizabeth G. Hopkins died March 25, 1857 ae 5 ys. 6 ms. 28 ds.
5. Moses S. son of Joshua F. & Elizabeth G. Hopkins died Sept. 22, 1850 ae 4 months

LOT #239 -- 1 Monument - 1 Stone - 2 Markers - 2 Footstones

1. Daniel C. McIntosh 1832-1912
  Rebecca B. McIntosh 1844-1915
2. Margaret E. Kane 1846-1937
3. Carolyne W. Flye 1863-1950
4. Sarah F. dau. of Daniel C. & Rebecca B. McIntosh died June 28, 1866 aged 8 mos. 2 days
5. Footstone - Mother

GIFFORD CEMETERY

LOT #239 (continued)

    6. Footstone - Father

LOT #240 -- 1 Monument - 5 Footstones

    1. Monument Front: Perez B. Rich 1828-1911
                            His wife Sarah W. 1830-1912
                            Edwin B. Rich 1850-1918
                            S. Louise his wife 1852-1886
                            Mary T. his wife 1862-(not cut)

       Monument Right: Samuel (Rich) 1853-1913

       Monument Left: Edwin W. (Rich) 1872-1873
                          Lizzie W. 1880-1895

    2. Footstone - Father

    3. Footstone - Mother

    4. Footstone - Wife - Baby

    5. Footstone - Samuel

    6. Footstone - Lizzie

LOT #241 -- 9 Stones

    1. Mary E. Lucas died Aug. 17, 1884 ae 5 mos. 25 das.

    2. John E. Lucas died Nov. 3, 1887 ae 5 yrs. 3 mos. 20 das.

    3. Gracie S. Lucas died Apr. 12, 1893 ae 13 yrs. 12 das.

    4. John Lucas 1847-1933
       Mary Lucas 1855-1940

    5. Mother - Barbara G. Rich died July 30, 1889 ae 62 yrs. 5 ms. 26 ds.

    6. Sylvester E. Rich died Feb. 18, 1862 ae 5 ms.

    7. Sylvester E. Rich died Dec. 21, 1861 ae 2 ys. 8 ms.

    8. Clara R. Young 1883-1904

    9. George E. Rich 1867-1943
       His wife Stella E. Rich 1860-1939
       George E. Jr. 1896-1896
       Sylvester E. 1830-1891
       His wife Barbara 1827-1889
       John 1865-1893 Died at sea

LOT #242 -- 4 Stones

    1. Capt. Joseph V. Foster died Feb. 18, 1853 ae 30 yrs. 9 ms.

    2. Emily wife of Joseph V. Foster died April 16, 1871 aged 40 yrs. 3 mos.

    3. Nathaniel W. Freeman Oct. 17, 1842 - Apr. 6, 1904
       Francina Freeman Nov. 26, 1850 - Feb. 18, 1922

GIFFORD CEMETERY

LOT #242 (continued)

    4. Edward J. Williams 1843-1909
       Adelaide P. his wife 1844-1924

LOT #243 -- 1 Stone - 1 Marker

    1. Almeda M. wife of Freeman W. Cobb died Feb. 11, 1871 ae 23 yrs. 4 ms. & 7 ds.

    2. Our Babe - Eddie A. son of F. W. & Abbie E. Cobb died Feb. 5, 1875 ae 3 mos.

LOT #244 -- No Stone

LOT #245 -- No Stone

LOT #246 -- 1 Monument - 4 Footstones

    1. Benjamin A. Atkins 1844-1912
       Theresa A. Cobb 1846-1900

    2. Footstone - Mother

    3. Footstone - Father

    4. Footstone - Bessie (Atkins) (no date)

    5. Footstone - Chester (Atkins) (no date)

LOT #247 -- 1 Monument - 1 Stone - 6 Footstones

    1. Monument Front: Capt. Phineas Paine died June 25, 1862 aged 56 yrs. 11 mos. 21 ds.
       Husband and Father
       Elizabeth M. widow of Phineas Paine died Oct. 11, 1876 aged 65 yrs. 8 mos. 28 ds.

       Monument Right: Mr. Jas. N. Hopkins born July 29, 1832 died June 25, 1861. Son and Brother

       Monument Left: Phineas C. son of Phineas & Elizabeth M. Paine died Jan. 3, 1845 aged 2 yrs. 10 ms.
       Salina T. dau. of Phineas & Elizabeth M. Paine died Jan. 16, 1849 aged 1 yr. 10 mos. 13 ds.
       Martha C. dau. of Phineas & Elizabeth M. Paine died Jan. 26, 1853 aged 2 yrs. 5 ms. 26 ds.

    2. Footstone - Phineas C. son of Phineas & Elizabeth M. Paine died Jan. 3, 1845 ae 2 ys. 10 mos.

    3. Footstone - Salina T. daughter of Phineas & Elizabeth M. Paine died Jan. 16, 1849 ae 1 yr. 10 ms. 13 ds.

    4. Footstone - Martha C. daughter of Phineas & Elizabeth M. Paine died Jan. 26, 1853 aged 2 yrs. 5 mos. 26 days

GIFFORD CEMETERY

LOT #247 (continued)

    5. Footstone - H. N. P.

    6. Footstone - P. P.

    7. Footstone - Mother

    8. Otis Horton Bramhall 1881-1916
       Helen Hilliard Bramhall 1877-1951

LOT #248 -- 1 Monument - 1 Marker - 7 Footstones

    1. Monument Front: Joshua E. Bowly died Apl. 3, 1883 ae 70 ys. 6 ms.
                      Jane C. wife of Joshua E. Bowly Apl. 14, 1883 ae 68 ys. 4 ms. 23 ds.

       Monument Right: Joshua E. Bowley Jr. died June 4, 1885 ae 37 ys. 7 ms. 3 ds.
                       Rebecca E. Bowly 1853-1911

       Monument Left: Priscilla M. Whorf 1878-1924

    2. Amos F. Whorf 1836-1896

    3. Betsey K. Whorf 1838-1905

    4. Footstone - Mother

    5. Footstone - Father

    6. Footstone - Rebecca

    7. Footstone - Joshua

    8. Footstone - Priscilla

    9. Stephen C. Whorf (no date)

LOT #249 -- 1 Monument - 1 Stone - 2 Footstones

    1. Artemas Paine 1815-1883
       Lucy J. Paine 1819-1906

    2. Mehitable Hinckley widow of Leander Stafford Jan. 29, 1802-Dec. 11, 1887 (Maiden name Lothrop)

    3. Footstone - A. P.

    4. Footstone - L. J. P.

LOT #250 -- 1 Stone - 4 Markers - 2 Footstones

    1. Willard T. Burkett 1847-1914
       Susan his wife 1848-1918

    2. Footstone - Mother

    3. Footstone - Father

    4. George P. Williams 1881-1949
       Hattie E. Williams 1886-1954

GIFFORD CEMETERY

LOT #250 (continued)

    5. Curly (surname unknown) 1943-1957

    6. Delia Pierce (no date)

    7. Birtie B. Pierce born Aug. 26, 1858 died Feb. 22, 1893 son of Mary & John Pierce

LOT #251 -- No Stone

INDEX TO PART TWO

PERSONS, PLACES & SHIPS BY LOT NUMBER

GIFFORD CEMETERY

ADAMS Adele (Proctor 15 Darrow 15 Harriet D 15 Infants 15 Jennie (Holmes) 15 John Darrow 15 Lavina 43
ALLEN Carrie H 215 Daniel 50 Donald M 50 Eunice T 105 Flora 50 George 105 George M 105 Georgie B 105 Gideon 105 Hattie P 105 Helen S 105 Polly 105 Tabitha 105 William 215
ASPLEY Chas 100 Lizzie J 100 Martha 100
ATKINS Albert W 127 Anna W 127 Asaph S 68 Benjamin A 246 Benjamin D 224 Benjamin E 68 Benjamin H 204 Bertha Evelyn 204 Bessie 246 Bessie E 196 Carrie O 130 Charles A 11 Charles Carroll 204 Charlie P 230 Chester 246 Christie (Kemp) 204 David H 127 Eliza L 204 Ellen F 127 Elry F (Baxter) 91 Emma W (Cook) 184 Enos N 20 Esther 127 Esther F 11 Frank K 184 Franklin 130 Hannah S (Higgins) 92 Hannah W 130 Hannah Y (Sparks) 224 Henry 127 Ida E 127 Ira B 91 Isaac F 130 James 92 James F 130 James T 130 Joseph R 22 Joshua 112 Joshua R 127 Lillian Russell 196 Lillie L 196 Lizzie Ainsworth 92 Lydia S 68 Margaret H 230 Maria E 130 Marion 68 Martha J 22 Martha W 22 Mary M 127 Mary Pauline 204 Mary T 130 Nancy A 159 Paul 230 Pauline Jennie Carroll 204 Rebecca W 112 Reuben 44 Roxanna 44 Ruhama H 130 Samuel K 184 Theresa A (Cobb) 246 Viola F 184 William T 196 Willie Lawson 68 Zaccheus R 22
ATWOOD Abbie (Ryder) 234 Abbie T 64 Adelia C 179 Alonzo F 64 231 Benajmin R 78 Bertha G 178 Betsey N 78 Charlie S 46 Doris 78 Edwin C 64 Elizabeth P 46 Fred S 78 George W 64 Harriet G 231 Ida Chester 64 Infant dau 64 John 64 John E 46 John W 64 Joseph S 78 Lizzie S 46 Lois N 78 Louisa M 46 Maria 46 Mary F (Sparks) 64 Myrick C 46 Nathaniel E 46 Rebecca M 64 Stephen F 179 Willie Lester 64

BAKER Charles 12 Ellie R 237 Leroy C 12 Lizzie P 12 Maud C 12 William F 237
BANGS Anne (Lyford) 121 Carrie F 126 Charles Dana 121 Elijah 121 Elijah Dana 121 Frank Sparks 121 Hattie N 121
BANNISTER Charlie 1 Chas F 1 Chas H 1 Emina C 1
BATT Leonard S 45 Stanley 45
BAUMGARTNER F Louise (Waldin) 44 Leslie 44
BAXTER Eliza C 44 Elry F 91 Florence M 44 Joseph B 91 Richard 44 Susan E (Morris) 91
BELL John 10 Zilpha 10
BENNETT Irene F 102 Jeremiah 139 Louis A 102 Louis F 205 Melissa F 102 Samuel A 102
BENT Emma F 175
BLACK Lucius A 62
BLUNDELL Henry 7 Mary 7 Willie F 7
BOWLEY/BOWLY Asa F 236 Jane C 248 Joshua E 248 Joshua E Jr 248 Marcia N (Franzen) 227 Rebecca E 248 William W 227
BRADSHAW Jerusha K 195 Sadie S 195 William M 195
BRAMHALL Helen Hilliard 247 Otis Horton 247
BROOKS Abby C 31 Lillian N 31 Maria 31 Newell C 31 Newell C 2nd 31 Newell C 3rd 31
BROWN (see also BROWNE) Abbie Hilliard 70 Adeline C (Hilliard 70 Albina F 31 Alfred N 16 Annetta N (Pierce) 16 Benjamin 70 Carrie L (Crooker) 16 Ira W 16 Reuben F 31
BROWNE (see also BROWN) Charles Ellsworth 146 Elsie Hadley 146
BUCKNAM Celeste 17 Celia T 17

-197-

GIFFORD CEMETERY

Walter E 17
BURCH Carrie T 143 Eben F 143
  Ida Bell 41 John M 143 Maria
  P 143 Nancy H 143 Theodora A
  143 Wallace A 143 Wallace F
  143
BURGESS Henrietta A (Lavender)
  188
BURKE Ada (Holmes) 42 James M 42
  John 42
BURKETT Susan 250 Willard T 250
BUSH Edith Linwood 173 Edwin
  Willis 173 Emma Linwood 173
  Mary W 173 Richard P 173
  Richard Perry 173

CAMPBELL Archibald 119A Hattie
  L 125 Infant 125 John W 125
CARD Sarah F 165 William A 165
CATE Charles F 22 Etta A 22
CATON Abbie B 207 Emanuel 207
  Joseph M 207 Matilda A 207
CAVANAGH Mary J 17 Michael J 17
  Sara A 17
CHASE Amelia A 53 Bessie Aldwell
  53 Joseph L 207 Josiah A 53
  Mariner H 207
CHILDS Abbie D 35
CHIPMAN Fannie H 179 Gladys 179
  Henry T 179 William H 139
CHISHOM Duncan 162 Mary (Matheson) 162 Roderick 162
CHRISTOPHER Edith (Dunham) 181
COBB Almeda M 243 Eddie A 243
  Theresa A 246
COLE Lou (Harding) 41
CONANT Bethia N 97 Oliver B 97
CONNELL Georgie M 185
CONWELL Almira B 23 Arrilla M 23
  R Eugene 180 Ruth S (Hedge)
  180 Walter L 23
COOK Abigail 215 Abigail R 219
  Addie 22 Adelaide Jones
  (Masten) 26A Adeline 80
  Almena Ellen (Hopkins) 145
  Annie W 111 Apphia D 156 Benjamin 159 Bertha 155 Betsey
  F 111 Betsey L 59 Caroline F
  54 Charles A 8 Charles D 103
  Charles E 103 Charlotte A
  (Hooton) 155 Cornelius 59 70
  Daniel C 70 Delia 129 Eddie

54 Effie L 145 Elisha 96
  Elisha H 129 Eliza S 129
  Eliza W 22 Ellen B 103 Emily
  A 184 Emma P 11 Emma W 184
  Ephraim 59 Francis P 111 Fred
  W 22 Frederick F 11 Freeman
  228 Grace Elliott 8 Hannah K
  228 Harvey A 155 Harvey S 155
  Henry 219 Horace W 54 Infant
  dau 219 Isaiah W 111 James
  184 James Bradford 145 Jesse
  Jr 80 Joanna R 54 John A 80
  184 Johnnie 54 Joshua 145
  Lemuel 103 Lemuel 2nd 111
  Lillian M 8 Marion F 8 Mary
  B 70 Olive Wadsworth 19
  Rebecca 54 Rebecca A 111
  Rebecca E 59 Rebekah 103
  Rubie 54 Sadie H 59 Sally 103
  Sarah H 96 Viola D (Fish) 184
  Walter S 111 William 54
COPELAND Susan E (Morris) 91
CORDES Charles 237 Charles F 237
  Cordelia E 106 John A 237
  Martha A (Paine) 237
COVELL Margaret W 180 Ruth S 81
CRAWFORD Harry B 109 Sadie (MacKenzie) 109
CREIGHTON Dora B 132
CRITCHETT Julia Frances 39
CROCKER Andrew 229 Benjamin I 229
  Benjamin T 229 David 229
  Elizabeth S 229 Francis 163
  George E 139 John Myrick 163
  Josephine 163 Joshua A 229
  Lillian A 229 Louisa W 186
  Rebecca N 229 Sarah 229
  Susanna 163 Waterman 186
CROOKER Carrie L 16
CROSBY Jane C 101 Jonathan 101
  Norman S K 101
CROWELL Bertha (Smith) 165
  Dorothy 165
CURREN Hannah 138 Hugh 138 Mary
  G 138 William 138
CUTTER Phineas S Jr 212 Rebecca
  F 212

DAGGETT (see also DOGGETT) Cora
  M 51 Frederick T 51 Helen F
  51 James 153 John L 51 Mary S
  153

-198-

DAVIS Clara N 34 Cora A 207
  Everett B 207 Frank A 34
  Frederick Walton 41 Ida Bell
  (Burch) 41 John Walton 41
  John Winthrop 41 Laura
  Talmadge 41 Mary W 205
DAWES Clara W 127
DEARBORN Addie A 131 Caroline
  F (Nickerson) 87 Fred H 131
DEARS Mary J 147
DICKSON Hannah W 58 Thaddeus P
  58
DIGGDON Jacob 5 Mary 5
DOANE Hattie P (Allen) 105
DODGE Sarah C (Patton) 96
DODS Amelia Jennie 40 Willie 40
DOGGETT (see also DAGGETT Frank-
  ie F 153 Janet 153 Lathrop
  153
DOWLING Albert H 98 Alex 1
  Archibald W 113 Archie F 1
  Bessie F 113 Blanche I 98
  Daniel W 98 Experience L
  113 Margaret (Kemp) 98 Sadie
  L 113
DUNHAM Abbie 181 Abbie F 181
  Austin R 181 Edith 181 Edwin
  W 181 George L 181 James B
  142 John A 181 John T 181
  Margaret A 181 Nathan 142
  Olive N 142
DYER Alley 65 Amasa S 3 Emily M
  185 Isaac Atkins 4 J Emmons
  185 James S 65 Lorena (Sparks)
  4 Martha 158 Mary E 3 Phebe
  185 Sadie G (Emery) 89 Sarah
  S 65

ELDER Salome A (Gifford) 86
  William A 86
ELLIOTT Elizabeth Hannum
  (Kenney) 19 Olive Wadsworth
  (Cook) 19 Russell Dunson 19
  Russell Dunson Jr 19 Russell
  Knox 19
ELLIS Adelia (Tuttle) 32 Minnie
  A 210
EMERY Alfred J 209 Eliza A 209
  Eva 209 Fred 209 James 88
  Joseph H 89 Mary 88 Mary A 89
  Mary P 88 Priscilla 88 Sadie
  G 89 Willis N 88

EWELL Ezra D 185 Josephine 185
  Melintha D 185

FARWELL J Ella 61
FIELD George Chester 26
FIFIELD Gilbert H 3 Susie W 3
FISH Viola D 184
FISHER Almera C 21 Caleb Eugene
  21 Elmira N (Pierce) 194
  Frances C 21 L Jane (Talbot)
  194 Samuel 194 Samuel O 194
FLYE Carolyne W 239
FORD Herbert A 8 Lillian M
  (Cook) 8
FOSS Howard W 32 Katie B 32
  Leonard R 32
FOSTER Anna 205 Charles A 205
  Emily 242 Joseph V 242 Lizzie
  B 205
FRANCIS Hannah 110
FRANZEN Arline M 227 Asa A 139
  Marcia N 227
FREEMAN Abigail 62 Annie E 114
  Apphia D (Cook) 156 Bathsheba
  168 Benjamin 63 Benjamin Jr
  63 Betsey 63 Betsey D 63
  Elisha 74 Elizabeth 122 Emily
  B 63 Flora M 156 Florence M
  185 Francina 242 George
  Everett 114 Hannah 114 Hatsuld
  156 Horace A 88 J Everett 114
  John 114 John T 71 Josiah C
  139 Lewis M 122 Mary (Emery)
  88 Mary H 114 Nathan 62
  Nathaniel W 242 Phebe 83
  Reuben 122 Reuben F 122
  Simeon N 73
FRELLICK Christopher L 131 George
  131
FULLER Charles A 9 Mary F (Sparks)
  64 Sarah D 9

GAUDIN James 100 Malvina C 100
GHEN Infant 195 Mehitable Cook
  69 Sadie S (Bradshaw) 195
GIBBONS Thomas J 139
GIFFORD Agnes 84/85 Annie 86
  Banjamin 84/85 Ellen S 165
  Frances C 86 Frederick A H 40
  Harriet C 86 Isaiah 84/85
  James 84/85 86 James Jr 86

GIFFORD CEMETERY

Laura 40 Lemuel 84/85 Marinda
 A 40 Mary E 40 Moses N 86
 Nabby 84/85 Nabby Y (Nickerson) 84/85 Nathaniel N 84/85
 225 Orra K 225 Rebecca A 86
 Rebekah A 84/85 Romenia 40
 Salome 84/85 Salome A 84/85
 86 Salome S 40 Stephen A P
 86 Thomas 86
GILES Charles H 6
GODFREY Francis 137
GOODRICH Annie Y (Shortle) 218
 C G 218
GORDON Abbie H 172 Willie T 172
GOSS Myra 57
GRAHAM Edmund 9 Rachel S 9
GROSS Amelia O 178 Bartholomew
 O 178 Bertha G (Atwood) 178
 Clarissa P 67 Edward Blake 39
 George Thomas 39 Julia Frances
 (Critchett) 39 Mattie Hanson
 39 Melville A 178 Susan B
 (Hopkins) 178 Sylvanus 67

HAMLIN Alexander 62 Mary E 62
 Minnie E 62 Sara A 62 Sarah
 A 62
HANNUM Chas A 61 J Ella (Farwell) 61 Olive N (Paine) 61
 William Porter 61
HARDING Elizabeth O 41 Lou 41
 Robert L 41
HARTFORD Abigail N 18 Barachias
 F 18 Elvira 18
HARVENDER Ada B 5 Bessie A 50
 Daniel R 50 Dwight H 50
 Edwin A 50 Florence W 50
 Fred M 5 Henry B 5 John P 5
 Maude B 50 Neoma 5 Sadie E
 5 William T 50
HASTING Pauline Jennie Carroll
 (Atkins) 204
HATCH Abbie D (Childs) 35 Benjamin F 35 Florence R 35
 Gertrude W 35 Jennie C 35
 Samuel T 35
HEALEY Adelaide Jones (Masten)
 26A Willis 26A
HEDGE Margaret W (Covell) 180
 Ruth S 180 William H 180
HEIM George E R 116A Infant dau

116A John C 116A Mary K 116A
HENDERSON Addie Bell 147 Benjamin
 S 147 Grace May 147 Mary J
 (Dears) 147
HIGGINS Bessie L 211 C Lothrop 57
 Charles Alden 211 Charles W
 43 Clara E 57 Ebenezer 100
 Elmer A 57 Hannah S 92
 Harriet N 57 Hattie L 57
 Isaac H 57 Josiah 43 Lavina
 (Adams) 43 Levi 54 Lucy J 211
 Malvina C 100 Mary Abbie 43
 Myra W 57 Nehemiah Y 211 Rotie
 Nye 57 Sarah (Hinks) 43
 Solomon R 139 Stephen W 57
 Susan B 43 Vine Adams 43
HILL Almira B 90 Clarence H 90
 George C 90 George C Jr 90
 Jonathan E 90 Jonathan Jr 90
 Rebecca H H 90 Susan K 90
 William G 90
HILLIARD Adeline C 70 Pauline 70
HINKS Sarah 43
HINMAN Alice (Kelley) 47
HOBBINS John W 139
HODGDON Charles D 132 Helena E
 132
HOLMES Ada 42 Carrie L 42 Emma M
 175 Flo M 42 James M 42 James
 P 42 Jennie 15 Salome C 42
 Sarah C 42
HOLWAY Rebekah A (Gifford) 84/85
 Susan A 3
HOOTON Annie Q 206 Charlotte A
 155 Joseph H 206
HOPKINS Almena Ellen 145 Annie
 (Gifford) 86 Charles S 238
 Charlotte S 238 Cora M
 (Daggett) 51 Elizabeth G
 (Sumner) 238 Howard R 51
 Isabel M 128 James N 247
 Joshua F 238 Mary A 128 Moses
 F 238 Moses S 238 Susan B 178
 William Stowell 128
HOTCKISS Christine (Rouse) 221
 Edwin Lyman 221
HOWES Emma F 184
HUCKINS Nellie D 99
HUGHES Maggie A 92
HUTCHINGS Margaret A 21
HUTCHINSON Anna Edith 169 Anna J
 169 Benjamin F 169 Frances

GIFFORD CEMETERY

Sturgis 169

JACOBS Abigail (Cook) 215 Thomas 215
JOHNSON Alice A 170 Charles E 170 Clara C 170 Lina B 170 Mary L 130
JORDAN Clarence B 77 Ida S 77

KANE Margaret E 239
KELLEY Alice 47 Benjamin 183 Charles P 9 Hannah C 9 Hernaldo H 183 Mertie C 183 Minerva B 47 Sherborn S 183 Susan C 183
KEMP Annie R 117 Christie 204 Daniel 117 Francis 117 Jane M 117 Jennie F 117 Katherine A R 117 Margaret 98 Margaret M 136 Murdock 136
KENDALL Almon 34 Clifford 34 Harriet 34 Jesse I 34 Maud 34 Nellie P 34
KENNEDY Andrew 123 Lillian M 123 Nettie P 123
KENNEY Elizabeth Hannum 19
KILBURN Asenath 91
KILEY Eleanor J (Rich) 133
KING George W 220 Hannah C 220 Joseph 139 Sarah 220
KNOWLES Adelia G 182 Ambrose D 182 Asenath (Kilburn) 91 Josiah F 182 Rebecca 182 Rebecca D 182 Ruth G 182

LANCY Helen (McBrien) 27 Henry J 27
LAVENDER Albertina 65 Allen 187 Elbridge 65 Henrietta A 188 Katie 187 Katie A 65 Katie Allen 65 Louise J 65 Mabel A 187 Maria Y 187 Robert M 65 Stephen A 187 Stephen S 187
LAW Edward M 79 Louis A 77 Mehitable 77 Mertie J 79 Nellie N 77 William H 77 William M 77 Willie B 77
LECOUNT Sarah 72
LEONARD Josephine W 45 William J 45 Willis F 45
LEWIS Alfred H 35 Bangs A 7 Betsey W 6 Daniel F 79 Edna 210 Elizabeth A 6 Emma R 7 Ensley 210 Frederick A 210 Hetty F 79 Isaac B 6 Janet W 166 Jennie C (Hatch) 35 Lloyd 210 Marguerite 210 Mattie A 166 Mercy M 79 Minnie A (Ellis) 210 Olive A 6 Susie E (Whitcomb) 108 Susie Warren 7 Thomas Julian 166
LIVINGSTON Alexander 131 Bessie M 131 Elizabeth I 131 Susan R 131
LOCKWOOD George 139
LOMBARD Arthur L 133
LORING Charles 112 Eugene W 28 Infant dau 112 Mary C 28 Rebecca W 112 William G 28
LOTHROP Mehitable Hinckley 249
LOWELL Romenia (Gifford) 40
LUCAS Gracie S 241 John 241 John E 241 Mary 241 Mary E 241
LURTEN Deborah M 38 Frank W 158 Freeman S 38 John C 139 Jonathan C 158 Martha E 158 Susan J 158 Susie K 158 William 158
LYFORD Anne 121

MCBRIEN Helen 27
MCDONALD (see also MACDONALD) Flora Jane 141 Jannie 141
MACDONALD (see also MCDONALD) Lorena D 66 Murdock 66
MCFADDEN (see also MCFADYEN/ MCFAYDEN) Ann 171 Dan 171 John 171
MCFADYEN (see also MCFADDEN/ MCFAYDEN) Ebbie Leonard 152 Hugh 152 Susan (West) 152
MCFAYDEN (see also MDFADDEN/ MCFADYEN) John 171
MCINTOSH Daniel 137 Daniel C 239 Isabella 137 John 137 Martha 137 Rebecca B 239 Roderick 162 Sarah 162 Sarah F 239
MCINTYRE Angus 128 Annabella 128 Duncan A 128 Katie Bell 128
MACK Lydia 160

GIFFORD CEMETERY

MACKAY Christie 221 Eli 132
    Isabelle 221 Louise R 217
    Mary W 132
MCKENZIE (see also MACKENZIE)
    Duncan 141 Lillian 144
    Margret 141
MACKENZIE (see also MCKENZIE)
    Ella 117 Lawrence 109 Maggie
    A 109 Norman 109 Sadie 109
    Sarah 109
MCKINNON Daniel 125 Margaret
    125 Sadie B 125
MCLEAN Alexander 137
MACLEOD Katherine 136
MACMILLAN John 66 Mary H 66
MACPHEE Donald F 132 Helen C
    132 William K 132
MCRITCHIE Ann Eliza 113 Eddie
    Burt 113 John A 113
MADDOCK Lawrence 28 Lydia A 28
    Martha J 28
MARSHALL George H 122
MARSTON Elmira N (Pierce) 194
MASTEN Adelaide Jones 26A
    Louisa Bangs 26A
MATHESON Addie J 208 Anabel 208
    Catherine 208 Christie (Mac-
    Kay) 221 Donald J 92 Duncan
    208 Ellen 208 Ida 221 John
    W. K. 221 Mary 162 Maud J
    208 Roderick 116 Sarah 116
    William H 208 William K 221
MAYO Adeline 124 Annie M 144
    Bernice R 144 Bessie F 21
    Bessie G 21 Betsey 124 Eliza
    L 124 Emily J 185 George R
    124 Herman L 144 Izetta F
    170 Jerome A 21 Joseph 124
    Joseph A 124 Joshua A 124
    Lizzie 124 Mary Franklin 124
    Nellie Florence 144 Phebe
    (Dyer) 185 Susan 124 Thomas
    185
MERRILL Antone P 45 Florence M
    45
MESSER Florence M (Whitcomb) 108
    Infant 108 Josephine W 108
MILLER Viola F (Atkins) 184
MOORE Huldah C 118 Joseph W 118
MORRIS Asenath (Kilburn) 91
    Charles 91 Hannah J 107 Susan
    E 91

MORROW Rebecca S 235 Robert 235
MOTT Annie C 161 Atwood 161
    Bertha 161 Eveline L 161
    George P 161 Phillis M 161
    Stephen 161
MULLINS Ada 224
MULREADY Robert 47 Violette 47

NEWCOMB Almena F 52 Annie Almena
    52 Charles F 52 Ella F 52
    Irma 209 Jonah 52 Mabel 52
    Melissa 52 Robert 55 Samuel
    F 52 Sarah 52 55 Susan S 209
    Thomas C 52 Warren T 52
    William 209 Willie 209
NICKERSON A Loretta 216 Abigail
    N 215 Addison 99 Alfred 87
    Anna S 168 Atkins 83
    Bathsheba (Freeman) 168
    Bethiah 223 Caleb 168 Caleb
    A 168 Caroline F 87 Charles
    H 168 Delia A 223 Elizabeth
    S 82 Ephraim 215 Francis 135
    Hannah J 83 Helen (Ryder) 234
    Henry P 168 Herbert M 83
    Infant dau 168 Infant son 168
    Jesse 99 216 Lavinia 216 Lewis
    222 223 Louisa Bangs (Masten)
    26A Luther 82 Malvina 135
    Malvina J 99 Mary 99 Mary A
    216 Mary H 87 Mary Lombard
    (Nickerson) 99 Mary R 81 Mary
    S 168 Moses P 87 Nabby Y 84/85
    Nehemiah 216 Nellie D V 216
    Polly 87 Rawlins A 216 Rebecca
    R 81 Reuben 215 Ruth S
    (Covell) 81 Sally 168 Sarah E
    222 Seth 81 Solomon D 223
    Stephen 81 Stephen T 81 Susan
    L 223 Thomas 87 Walter I 83
    William K 216

PAINE Annie Putnam 147 Artemas
    249 Elizabeth M 247 Emily K
    16 Eugene Willard 147 Joshua
    S 173 Lizzie 146 Lucy J 249
    Lysander N 173 Martha A 237
    Martha C 247 Martha H 147
    Olive N 61 Phineas 247
    Phineas C 247 Rebecca S 173

-202-

GIFFORD CEMETERY

Salina T 247 Samuel T 139
Thomas K 146 Thomas N 147
Willard H 147
PARKER Mehitable Cook (Ghen) 69
Samuel 69
PASCHAL Carrie E 126 Joshua 126
Rebecca 126
PATRICK Manuel 55 Sadie M 55
PATTON Bertie 96 H Egbert 96
Mary S 96 Melissa C 96 Minnie
96 Robert H 96 Sarah C 96
PEALE Louise (Watson) 176
PETTES/PETTIS Elsiaida B 233
George W 233 Samuel 233
PIERCE Annetta N 16 Birtie B
250 Delia 250 Elizabeth E
16 Elmira N 194 Mary Carrie
142 Stephen D 142
PINE Grace I 95 J Emerson 95
Joseph S 95 Mary R 95
PLACES Alabama Mobile 113; East
Indies 63; Florida Coral
Gables 184 Fernandina 73;
Grand Banks 174; Illinois
Quincy 44; Japan Tokio (sic)
43 Yokohama 43; Korea 45;
Maine Clinton 69; Maryland
Greensboro 69; Massachusetts
Attleboro 145 Boston 69 167
Bourne 26A Bridgewater 204
Chatham 69 Cohasset 69 East
Boston 72 Eastham 93
Gloucester 128 Medfield 26A
Middleboro 196 Provincetown
69 127 139 Truro 145; Michigan
Lansing 205; New Hampshire
Fremont 43 Isles of Shoals
53 Manchester 6; Nova Scotia
Liverpool 65 Yarmouth 65;
South Atlantic 148; Virginia
Northumberland County 69;
West Africa Monrovia 53; West
Indies Carriacou 68 St Gago
De Cuba 103
POWE Andrew T 196 Bessie E 196
PRINCE Hannah M 119
PROCTOR Adele 15 Beatrice H 56
PUTNAM A Louis 219 Abbie C 219
Adelaide O 219 Luella W 235
Nellie F 219

RAMSEY Malcom 29 Mary G 29
REMINGTON Orie M 56 Orie P 56
William F 56 Willie S 56
REYNOLDS Jessie M 50
RICH Allen O 75 Allen W 75 Amelia
O (Gross) 178 Austin W 125
Barbara G 241 Basil E 95
Chester A 75 Cordelia E
(Cordes) 106 David 160 Edwin
B 240 Edwin W 240 Eleanor J
133 Elisha 160 Elisha T 160
Eunice S 75 George E 241
George E. Jr 241 Georgianna F
160 Grace Elliot (Cook) 8
Herbert Woodbury 8 Izetta F
(Mayo) 170 James E 134
Jeremiah A 166 John 241 John
B 106 John L 178 Julia F 106
Lizzie W 240 Lombard 166
Lydia N 166 Manie Steele 68
Margery T 133 Martha J 166
Mary E 68 125 Mary R 160 Mary
T 240 Nathaniel 125 Perez B
240 Priscilla K 160 Rebecca A
100 134 S Louise 240 Samuel
240 Sarah W 240 Sophronia B
125 Stella E 241 Sylvester E
241 Xenophon S 68 Z Thomas
133 Zephaniah 133
RICHARDSON Nettie C 228 Osman D
228 Susan Emma 228
ROBERTS Edward 16 Elizabeth E
(Pierce) 16 Emily K (Paine)
16 William 16
RODGERS (see also ROGERS) Clara
20 Elijah 20 Honorah A 20
Mary J 20 Neadom 20
ROGERS (see also RODGERS) Emerson F 110 Frances E 110 Frank
M 110 Hannah F 110 Joseph F
110 Lillian E 110
ROOD Elizabeth N 82 Jacob 82
Luther Colby 82 R Dora 82
ROOP Elvira (Hartford) 18
ROSS Infant male 58
ROUSE Christine 221 Edwin W Jr
221 Ida (Matheson) 221
RYDER Aaron 160 Abbie 234 Anna
78 Benjamin 78 Eddie 234
Ephraim Henry 78 Helen 234
Henry B 234 Janet 78 Lucy A
78

SEARS Edwin 109 Elizabeth 109
    Emma F 2 Frank I 109 Infant
    2 Manuel 2 Mary E 109
SHIPS C E Trumbull 127 C H Hodg-
    don 119A Carrie D Knowles 148
    James Porter 174 Joseph H
    Chandler 128
SHORTLE Annie Y 218 Henry 218
    Mary N 218
SMALL Abraham 101 Ann Simmons 30
    Arnold 56 Arnold O 56 Bertha
    F 94 Catherine T 167 D Fran-
    cis 186 Daniel 30 Daniel F
    186 Eliza S 106 Esther D 56
    Esther F 56 Francis 167
    George 186 George W 186 Hannah
    94 Hannah G 30 Infant son 106
    Ira K 106 Ira Kilburn 106
    Isaac 3rd 94 James H 120 Jane
    C 101 John W 3 139 John Wells
    3 Josephine T 56 Leonora S
    186 Lot 94 Lydia B 167 Lydia
    S 56 Maria C 186 Mary E 101
    Norman S K 101 Rachel S 3
    Reuben C 167 Sally 30 Susan
    A (Holway) 3 Taylor Jr 139
    Uriah 106 Waterman C 186
    Winnifred S 94
SMITH (see also SMYTH) Abbie H
    164 Alma F 164 Amanda M 169
    Bertha 165 Catherine 175
    Charles K 151 Clara 176
    Edmund 69 Elijah 169 Eliza-
    beth B 164 Elkanah 139 Emma
    M (Holmes) 175 Emily A 112
    Emily E 165 Ethel B 164
    Eva M 175 Fidelia P 33 Fran-
    cis P 33 Francis P Jr 33
    Frankie C 151 Franklin N 175
    Gamaliel B 72 H Merrill 175
    Henry A 139 Infant 33 James
    134 James H 134 Jerome S 164
    John 112 187 John R 139
    Joseph H 94 Katie N 164 Lydia
    169 Maria D 151 Mary E 187
    Mary M 134 Mother 72 Obadiah
    151 Ouvra K 220 Rebecca 134
    Sadie J 112 Sadie W 112 Sally
    M 93 Samuel S 165 Sarah A 165
    Sarah C 94 Sarah J 112 Sarah
    (King) 220 Sarah (LeCount)
    72 Simeon C 112 Simeon C Jr
    112 Stephen H 112

SMYTH (see also SMITH) Alonzo 69
    Edmund 69 John 69 John Thomas
    69 Mehitable Cook (Ghen) 69
SNOW Atkins D 146 Betsey D 217
    David F 153 Eleanor C 215
    Elijah Olin 107 Eugene C 232
    Hattie A 146 Herman Holden 217
    Joanna 232 Joseph W 217 Joshua
    A 34 Louis M 107 Lucy E 146
    Mabel F 107 Mary E 107 Nellie
    P (Kendall) 34 Obadiah 107
    Olin B 146 Sadie A 232 Sarah
    M 107 Wilfred C 215 William C
    215 William N 232 Woodbridge
    C 232
SPARKS Ada (Mullins) 224 Charles
    A 224 Charles P 224 Frederick
    A 226 George Q 222 Hannah C
    224 Hannah Y 224 James T 97
    Lorena 4 Mary F 64 Mattie (see
    also Unknown) 97 Rebecca 4
    Sarah A 97 Serviah 222 Thomas
    W 224
SPARROW Clara C 67 Harvey O 67
    Harvey O Jr 67 Herbert C 67
    Mary E (Williams) 174 Orianna
    C 67 Osborne M 208 William
    Chester 174
SPEAR Charles J 157 Harriet F 157
SPINNEY Leslie A 131 Nellie B 131
STAFFORD Mehitable Hinckley
    (Lothrop) 249
STANDISH Ann C 132 George W 132
STEVENSON Collin A 148
STONE Hazel Y 11
STID Mary 104 Wm J 104
SUMNER Elizabeth G 238 Enoch N
    119 Hannah F 138 Hannah J 138
    Hannah M (Prince) 119 Hulda C
    138 Josiah T 119 Moses 138
    Sophronia A 119
SWEETSER Malvina J (Nickerson) 99
SWENSON Nellie (Swift) 154
SWIFT Betsey C 129 Delia (Cook)
    129 Ellen A 154 Helen May 93
    John 129 John N 129 Josiah 129
    Leon S 154 Maria Francis 93
    Mary E 93 Mattie Hanson
    (Gross) 39 Nellie 154 Rebecca
    P 93 Reuben 93 Reuben W 93
    Sally M 93 Sally M (Smith) 93
    Samuel S 154 Sarah J 129
    Theodore Winthrop 39

TALBOT L Jane 194
TAYLOR Ama S 126 Charles 115
　Hannah 115 Mary W 115 Sally
　126
TILLSON E H 167 Elisha 73 John
　A 73 Martha A 167 Mary C 167
　Mary L 73 Tamsin 73
TUCK Charles U 26
TUPPER William E 139
TUTTLE Adelia 32

UNIDENTIFIED No Stones or Empty
　Lots 13 14 24 25 36 37 48 49
　60 71 119A 120 148 156 189
　190 191 197 198 199 200 201
　202 203 213 214 244 245 251
UNKNOWN Curly 250 Mattie 97

VINTON Albert J 4 Porter Monroe
　4 Rebecca (Sparks) 4 Sherman E 4 William M 4

WALDIN F Louise 44 Florence M
　(Baxter) 44 Reinhold 44
WALRADT Elnora F 122 Henry M
　122
WATSON Clara (Smith) 176 Effie
　Y 176 Eldridge Rich 176
　Eleanor Louise 176 Eugene W
　176 Horace H 176 Horace S
　176 Louise 176 Rebecca T 176
WEEKS Carrie A 157 Charlotte
　Mary 157 Harold Stillman 188
　Isadore L 188 John C 157 John
　C Jr 157 Joseph E 188 Joseph
　H 157
WELDON (see also WHELDEN) Anna
　(Foster) 205
WEST Eliza 76 Elizabeth A 115
　Hattie M 76 Henry N 181 May
　115 Newton P 115 Phebe A
　152 Rebecca P 181 Robert L
　152 Simeon L 76 Susan 152
WHELDEN (see also WELDON)
　Adelaide H 183 Elmer G 183
　George M 183 George M Jr 183
　John G 183 Mercie F 183
WHITCOMB Emma J 108 Florence M
　108 Joseph 108 Levenia C 108
　Susie E 108
WHITE Harriet S 68 Ira Bidwell
　68 Nicholas 68
WHITNEY George R 70 Pauline
　(Hilliard) 70
WHORF Amos F 248 Betsey K 248
　James 123 Josiah F 123
　Lucinda F 123 Lucinda W 123
　Phebe M 123 Priscilla M 248
　Stephen C 248 Warren H 111
WILLIAMS Adelaide P 242 Andrew
　174 Andrew T 174 Augusta R
　233 Edward J 242 Eliza Ann
　174 Emanuel 205 Eveline N
　174 George P 250 Hattie E
　250 Joan 205 Louise B 8
　Louvisa 174 Mary E 174 Nina
　Soper 174 Sarah 174 Sarah
　Eldridge 174 William 8
WINSLOW J Emmons 2
WITHAM Nicholas B 188
WORTH Albert V 28 Ethel 7
　George L 28 Georgie 7 James E
　7 John 28 Nellie P 7

YOUNG Abbie 177 Betsey A 193
　Clara R 241 Elizabeth H 118
　Infant 118 193 Isaiah 193
　James 76 Josiah L 192 Lizzie
　B 172 Lucena M 192 Mary A 76
　Millie W 177 Nathan 177
　Stanley M 172 Susan M 192
　Willie F 193

PART THREE

HAMILTON CEMETERY

HAMILTON CEMETERY

LOT #1 -- 8 Stones - 1 Marker

1. Capt. Amos Whorf died Oct. 20, 1849 ae 31 ys. 4 ms.
2. Susan L. widow of Amos Whorf and wife of James Chandler died Aug. 5, 1858 ae 38 ys. 7 ms.
   Also her two babes died Aug. 15
3. Susan M. Whorf died Nov. 20, 1861 aged 15 ys. 1 mo. 17 ds.
4. Mrs. Lucinda wife of James Chandler died March 26, 1850 ae 35 years
5. Betsey F. daughter of James & Lucinda Chandler died Aug. 26, 1842 ae 19 ms. 13 ds.
6. Franklin D. son of James & Lucinda Chandler died Oct. 19, 1849 ae 2 ys. 2 ms.
7. Lucinda wife of Charles W. Howe died July 11, 1868 ae 25 years daughter of James & Lucinda Chandler
8. Abbie E. daughter of John & Sarah Talbort died May 4, 1865 ae 19 ys. 8 ms.
9. Marker - Little Freddie (VR: died April 28, 1864 ae 2 yrs. son of James & Amelia Chandler)

LOT #2 -- 8 Stones - 1 Marker - 2 Footstones

1. Front: Benjamin Small born Dec. 20, 1802 died Dec. 30, 1890
   Right: George Bond Crane 1872-1935
          Abbie Dora Leach Crane 1868-1940
2. Footstone - Abbie
3. Footstone - George
4. Marker - Drusilla Small 1834-1923
5. Jonah G. Small died Dec. 13, 1882 ae 55 yrs. 5 mos. 27 dys.
6. Taylor Small died March 4, 1865 ae 72 ys. 8 ms. 26 ds.
   Taylor Small Jr. died in Danville Prison (Virginia) Feb. 5, 1865 ae 27 ys. 1 mo. 20 ds.

HAMILTON CEMETERY

LOT #2 (continued)

7. Abigail C. wife of Taylor Small died May 19, 1886 ae 81 ys. 5 ms. 2 ds.

8. Abby daughter of Taylor & Abigail C. Small died April 12, 1859 ae 23 years 7 mos. 22 days

9. Simeon C. son of Taylor & Abigail Small died March 25, 1848 aged 5 years 9 ms. 2 ds.

10. Benjamin L. Small died May 9, 1865 ae 35 ys. 11 ms. 23 ds.

11. Whipple A. Leach 1837-1877 Buried at sea
    Mary D. Leach 1839-1919

LOT #3 -- 1 Monument - 7 Footstones

1. Monument Front: R. (Richard E. - VR) E. Nickerson died Mar. 7, 1894 ae 63 yrs. 10 mos. 6 ds.
   Bethia M. wife of R. E. Nickerson died September 18, 1879 ae 46 yrs. 4 ms. 13 ds.

   Monument Rear: Charles Elliot (Nickerson) Oct. 5, 1857 - April 17, 1901
   His wife Alice L. Feb. 27, 1860 - Dec. 13, 1944

   Monument Left: Infant daughter died September 16, 1862
   Clara D. died March 19, 1865 ae 1 yr. 4 ms. 22 ds.
   Freddie J. died August 7, 1866 ae 2 mos. 16 ds.

2. Footstone - "Elliot" 1830-1894, back: R. E. N.

3. Footstone - Bethia

4. Footstone - Charles

5. Footstone - Alice L. Nickerson wife of Charles E. Nickerson died Dec. 13, 1944 aged 84 years 9 months 15 days

6. Footstone - Clara D. Nickerson died March 19th 1865 aged 1 year 4 mos. 22 days

7. Footstone - Infant daughter born Sept. 16, 1862

8. Footstone - Freddie J. Nickerson, twin son, died Aug. 7th 1866 aged 2 mos. 16 days

LOT #4 -- 1 Monument - 6 Stones

1. Monument Front: Lucy N. wife of John Francis died Dec. 31, 1873 aged 55 yrs.

   Monument Left: Pamelia S. wife of John Francis died Jan. 16, 1887 aged 60 yrs. 5 mos. 5 dys.

2. Chandler S. Covell March 13, 1825 - March 22, 1915

HAMILTON CEMETERY

LOT #4 (continued)

    3. Mr. Joshua D. Covell died Nov. 6, 1846 ae 26 years

    4. Nathaniel Covell died Dec. 9, 1862 ae 69 ys. 7 ms.

    5. Ruth wife of Nathaniel Covell died Aug. 4, 1873 ae 79 ys. 10 ms. 15 ds.

    6. Elijah D. son of Nathaniel & Ruth Covell died Jan. 6, 1840 ae 3 yrs.

    7. Edith V. daughter of Nathaniel & Ruth G. Covell died Oct. 14, 1872 aged 4 ms.

LOT #5 -- 1 Monument - 2 Stones - 5 Footstones

    1. Monument Front: Capt. Nathan Small died at sea on a whaling voyage April 30, 1860 aged 47 yrs. 8 mo. 11 days
Jane wife of Nathan Small died Feb. 16, 1895 aged 77 yrs. 9 mos. 21 das.

       Monument Left: Charles G. son of Nathan & Jane Small died Apl. 30, 1875 ae 24 yrs. 10 ds.
Ellen M. Small 1855-1915

       Monument Right: Jane L. born Aug. 28 died Sept. 14, 1838 aged 17 days
Nathan born July 14, 1845 died Oct. 5, 1846 aged 1 year 2 mo. & 26 days
Ellen M. born Sept. 10, 1849 died Aug. 10, 1850 aged 11 mos.
Children of Capt. Nathan and Jane Small

           "Sweet is the memory of our little ones"

           Everett Small 1840-1936
Hattie E. Small 1839-1926

       Monument Rear: Seneca G. Ewell 1837-1916
Jane N. Ewell 1842-1908

    2. Pamelia C. wife of Everett Small died Sept. 24, 1867 aged 35 years

    3. Hattie L. daughter of Seneca G. & Jane N. Ewell died Oct. 3, 1870 aged 5 ms. 9 ds.

    4. Footstone - Father

    5. Footstone - Mother - Jane N. Ewell

    6. Footstone - Ellie

    7. Footstone - Hattie

    8. Footstone - Everett

HAMILTON CEMETERY

LOT #6 -- 1 Monument - 2 Footstones

   1. Monument Front: Benj. Lancy Jr. born Sept. 23, 1810 died
                         Aug. 26, 1859 aged 48 yrs. 11 mos. 3 ds.
                         Nabby Cook his wife 1812-1896
                         Benjamin Lancy 1847-1923
                         Maria Lancy 1841-1922

   2. Footstone - Mother

   3. Footstone - Father

LOT #7 -- 1 Monument

   1. Monument Front: Benjamin Lancy died Aug. 4, 1863 ae 83 ys.
                         Jane Lancy wife of Benj. Lancy died
                         July 16, 1868 aged 82 yrs.

     Monument Right: Jane daughter of B. & J. Lancy died Aug.
                       15, 1816 aged 9 yrs. 6 ms.
                       Ellen M. wife of Henry Young and daughter
                       of B. & J. Lancy died Sept. 20, 1861
                       aged 39 yrs.

LOT #8 -- 1 Monument

   1. Monument Front: Capt. Seth N. Lancy died Sept. 6, 1863
                         aged 49 yrs.
                         Phebe Lancy died Feb. 26, 1893 aged 75 yrs.
                         1 mo. 10 dys.

     Monument Left: Seth N. son of Seth N. & Phebe Lancy died
                      Aug. 14, 1846 aged 1 yr. 2 ms.

                      "His head is pillowed on Jesus' breast
                      Dear little babe, he is sweetly at rest"

LOT #9 -- 2 Stones

   1. Our Father - Capt. Nathan Smith died July 1, 1870 aged
      56 years 8 mos. 28 dys.

   2. Our Mother - Winifred Smith died March 14, 1885 aged
      69 yrs. 2 mos. 22 ds.

LOT #10 -- No Stone (Cem. records - lot listed under name of
                 Simeon L. Nickerson)

LOT #11 -- 1 Stone

   1. Annabella Morrison 1844-1939

      (Ed. note: Children of Murdock & Annie Morrison)
     Mary J. Judkins 1867-1895
     Allen P. 1870-1919
     John F. 1871-1930
     Henry J. 1875-1897
     Nathan H. 1878-1879
     Duncan M. 1884-1884

HAMILTON CEMETERY

LOT #12 -- 1 Stone - 5 Footstones

   1. Front: Capt. John A. Matheson 1856-1941
            Thankie C. Matheson 1859-1940

      Right: William B. (Matheson) 1881-1922
            Raymond P. Silva 1921-1954

      Rear: Capt. Frank W. McKay 1836-1877 Lost at sea
           Annie McKay 1842-1916
           William F. 1860-1884
           Angus S. 1863-1864
           Frank S. 1866-1868
           Frank D. 1869-1893

      Left: Leon J. Silva 1893-1963
           Elizabeth Matheson Silva 1892-1942

   2. Footstone - Mother

   3. Footstone - Father

   4. Footstone - Elizabeth

   5. Footstone - Leon husband of Elizabeth

   6. Footstone - Raymond

LOT #13 -- 1 Stone - 8 Footstones

   1. Front: John Kiley 1814-1897
           Sally K. Rich 1818-1893

      Right: John (Kiley) 1839-1886
            Mary M. 1843-1878

      Rear: Samuel J. Rich 1842-1914
           Thankful J. Kiley 1844-1939
           Infant

      Left: Thankful J. (Rich)
           Rosilla R. (Rich)
           Samuel R. (Rich)

   2. Footstone - Father

   3. Footstone - Mother

   4. Footstone - John

   5. Footstone - Mary

   6. Footstone - Infants

   7. Footstone - Thankful

   8. Footstone - Thankful

   9. Footstone - Samuel

LOT #14 -- 1 Monument - 1 Stone - 3 Footstones

   1. Monument Front: James Rich Oct. 16, 1820 - July 18, 1893

HAMILTON CEMETERY

LOT #14 (continued)

      Peggy S. Rich Sept. 22, 1821 - Oct. 8, 1902

  Monument Right: Benj. F. Rich Aug. 18, 1849 - March 17, 1864

  Monument Rear: James A. Rich 1842-1908

 2. Stephen Chapman 1821-1880
   Thankful R. his wife 1824-1908

 3. Footstone - Father

 4. Footstone - Mother

 5. Footstone - Benjamin

LOT #15 -- 2 Stones

 1. Capt. Isaac Cook 1777-1861
   Martha Cook 1784-1868

 2. Caroline W. daughter of Josiah & Caroline Cook born April
   10, 1843 died Aug. 25, 1857

LOT #16 -- 1 Stone

 1. Front: Capt. John J. Cook 1817-1907
     Elizabeth S. Cook 1826-1911
     Richard W. 1849-1924
     Fred W. 1858-1906
     Elizabeth K. 1866-1948
     John J. 1863-1864
     Martha 1852-1857

   Right: George B. Young 1852-1936

   Rear: Charles H. Holbrook 44th Mass. Vols. 1842-1904
      Emma B. Cook (no date)

LOTS #17 & #18 -- 1 Monument - 4 Stones - 2 Markers - 6 Footstones

 1. Monument Front: Thomas Lothrop died July 19th 1881 aged
        81 years 4 mos. 24 days
       Rebecca Lothrop died Nov. 2nd 1892 aged
        86 years 3 mos. 25 days

  Monument Right: Salome C. died July 20, 1891 aged 63 ys.
        5 ms. 11 ds.

  Monument Left: Eben died Sept. 19, 1900 aged 70 ys. 3 ms.
        8 ds.
        Sarah F. Apr. 2, 1839 - Oct. 17, 1914
        Adeline Dec. 16, 1832 - Oct. 22, 1909

 2. Footstone - T. L. 1800-1881

 3. Footstone - R. L. 1806-1892

 4. Footstone - Salome 1828-1891

 5. Footstone - Eben 1830-1900

HAMILTON CEMETERY

LOTS #17 & #18 (continued)

    6. Footstone - Sarah 1839-1914

    7. Footstone - Adeline 1832-1909

    8. Rosetta L. Cook Feb. 5, 1842 - March 13, 1933

    9. Amaziah Baker died Sept. 12, 1873 aged 48

    10. Warren son of Amos P. and Betsey A. Fielding Oct. 3, 1841 - Feb. 21, 1905

    11. Rebecca wife of Warren Fielding & daughter of Thomas & Rebecca Lothrop Jan. 23, 1845 - Aug. 12, 1914

    12. Grace L. F. Hall daughter of Warren Fielding and Rebecca Lothrop Fielding March 21, 1867 - Nov. 17, 1948

    13. Marker - (Lothrop) Marcus M. (VR: died Sept. 1, 1847 ae 3 mos.); Rosetta C.; Eben; Thomas

LOT #18 (see LOT #17)

LOT #19 -- 1 Monument - 1 Stone - 3 Footstones

    (Monument erected 1884) (Stephen A. & Catherine M. W. Paine)

    1. Monument Front: S. A. Paine M.D. died Sept. 3d 1869 aged 63 years
        C. M. W. Paine wife of S. A. Paine died Jan. 6, 1889 aged 79 years

    2. Footstone - S. A. Paine

    3. Footstone - C. M. W. Paine

    4. Footstone - Charles G.

    5. James A. adopted son of Dr. S. A. & C. M. W. Paine died March 20, 1862 aged 20 yrs. 10 ms. 23 days

LOT #20 -- 1 Monument - 4 Footstones

    (Monument erected 1860)

    1. Monument Front: Erected in memory of Capt. Henry Paine who died at Kurrachee, India, Sept. 17, 1859 aged 50 years

    Monument Right: Rebecca Francis wife of Henry Paine died Jan. 3, 1891 ae 80 yrs.

    Monument Left: Nehemiah H. Young died Dec. 15, 1851 ae 37 yrs. 6 mos. 5 dys.
    Sarah H. Paine died Dec. 23, 1865 ae 35 ys. 11 mos. 18 dys.

    2. Footstone - Wife

    3. Footstone - Sarah

    4. Footstone - Mother

HAMILTON CEMETERY

LOT #20 (continued)

    5. Footstone - Brother

LOT #21 -- 1 Monument - 2 Footstones (large)

    1. Monument Front: Capt. John Nickerson died May 3, 1869 aged 73 ys. 9 mos.
        Elizabeth wife of Capt. John Nickerson died Sept. 26, 1863 aet 61 yrs.

    2. Footstone - Capt. John Nickerson

    3. Footstone - Elisabeth (sic) Nickerson

LOT #22 -- 1 Monument - 5 Footstones (large)

    1. Monument Front: Capt. Eldridge Nickerson died Nov. 22, 1865 aet 68 ys. 10 mos.
        Eunice his wife died Sept. 23, 1873 aet 74 ys. 10 ms. 27 ds.

       Monument Right: Eldridge son of Eldridge & Eunice Nickerson died Dec. 17, 1834 aet 1 yr. 3 mos. 18 ds.

       Monument Left: Eunice S. daughter of Eldridge & Eunice Nickerson died Feb. 14, 1893 ae 66 ys. 11 mos. 9 ds.
        Marinda J. Nickerson born Oct. 17, 1829 died Apr. 15, 1898

    2. Footstone - Mother

    3. Footstone - Father

    4. Footstone - Eunice

    5. Footstone - Marinda

    6. Footstone - Eldridge

LOT #23 -- 1 Monument - 7 Footstones (large)

    1. Monument Front: Capt. Jesse Cook died July 9, 1871 aged 88 yrs. & 21 ds.
        Thankful H. wife of Capt. Jesse Cook died March 10, 1863 aet 77 ys. 10 ms.

       Monument Right: Harriet Cook born July 29, 1817 died Dec. 6, 1887
        Sarah S. Cook born July 31, 1825 died Oct. 4, 1886

       Monument Rear: Emeline Cook born March 23, 1811 died March 14, 1812

       Monument Left: Ephraim S. Cook born Sept. 6, 1807 died June 15, 1867
        Emeline Cook born Dec. 8, 1812 died Jan. 12, 1870

HAMILTON CEMETERY

LOT #23 (continued)

    2. Footstone - Capt. Jesse Cook

    3. Footstone - Thankful H. Cook

    4. Footstone - Ephraim S. Cook

    5. Footstone - Emeline Cook

    6. Footstone - Harriet Cook

    7. Footstone - Sarah S. Cook

    8. Footstone - Emeline

LOT #24 -- 1 Monument - 5 Stones - 2 Footstones

    1. Monument Front: Capt. Stephen Mills died at Matanzas, W.I. August 1822 aet 44 yrs. also, his wife Rebecca who subsequently married Capt. David Brown and died Jan. 15, 1857 aet 63 yrs. 3 mos.

        Delia A. dau. of Stephen & Rebecca Mills born in Truro, Mass. March 27, 1821 and died in Rutland, VT. Jan. 21, 1892

       Monument Left: Elizabeth Fernald daughter of Stephen & Rebecca Mills was born in Truro, March 25, 1813 and died August 1815

    2. Footstone - Mother

    3. Footstone - Delia

    4. Rev. Osborne Myrick died in Rutland, Vermont, January 15, 1892 aged 73 yrs. 4 months 19 days.

       Back of Stone: Born in Orleans, Mass. August 27, 1818, was graduated from Middlebury College 1842, ordained Feb. 1846. Pastor of Cong'l Church at Provincetown, Mass. 1846-1866. Pastor of Cong'l Church at Middletown Springs, Vt. 1866-1890.

    5. Joanna C. Mills wife of Rev. Osborne Myrick born in North Truro, Mass. Feb. 7, 1819 died in Rutland, Vt. May 26, 1896

    6. Osborne son of Rev. O. & Mrs. J. C. Myrick died Sept. 6, 1883 aged 30 yrs. & 28 ds.

    7. Joseph son of Rev. O. & Mrs. J. C. Myrick died July 19, 1864 aged 12 yrs. 11 mos. 28 ds.

    8. J. Josephine daughter of Rev. O. & Mrs. J. C. Myrick died Sept. 20, 1849 aged 2 yrs. 10 mos. 15 ds.

LOT #25 -- 1 Monument - 6 Footstones

    1. Monument Front: Francis B. Tuck died Dec. 27, 1862 ae 36 yrs. 2 mos. 20 dys.
        Lydia S. Tuck 1828-1905

HAMILTON CEMETERY

LOT #25 (continued)

                                  Enoch F. Tuck died July 13, 1852 ae 1 yr. 10 ms. 13 dys.

    Monument Left: Enoch Nickerson died Oct. 3, 1886 ae 81 ys. 1 mo. 21 dys.
                         Eliza P. Nickerson died March 8, 1893 ae 86 yrs. 3 ms. 9 dys.
                         Richard F. Nickerson died Sept. 21, 1839 ae 3 yrs. 3 mos. 17 dys.

    Monument Right: Charles Upham Tuck 1856-1901
                          Mary Louise Tuck 1862-1904

2. Footstone - F. B. T. 1826-1862

3. Footstone - Frank

4. Footstone - E. N. 1805-1886

5. Footstone - E. P. N. 1806-1893

6. Footstone - R. F. N.

7. Footstone - Louise

LOT #26 -- 6 Stones

1. Charles Nickerson 1807-1887

2. Eleanor Nickerson 1809-1893
Wife of Charles Nickerson and daughter of Jesse & Thankful H. Cook

3. Ellen C. Nickerson 1840-1886
Daughter of Charles and Eleanor Nickerson

4. Emeline C. Nickerson 1843-1907
Daughter of Charles and Eleanor Nickerson

5. Capt. Josiah A. Hannum died May 2, 1880 aged 56 years 4 mos. 7 das.
"One less to love on earth, one more to meet in Heaven"

6. Lucy Maria wife of Capt. Josiah A. Hannum died April 8, 1857 aged 21 years & 3 months

LOT #27 -- 1 Monument - 8 Footstones

(Monument erected 1864)

    1. Monument Front: Lucy L. wife of Jas. C. N. Paine born Aug. 3, 1821 died Oct. 27, 1856
                            Jas. C. N. Paine 1818-1905
                            Phebe A. 1836-1923

       Monument Right: Lucy A. Paine 1845-1903
                            Louise C. Paine 1860-1951

       Monument Rear: Heman S. Cook 1840-1927
                          Hannah C. Cook 1837-1923

HAMILTON CEMETERY

LOT #27 (continued)

    Monument Left: Clara Holmes daughter of James C. & Phebe A. Paine born Nov. 6, 1863 died Nov. 6, 1868 aged 5 years

  2. Footstone - James

  3. Footstone - Lucy L.

  4. Footstone - Clara

  5. Footstone - Phebe

  6. Footstone - Lucy

  7. Footstone - Louise C. Paine

  8. Footstone - Heman

  9. Footstone - Hannah

LOT #28 -- 1 Monument - 5 Stones - 5 Footstones

    (Monument erected 1859)

  1. Monument Front: Jairus H. Hilliard sailed from this port Dec. 13, 1851 in Schooner Sunbeam for St. Thomas, West Indies, from whom there has been no tidings. Aged 41 years 6 ms. & 24 ds.

    Monument Right: Jairus Howard son of Jairus H. and Emily Hilliard died July 4, 1856 aged 7 years & 23 days

    Monument Rear: Almeda Ann dau. of Jairus H. & Emily Hilliard died Nov. 19, 1842 aged 10 mos. & 14 dys.
        Emily Cook dau. of Jairus H. & Emily Hilliard died July 3, 1840 aged 3 mos. & 18 days

    Monument Left: An infant son of Jairus H. & Emily Hilliard died Jan. 8, 1839 aged 3 days
        An infant son of Jairus H. & Emily Hilliard died July 6, 1845 aged 14 days

  2. Footstone - Jairus Howard

  3. Footstone - Almeda Ann

  4. Footstone - Emily Cook

  5. Footstone - An infant son

  6. Footstone - An infant son

  7. Mother - Emily Hilliard died Mar. 29, 1886 aged 70 yrs. 5 ms. 17 ds.

  8. John D. Hilliard 1836-1906
    Lizzie H. P. Hilliard 1843-1909

HAMILTON CEMETERY

LOT #28 (continued)

    9. Rebecca Helen wife of John D. Hilliard died Sept. 10, 1867 aged 29 yrs. 3 ds.

   10. Nellie B. Hilliard died May 12, 1937 aged 76 yrs. 6 mos. 1 day

   11. Alice S. Hilliard died Dec. 18, 1892 aged 27 yrs. 5 mos. 12 days

LOT #29 -- 1 Stone - 7 Footstones

    1. Front: Isaiah A. Whorf May 28, 1848 - May 3, 1901
           Thannie A. Whorf Dec. 9, 1846 - Jan. 31, 1922

       Right: Henry Whorf June 15, 1813 - Port au Prince Dec. 5, 1853
           Sally Whorf June 27, 1818 - Dec. 15, 1893

       Rear: Henry S. Whorf Aug. 16, 1845 - Jan. 10, 1918
           Sarah M. Whorf April 22, 1847 - April 30, 1910

       Left: Edgar J. Whorf Feb. 11, 1876 - April 28, 1910

    2. Footstone - Isaiah

    3. Footstone - Thannie

    4. Footstone - Henry

    5. Footstone - Sarah

    6. Footstone - Sally

    7. Footstone - Baby

    8. Footstone - Edgar

LOT #30 -- 1 Stone

    1. William Bush 1822-1871
       Rebecca C. his wife 1825-1909
       Justine E. 1854-1887

LOT #31 -- 3 Stones

    1. Father - Paul L. Bangs August 10, 1828 - October 25, 1892
       Mother - His wife Ann E. Bangs January 10, 1830 - June 13, 1892

    2. Paul L. Bangs died Aug. 10, 1862 aged 64 years 2 mos. & 20 days

    3. Peggy wife of Paul L. Bangs died Apr. 30, 1883 aged 82 yrs. 8 mos. & 8 days

LOT #32 -- 2 Stones

    1. John B. Bangs 1834-1882
       Rebecca Bangs 1840-1909
       Lena M. Bangs 1873-1948

HAMILTON CEMETERY

LOT #32 (continued)

    John B. Bangs 1873-1955

  2. Banjamin A. Dyer 1864-1929
     His wife Annie M. Bangs 1866-1945

LOT #33 -- 3 Stones

  1. Father - Stephen A. Ryder died Dec. 21, 1882 ae 53 ys. 3 ms.
     Mother - Clara C. Ryder died Apr. 2, 1881 ae 49 ys. 1 mo. 11 ds.
     Frank B. Ryder lost at sea May 4, 1876 ae 20 ys. 8 ms. 8 ds.

  2. Charles Gott 1887-1938
     Gladys Baker Gott Armstrong 1889-1973

  3. Lewis H. Baker 1842-1905
     Clara A. Baker 1860-1940

LOT #34 -- 1 Monument - 1 Stone - 3 Footstones

  1. Monument Front: Capt. Augustus L. Ditson drowned in Troy, N. Y. Sept. 9, 1865 aged 50 yrs.

     Monument Right: George Lockwood, Co. A 2d Reg't Mass. H. A. died at Newburn, N. C. Nov. 28, 1864 aged 38 yrs. 6 ms.

     Monument Left: Tamsin Ann wife of Capt. A. L. Ditson died Feb. 2, 1851 aged 30 yrs. 8 ms.
     Sarah D. P. wife of A. L. Ditson died May 16, 1883 ae 64 yrs. 3 ms. 13 ds.

  2. Tamsin A. wife of Augustus L. Ditson born June 12, 1820 died Feb. 2, 1851

  3. Footstone - Augustus L.

  4. Footstone - Sarah D. P.

  5. Footstone - Husband

LOT #35 -- 1 Stone - 1 Marker

  1. Hellen F. wife of Thos. Bush died June 20, 1863 aet 28 ys. 7 ms.
     An infant son ae 5 days

  2. Annie dau. of Thos. & Hellen Bush died Aug. 17, 1863 aged 3 ys. 6 ms.

LOT #36 -- 3 Stones

  1. John M. Graham died Nov. 23, 1905 ae 80 yrs. 7 mos. 27 ds.

  2. Rebecca A. wife of John M. Graham died Oct. 24, 1885 ae 57 yrs. 4 mos. 16 dys.

  3. Augustus E. Rich 1862-1935
     His wife Melissa N. 1872-1901

HAMILTON CEMETERY

LOTS #37 & #38 -- 1 Monument - 5 Stones - 7 Footstones

   1. Monument Front: Stephen Cook died Sept. 3, 1888 aged 71 years 3 mos. 14 days

      Monument Right: Lucy Ann wife of Stephen Cook Jr., daughter of Rev. Ephraim and Rebecca E. Wiley, died May 27, 1847 aet 24 yrs. 8 mos. 16 ds.
Lucy Ann daughter of Stephen & Lucy A. Cook died Aug. 25, 1847 aet 3 ms. 6 ds.

      Monument Rear: Mary A. wife of Stephen Cook Jr., daughter of Rev. Josiah & Sarah Higgins, died Jan. 31, 1864 aet 33 yrs. 5 mos. & 15 ds.
Charles H. son of Stephen & Mary A. Cook died April 6, 1864 aet 6 yrs. 1 mo. 20 ds.

      Monument Left: Julia F. wife of Stephen Cook, daughter of Ebenezer & Ruth Higgins died Sep. (sic) 8, 1865 aet 37 yrs. 7 ms. 26 ds.
Jennie E. wife of Stephen Cook, daughter of John & Eliza Churchill died Feb. 15, 1912 aet 71 yrs. 8 mos. 1 day

   2. Footstone - Charlie

   3. Footstone - Mary

   4. Footstone - Julia

   5. Footstone - Jennie

   6. Footstone - Stephen

   7. Footstone - Lucy

   8. Footstone - Babe

   9. Capt. Stephen Cook died Jan. 8, 1859 ae 72 yrs. 2 mos. & 10 days

  10. Mrs. Delia wife of Capt. Stephen Cook died Sept. 24, 1872 ae 83 yrs. & 9 mos.

  11. Father - Leonard Cook born Sept. 5, 1809 died Dec. 25, 1882

  12. Sally daughter of Capt. Stephen & Delia Cook died Aug. 30, 1825 ae 13 yrs. & 7 mos.

  13. Betsey Kibby daughter of Capt. Stephen & Delia Cook died July 28, 1832 ae 4 yrs. 2 mos.

LOT #38 (see LOT #37)

LOT #39 -- 4 Stones

   1. Eleazer Young 1820-1880
Phebe N. Young 1828-1914

HAMILTON CEMETERY

LOT #39 (continued)

    2. A. Waldo Young Oct. 21, 1851 - Mar. 7, 1920
       Mercy H. Young Sept. 26, 1853 - Aug. 31, 1907

    3. Prince I. Freeman 1851-1927
       Dorinda C. Freeman 1854-1899
       Arthur C. 1877-1886

    4. Jennie Y. Freeman 1879-1951 Buried in Glendale, Cal.
       Faustina Freeman 1886-(not cut - living in 1979)
       A. Irving Freeman 1875-1960

LOT #40 -- 1 Monument - 7 Footstones

    1. Monument Front: Capt. Jonathan Kilburn died at Isle of Sal.,
                    Cape Verde, Jan. 15, 1865 aged 47 yrs.
                    Hannah Soule Jan. 20, 1820 - Jan. 5, 1913

       Monument Right: William Palmer died Sept. 17, 1833 aged
                    44 yrs.
                   Margarett wife of William Palmer died
                   Jan. 20, 1863 aged 74 yrs.

       Monument Rear: Seth N. Hartford 1848-1913
                  Hattie M. his wife 1848-1917

       Monument Left: Samuel T. Kilburn died June 29, 1881
                  ae 66 yrs. 5 ms. 7 ds.
                  Harriet P. his wife May 3, 1821 - July 15,
                  1891

    2. Footstone - Father

    3. Footstone - Mother

    4. Footstone - Hannah

    5. Footstone - Father (Palmer)

    6. Footstone - Mother (Palmer)

    7. Footstone - S. N. H.

    8. Footstone - H. M. H.

LOT #41 -- 3 Stones

    1. George H. Holmes 1833-1905
       Rebecca E. his wife 1838-1928
       Clara T. 1859-1864
       Caroline B. 1860-1907
       Lottie E. 1861-1864
       Blanche A. 1871-1956

    2. Capt. Tilton Cook 1810-1893
       Clarinda Cook 1818-1889

    3. Clarinda Tilton daughter of Capt. Tilton & Clarinda Cook
       died Aug. 31, 1854 aged 8 ys. 3 ms. 16 ds.

HAMILTON CEMETERY

LOT #42 -- 6 Stones

1. Capt. Jonathan Cook died April 26, 1862 aged 82 yrs. 2 mos. & 4 days

2. Sabra wife of Jonathan Cook died Aug. 20, 1872 aged 89 yrs. 5 mos. 5 days

3. Sacred to the memory of Mr. Jonathan Cook 3d son of Mr. Jonathan Cook Jun. & Sabra, his wife, who died Oct. 7, 1825 aged 20 years & 7 days

4. Sacred to the memory of Mr. Edward Cook son of Mr. Jonathan Cook Jun. & Sabra, his wife, who died Oct. 2, 1825 aged 21 years & 10 mon.

5. Capt. Jonathan H. Young died Jan. 29, 1861 aged 41 yrs. & 3 mos.

6. Abbie H. wife of E. G. Loring died May 13, 1866 aet 35 yrs. 11 mos.

LOT #43 -- 3 Stones

1. Bethiah widow of Isaac Nickerson died April 24, 1861 ae 73 ys. 9 ms.

2. Benjamin Ryder 2nd 1832-1871
A. Maria his wife 1831-(not cut)
Angie 1863-1864
Ella K. 1868-1874
Susie C. 1870-1874

3. Ebenezer Cook Feb. 2, 1811 - Oct. 10, 1898
Sarah R. Cook July 15, 1819 - Mar. 24, 1887
Eben A. Feb. 22, 1841 - Feb. 4, 1873

LOT #44 -- 4 Stones

1. Capt. Samuel Cook born Oct. 17, 1781 died Jan. 11, 1867

2. Tamsin wife of Capt. Samuel Cook born April 16, 1785 died October 7, 1851

3. Jonathan Cook died Dec. 7, 1884 ae 59 yrs. 1 mo. 9 dys.

4. Nathan Cook died July 24, 1874 aet 65 yrs. 9 mos. 21 days

LOT #45 -- 1 Monument - 4 Footstones - 3 Stones

1. Monument Front: Sylvanus Cook April 13, 1812 - Jan. 6, 1892
                 Louisa wife of Sylvanus Cook Nov. 27, 1822-
                 Mar. 26, 1897

   Monument Left: Byley Lyford 1832-1913
               Hannah Lyford 1845-1915

2. Footstone - Mother

3. Footstone - Father

4. Footstone - Husband

5. Footstone - Wife

HAMILTON CEMETERY

LOT #45 (continued)

    6. Eddie C. and Baby: Infant children of Capt. Joseph B. & Hannah L. Dyer

    7. Artie C. son of Capt. Joseph B. & Hannah L. Dyer born June 30, 1865 died Feb. 22, 1877 ae 11 ys. 7 ms. 22 ds.

    8. Laura daughter of Sylvanus & Louisa Cook died Nov. 1, 1849 ae 2 yrs.

LOT #46 -- 9 Stones - 1 Footstone

    1. Enos Nickerson died Feb. 27, 1867 aged 71 ys. 28 ds. "A noble type of Christian manhood"

    2. Rebekah wife of Enos Nickerson died June 18, 1852 ae 56 ys.

    3. Ruth wife of Enos Nickerson died Oct. 1, 1861 ae 58 yrs.

    4. In memory of Mrs. Lucy wife of Capt. Enos Nickerson who died Aug. 26, 1834 aet 62

    5. Footstone - L. N.

    6. Sacred to the memory of Enos Nickerson who died June 22, 1825 aet 54

    7. Henry Paine died Jan. 12, 1861 ae 66 yrs. 5 mos. 13 dys.

    8. Lucy Paine died April 16, 1880 ae 79 yrs. 7 mos. 22 dys.

    9. Father - Ellis H. Holmes born Mar. 18, 1818 died Oct. 30, 1888

    10. Mother - Clarissa Holmes born Dec. 20, 1823 died July 28, 1891

LOT #47 -- 1 Monument - 3 Footstones

    1. Monument Front: David Cook 1859 (date monument erected)

    Monument Right: David Cook Jr. was lost at sea on the passage from Boston to Port au Prince about Jan. 26, 1839 aged 30 years & 2 mos.
Louisa Cook died Nov. 2, 1861 ae 49 yrs. 10 mos.

    Monument Left: Children of David Jr. & Louisa Cook:
Louise R. died Jan. 12, 1859 ae 27 yrs. 5 mos. & 3 dys.
Salome A. died Nov. 1, 1856 ae 21 yrs. 3 mos. & 16 days
An infant son died May 1833

"Rest husband and children dear
Beneath the billow and the sod
Your wife and mother hopes to meet you,
In mansions of our God"

HAMILTON CEMETERY

LOT #47 (continued)

    2. Footstone - Mother

    3. Footstone - David Cook

    4. Footstone - Salome A.

LOT #48 -- 9 Stones

    1. Capt. Joseph Atkins born Oct. 14, 1766 died Jan. 22, 1851

    2. Mrs. Ruth wife of Capt. Joseph Atkins born June 4, 1770 died June 22, 1854

    3. Wm. A. Atkins June 8, 1818 - April 7, 1897

    4. Abigail N. died Aug. 25, 1842 ae 22 yrs.
Jane F. died July 3, 1886 ae 67 yrs.
Wives of William A. Atkins

    5. William N. F. son of William A. & Abigail Atkins died Aug. 5, 1842 ae 2 ms.

    6. Helena G. daughter of William A. & Jane F. Atkins died Sept. 28, 1849 ae 11 ms.

    7. Helena P. daughter of William A. & Jane F. Atkins died July 14, 1848 ae 2 yrs. 3 mos.

    8. Eddie (Atkins)

    9. Rebecca A. Grozier 1829-1917 (Maiden name Atkins)

LOT #49 -- 6 Stones

    1. Capt. Alfred Cook died May 16, 1897 aged 80 yrs. 9 mos. 4 dys.

    2. Rebecca M. wife of Capt. Alfred Cook died Dec. 17, 1879 aet 50 yrs. 3 mos.

    3. Caroline E. wife of Capt. Alfred Cook died Sept. 17, 1879 aged 46 yrs. 2 mos. 28 ds.

    4. Edwin E. son of Alfred & Rebecca M. Cook born Sept. 12, 1843 died Oct. 23, 1852

    5. Clarence A. Cook 1855-1916
Cassie C. his wife 1857-1931

    6. Carrie Reba dau. of Clarence A. & Cassie C. Cook died Oct. 19, 1891 aged 7 yrs. 3 mos. 22 dys.

LOT #50 -- 3 Stones

    1. Nathaniel N. Cook Nov. 10, 1821 - July 12, 1888
Louisa Cook Sept. 20, 1823 - Dec. 18, 1890

    2. Nattie son of Nathaniel & Louisa Cook died June 12, 1852 aged 1 yr. 6 mos. 9 dys.

    3. Albertina F. - "Tenie" - wife of Josiah F. Knowles died

HAMILTON CEMETERY

LOT #50 (continued)
    Oct. 27, 1874 aged 28 ys.

LOTS #51 & #52 -- 1 Monument - 7 Footstones
    (Monument erected 1860)
    1. Monument Front: Capt. Francis Fluker died June 17, 1871
                      aged 69 years
                      Temperance wife of Capt. Francis Fluker
                      died Dec. 10, 1876 aged 73 yrs.

       Monument Rear: Adeline P. wife of Warren Hunt & daughter
                    of Francis & Temperance Fluker died Oct. 1,
                    1859 ae 24 yrs. 8 mos. & 24 days

       Monument Left: Josiah C. Fluker 1833-1912
                    William T. son of Francis & Temperance
                        Fluker was lost at sea from Brig Rienza
                      Sept. 16, 1846 ae 20 yrs. & 3 dys.

    2. Footstone - Father

    3. Footstone - Mother

    4. Footstone - Josiah C.

    5. Footstone - Warren F. Hunt

    6. Footstone - Adeline P. Hunt

    7. Footstone - Howard E. (Fluker) (VR: died July 21, 1854
        ae 8 months)

    8. Footstone - Adeline P. (Fluker) (VR: died Aug. 2, 1856
        ae 1 yr. 2 mos.)

LOT #52 -- (see LOT #51)

LOT #53 -- 1 Monument - 1 Marker
    1. Front only: Francis M. Freeman 1830-1913
                  His wife Mary J. 1822-1860
                  Dau. Mary F. 1860-1860
                  His wife Mary L. 1842-1926
                  Son Francis M. 1874-1875
                  Dau. Mabel F. 1876-1876
                  Clarence N. 1871-1913
                  Eldredge C. 1872-1906
                  Marion L. 1878-1919

    2. Chester C. (Freeman) 1883-1923

LOT #54 -- 7 Stones
    1. Elisha Dyer died Feb. 23, 1871 ae 78 ys. 8 ms. 6 ds.
    2. Huldah wife of Elisha Dyer died March 27, 1864
       ae 73 ys. 7 ms. 18 ds.

HAMILTON CEMETERY

LOT #54 (continued)

 3. Father - Thomas W. Dyer Sept. 14, 1826 - Oct. 22, 1900

 4. Mother - Lydia J. Dyer Nov. 30, 1827 - Oct. 11, 1903

 5. Elisha L. son of Thomas W. & Lydia J. Dyer May 8, 1851 - Mar. 22, 1897

 6. Lizzie B. dau. of Mr. & Mrs. Thomas W. Dyer ae 13 ys. 11 ms. 4 ds. Passed away Mch. 9, 1889

 7. David H. son of Thomas W. & Lydia J. Dyer died Oct. 8, 1860 ae 1 year 8 mo. & 25 days

LOT #55 -- 3 Stones

 1. John P. Lucas died August 23, 1864 aged 35 years

 2. Philip Freeman 1847-1923
  Mary Freeman 1853-(not cut)
  William (no date) (Freeman)
  John (no date) (Freeman)
  Grace (no date) (Freeman)

 3. John Cockett 21st Unattached Co. M. V. died May 8, 1865 ae 31 yrs. Native of Blackburn, England

LOT #56 -- 3 Stones - 5 Footstones

 1. J. Arthur Lucas 1851-1910
  Sarah E. Edwards 1866-1932

 2. Father - Antone Joseph Lucas died March 21, 1895 in his 75th year

 3. Mother - Margaret Jane wife of Antone Joseph Lucas died June 21, 1892 in her 60th year

 4. Little Charlie son of Antone & Margaret J. Lucas aged 3 ys. 2 ms. (VR: died June 26, 1857)

  Sarah Alletha aged 4 wks. (VR: died March 25, 1856)

 5. Footstone - Sarah E. (Ed. note - wife of J. Arthur Lucas)

 6. Mary M. (VR: dau. of Antone J. and Margaret J. Lucas died July 10, 1859)
  Also an infant (Child of Antone J. and Margaret J. Lucas)

 7. Mamie E. C. dau. of John & Ellen D. Days died May 11, 1880 ae 4 yrs. 9 mos. 11 ds.

 8. Margaret 1882 dau. of J. (Jackson) & M. (Minnie) Williams ae 16 ds. (VR: died Oct. 23, 1882)

LOT #57 -- 3 Stones

 1. John Fraleck died Jan. 12, 1869 ae 47 ys. 4 ms.

 2. Mary E. wife of John Fraleck died April 5, 1852 ae 27 ys. 1 mo.

HAMILTON CEMETERY

LOT #57 (continued)

   3. Joseph Arthur son of John & Mary E. Fraleck died Feb. 20, 1864 ae 12 ys. 2 ms.

LOT #58 -- 5 Stones - 1 Marker

   1. Benjamin Long born Apl. 18, 1797 died Apl. 26, 1874 aged 77 yrs. 8 dys.

   2. Thomas A. Long May 15, 1801 - Oct. 11, 1883
      Betsey C. Long June 10, 1807 - June 29, 1888

   3. Samuel T. Long 1830-1904
      Melissa V. Long 1832-1917

   4. Betsey C. Long 1837-1908

   5. Capt. Charles H. Long 1833-1912
      Sylvia C. Long 1836-1915
      Elsie F. Long 1866-1954

   6. Little May (VR: dau. of Charles H. and Sylvia C. Long died Sept. 9, 1864 ae 2 years)

LOT #59 -- 1 Stone

   1. Capt. Thomas Sparks 1805-1895
      Hannah his wife 1808-1833
      Anna his wife 1808-1836
      Lurana his wife 1819-1862
      Lydia K. his wife 1816-1890
      David H. 1831-1832
      Hannah Y. 1833-1833
      David H. 1835-1836
      Mary W. 1847-1847

LOT #60 -- 1 Monument - 3 Stones - 2 Footstones

   1. Monument Front: Capt. Eleazer H. Rich died Mar. 12, 1875
                      aged 61 yrs. 9 ms. 10 ds.
               Mercy wife of E. H. Rich died Mar. 26, 1884
                      aged 70 yrs. 5 ms. 22 ds.

      Monument Right: Capt. Joseph S. Hopkins died at sea Aug. 31, 1871 aged 37 yrs. 7 ms. 17 ds.

   2. Eleazer Osborn son of Eleazer H. & Mercy Rich died Oct. 12, 1860 ae 16 ys. 5 ms.

   3. Footstone - Mother

   4. Footstone - Father

   5. Maria C. daughter of Eleazer H. & Mercy Rich died Aug. 20, 1842 ae 1 yr. 6 ms. 22 ds.

   6. Elizabeth H. daughter of Eleazer H. & Mercy Rich died April 25, 1849 ae 2 ys. 5 ms. 6 ds.

HAMILTON CEMETERY

LOT #61 -- 1 Stone

   1. Front: Jesse Small 1814-1876
            Seviah H. Small 1821-1852
            Ruth E. Small 1826-1909

     Left: James L. 1858-1882

     Right: Jesse 1856-1876

LOT #62 -- 1 Stone

   1. Front: Josiah F. Small 1829-1897
            Adelaide L. Small 1834-1917

     Right: Adelaide F. (Small) 1858-1858
            Emma A. (Small) 1859-1917
            Edith S. Crawford 1860-1917 (Maiden name Small)
            Frederick W. (Small) 1864-1867

     Rear: Aylmer F. Small 1857-1932
            Katherine A. Small 1857-1923
            Stanley S. 1885-1900

LOT #63 -- 1 Monument - 3 Stones

   1. Monument Front: Louisa A. wife of Capt. Ephraim A. Nickerson and daughter of Seth & Ruth Nickerson, lost at sea in the Schooner Argo Naves, which was capsized on her passage from Jacmel to Boston, Nov. 18, 1852, Latt. 31.00, Long. 24.00, aged 25 ys. 7 ms.

        "The sea, the lo-(illegible) sea hath one;
        She lies where pearls lie deep;
        She was the loved of all, yet none
        O'er her low grave can weep"

     Monument Left: Ruth wife of Seth Nickerson died Feb. 15, 1875 ae 81 ys. 11 ms. 20 ds.

   2. In memory of Seth Nickerson 2d born Feb. 23, 1791 died Aug. 23, 1876

   3. In memory of Ruth wife of Seth Nickerson 2d born Feb. 25, 1793 died Feb. 15, 1875

   4. Alexander McKennon 1817-1895
     Ruth N. his wife 1821-1898
     Louise A. Paine 1852-1922 (Maiden name McKennon)
     Annie W. (McKennon) 1866-1945
     Capt. John W. Atkins 1844-1887
     Eugenia A. McK. his wife 1847-1926
     E. Wilfred (Atkins) 1874-1935
     Calista Cook 1817-1892 (VR: surname Cook)

HAMILTON CEMETERY

LOT #64 -- 4 Stones

1. William Matheson 1833-1868
   Kenneth MacPhee 1843-1883
   Mary Matheson MacPhee 1836-1916

2. Brother - Donald Cameron died May 16, 1865 ae 25 yrs. 3 mo. 2 dys.

3. Donald McDonald died May 21, 1872 aged 22 yrs. 5 ms. 7 ds.

4. Alexander McPhie died in Baltimore, Md., Aug. 14, 1879 aged 29 ys. 8 ms. 14 ds.

LOT #65 -- 1 Monument - 1 Stone

1. Monument Front: Obed Wyer born Dec. 9, 1791 died Oct. 14, 1861
   Lydia Stull his wife born June 25, 1804 died Feb. 3, 1890

   Monument Right: Thomas Stull died at sea Oct. 12, 1823 aged 21 yrs.
   Moses P. Stull died in Florida Jan. 15, 1837 aged 30 yrs.

   Monument Left: William W. Wyer born June 5, 1835 died June 14, 1863
   Rev. William C. Stull died Oct. 15, 1842 aged 24 years

2. Rev'd William C. Stull died Oct. 15, 1842 aet 24 yrs.
   Thomas Stull died at sea Oct. 12, 1823 aged 21 yrs.
   Moses P. Stull died at St. Joseph's, Fa., Jan'y 15, 1837 aet 30 yrs.

LOT #66 -- 5 Stones - 2 Footstones

1. Husband - Marshall L. Adams Dec. 4, 1842 - Sept. 30, 1904

2. Wife - Mary A. Adams July 5, 1840 - Mch. 19, 1900

3. Clarina Ardelle wife of M. L. Adams 1852-1907

4. Lizzie E. daughter of Marshall L. & Mary A. Adams died Sept. 4, 1864 aged 9 ms. 28 ds.

5. Capt. Calvin N. Freeman died at sea Jan. 10, 1872 aet 43 yrs.
   Lizzie J. his wife died Sept. 24, 1872 aet 31 yrs.

6. Footstone - Willie (Freeman) (no date)

7. Footstone - Annie M. Freeman Nov. 10, 1907 (VR: died in Boston ae 43 yrs. 1 mo. 21 dys.)

LOT #67 -- 1 Stone - 8 Footstones

1. Front: Charles A. Cook July 14, 1822 - October 8, 1891
   Sarah H. Dunham his wife October 20, 1825 - Feb. 9, 1848

-231-

HAMILTON CEMETERY

LOT #67 (continued)

          Olive Atkins his wife Nov. 23, 1828 - Aug. 12, 1917

    Right: Lizzie B. Atkins Nov. 16, 1832 - Dec. 6, 1896
             Jona. Y. Cook Oct. 4, 1847 - Jan. 1, 1929

    Left: George P. Cook April 9, 1874 - Dec. 7, 1893

    Rear: James W. Fuller 1851-1941
           Angie Y. his wife 1866-1944

2. Footstone - Mother

3. Footstone - Father

4. Footstone - Mother

5. Footstone - J. Wallace

6. Footstone - Angie

7. Footstone - George

8. Footstone - Lizzie

9. Footstone - John

LOT #68 -- 1 Stone

1. Front: Capt. William Martin 1814-1898
         Louisa A. Martin 1829-1914
         William Jr. 1854-1881
         Matty (no date) (VR: died Aug. 20, 1881 ae 2 ms.)

    Left: John L. (Martin) 1861-1933
          Bessie M. 1872-1959
          John L. Smith 1825-1850
          Sarah L. (no date)

    Right: Sarah M his wife 1818-1849 (first wife of Capt. Wm. Martin)
           William G. (Martin) (no date) (died c.1849)

LOT #69 -- 2 Stones - 5 Footstones

1. Hattie N. wife of Basset Chase died Feb. 20, 1865 aged 28 ys. 5 ms. & 15 days

2. Front: Thomas S. Taylor 1840-1919
         Josephine E. Taylor 1843-1917

    Rear: Children of Thomas S. & Josephine E. Taylor
         E. Thomas Taylor May 14, 1871 - October 28, 1895
         Charles N. Taylor June 3, 1866 - October 16, 1897
         Abby C. S. Taylor 1857-1926

3. Footstone - Mother

4. Footstone - Father

5. Footstone - Thomas

HAMILTON CEMETERY

LOT #69 (continued)

    6. Footstone - Abby

    7. Footstone - Charles

LOT #70 -- 4 Stones

    1. Front: Isaac G. Fisher Aug. 24, 1837 - Sept. 18, 1901
           Julia D. Fisher June 16, 1846 - Feb. 12, 1924

       Right: Susie M. wife of C. F. Dean 1866-1930

    2. Helena F. wife of Isaac G. Fisher died May 15, 1861
        ae 24 ys. 3 ms.
       Helena A. her daut. died May 24, 1861 ae 10 ms.

    3. Wife - Evelyn W. Fisher wife of J. Frank Boardman July 3, 1874 - Aug. 22, 1902

    4. Joseph W. Jordan Feb. 28, 1856 - Jan. 18, 1898

LOT #71 -- 1 Stone - 4 Footstones

    1. Front: James Cobb 1827-1891
           James E. Cobb 1865-1888

       Right: Betsey Cobb 1832-1915
       Left: Willie F. Cobb 1858-1863

    2. Footstone - Husband

    3. Footstone - Wife

    4. Footstone - Ellie

    5. Footstone - Willie

LOT #72 -- 1 Monument - 2 Footstone Bases (stones missing)

    1. Monument Front: Samuel T. Soper Nov. 23, 1823 - Feb. 4, 1898
                     Abby W. wife of Samuel T. Soper June 15, 1825 - Feb. 28, 1895

LOT #73 -- 1 Monument - 2 Stones - 3 Markers - 6 Footstones

    1. Monument Front: Isaiah Turner died May 9, 1875 ae 60 ys. 11 ms. 9 ds.
                     Deborah P. Turner died Dec. 26, 1887 ae 70 ys. 1 mo. 1 dy.

       Monument Left: James R. Turner born July 29, 1841 lost at sea Nov. 27, 1858 son of Isaiah & Deborah Turner

       Monument Rear: Isaiah Turner May 26, 1843 - June 21, 1915
                      Mary Turner 1847-1932

       Monument Right: George W. Rich 1842-1916
                       Rosilla B. Rich 1846-1922

HAMILTON CEMETERY

LOT #73 (continued)

    2. Footstone - Father

    3. Footstone - Mother

    4. Footstone - Isaiah

    5. Footstone - Mary

    6. Footstone - Rosilla

    7. Footstone - George

    8. Marker - James R. Turner 1873-1953

    9. Marker - Jennie B. Turner 1875-1958

    10. Marker - Sadie W. dau. of Geo. W. & Rosilla B. Rich died Aug. 7, 1874 aged 1 yr. 10 ms. & 27 dys.

    11. Mr. Ebenezer Turner died Nov. 29, 1854 ae 72 years

    12. Mrs. Hannah widow of Ebenezer Turner died June 28, 1855 ae 68 ys. 6 ms.

LOT #74 -- 1 Monument - 1 Marker - 4 Footstones

    1. Monument Front: Capt. Nath'l Holmes died Feb'y 15, 1865 aet 64 yrs.
    Sarah G. Holmes died Jan. 29, 1892 aet 88 yrs. 5 ms.

    Monument Right: N. Porter Holmes June 23, 1830 - April 12, 1906
    H. Maria Holmes Feb. 2, 1835 - Aug. 9, 1908
    Mary A. July 15, 1863 - June 20, 1864

    2. Footstone - Father

    3. Footstone - Mother

    4. Footstone - N. P. Holmes

    5. Footstone - H. M. Holmes

    6. Marker - Mamie (VR: Mary A. Holmes daughter of Nathaniel P. & H. Maria Holmes died June 20, 1864 ae 11 mos. 5 ds.)

LOT #75 -- 2 Stones - 2 Markers

    1. Father - Joshua Hutchings died Mch. 23, 1889 ae 73 yrs. 10 mos. 8 das.
    Mother - Hannah W. Hutchings died Feb. 28, 1864 ae 47 yrs. 10 ms. 9 ds.
    Thomas W. Hutchings lost at sea Jan. 23, 1869 ae 27 yrs. 4 mos. 11 das.

    2. John Dolan 1846-1910
    Olive Dolan 1847-1896

    3. Anna M. Dolan 1874-1946

    4. Charles W. Dolan 1872-1873

HAMILTON CEMETERY

LOT #76 -- 1 Stone

1. Front: Alexander Gayland 1828-1906
          Rebecca Gayland 1828-1899
   Rear: Henry B. Gayland 1868-1892

LOT #77 -- 2 Stones - 1 Marker

1. James Downer 1820-1897
   Hanna (sp. on stone) Downer 1820-1904

2. Elizabeth daughter of James & Hannah Downer born Aug. 22, 1855 died Sept. 18, 1855

3. Almena E. daughter of James & Hammah Downer born Dec. 6, 1857 died Dec. 29, 1857

LOT #78 -- 4 Stones

1. Front: Father - Joseph Collins died Jan. 24, 1887 aged 75 years
          Mother - Sarah K. wife of Joseph Collins died Aug. 3, 1887 aged 73 years
   Rear: Sebrena S. Llanos 1839-1909

2. Elisha N. Taylor 1834-1880
   Jerusha S. his wife 1835-1905

3. Apphia C. Childs 1853-1914

4. Nellie C. wife of A. A. Mack died Oct. 12, 1884 ae 17 yrs. 2 ms. 16 ds.
   Effie an infant daughter aged 1 year (died 1884, Jamaica Plain, Mass.)

LOT #79 -- 1 Monument - 1 Stone - 3 Footstones
          (Monument erected 1881)

1. Monument Front: To the memory of my wife, Susie J. (see #2 Stone)
                   Capt. Daniel C. Cobb Jr. lost at sea on a passage from Portland, Me. for Martinique, W. I. Dec. 1st 1883 aged 33 years
   Monument Left: Daniel C. Cobb Nov. 1, 1819 - Sept. 9, 1902
                   Betsey Cobb Oct. 25, 1820 - Sept. 3, 1910

2. Susie J. wife of Daniel C. Cobb Jr. died Sept. 4, 1879 ae 27 yrs. 1 mo. 11 ds.

3. Footstone - Mother

4. Footstone - Father

5. John Pidgeon 1850-1928
   Louise M. his wife 1858-1929

LOT #80 -- 4 Stones - 1 Marker

1. James B. Pratt died May 25, 1876 ae 65 yrs. 3 mos. 10 ds.

-235-

HAMILTON CEMETERY

LOT #80 (continued)

    Lydia R. wife of James B. Pratt died Feb. 18, 1845 aged 29 years

  2. Hannah B. wife of James B. Pratt died July 3, 1899 ae 76 yrs. 9 ms. 12 ds.

  3. Ezra T. Pratt died Apl. 7, 1886 ae 35 yrs. 1 mo. 15 dys.

  4. Moses P. Newcomb Sept. 4, 1842 - Dec. 27, 1905
    Lydia F. Newcomb Jan. 1, 1849 - Sept. 25, 1925

  5. James F. Pratt 1846-1926

LOT #81 -- 1 Monument - 2 Stones - 5 Footstones

  1. Monument Front: Lysander D. Mayo born Jan. 8, 1826 died Mar. 24, 1895
                  Elizabeth Mayo born Nov. 23, 1832 died Nov. 16, 1897

     Monument Right: S. Frank Mayo born Nov. 23, 1852 died Nov. 30, 1880 ae 28 yrs. 7 ds.

        "A member of the crew of the U. S. L. S. Station No. 7. Lost while attempting the rescue of shipwrecked sailors. He died for his fellow man"

     Monument Left: Fred W. Daggett 1863-1924
                 Nettie B. his wife 1866-1915
                 Mabel F. 1888-1893

  2. Footstone - Mabel Freeman beloved daughter of Fred W. & Nettie B. Daggett died March 5, 1893 aged 4 yrs. 6 mos. 22 days

  3. Footstone - Mother

  4. Footstone - Father

  5. Footstone - Mother

  6. Footstone - Father

  7. Nathaniel Freeman died Jan. 13, 1882 aged 53 yrs. 1 mo. 26 ds.

  8. Laura A. wife of Nathaniel Freeman died Sept. 23, 1878 ae 41 ys. 11 ms.

LOT #82 -- 1 Stone

  1. Front: Edwin Curtis Mayo 1835-1889
          Alexandrina M. Mayo 1842-1920
          Elmira C. 1869-1898
          Carrie E. M. Adams 1865-1936 (Maiden name Mayo)

     Rear: Ella Mayo Perry 1863-1923 (Maiden name Mayo)
          Louise A. Perry 1896-1896
          Edwin T. Perry 1899-1911 Buried in Malden

HAMILTON CEMETERY

LOT #83 -- 1 Stone - 2 Markers - 7 Footstones

1. Front: J. Harvey Dearborn, Co. G 16th N. H. Vol. Inf.
    1831-1908
    Emily T. his wife 1835-1922
    Elizabeth 1872-1915

   Right: Clara W. 1861-1863

   Rear: Dora A. Hill 1889-1918

   Left: Winthrop D. Cook 1808-1849
    Sarah W. Cook 1812-1886
    Joseph W. 1832-1849

2. Footstone - Father

3. Footstone - Mother

4. Footstone - Lizzie

5. Footstone - S. W. C.

6. Footstone - Clara

7. Footstone - Dora

8. Herman W. Wells 1872-1939

9. Bertha J. wife of H. W. Wells 1878-1932

10. Baby - Helen C. Wells -1906-

LOT #84 -- 3 Stones

1. Jesse Freeman died April 6, 1865 ae 64 ys. 6 ms.
   Josiah C. Freeman killed on board U. S. Ship Cumberland
     March 8, 1862 ae 34 years

2. Hannah N. widow of Jesse Freeman died Jan. 5, 1868 ae
   66 ys. 2 ms. 22 ds.

3. Henry Baxter 1819-1882
   Hannah D. his wife 1811-1906
   Henry F. 1851-1908
   John D. 1856-1864

LOT #85 -- 2 Stones - 1 Footstone

1. Father - Joseph Pinckney Sept. 15, 1819 - Apr. 2, 1889
   Mother - Elizabeth Pinckney May 21, 1830 - Aug. 29, 1901

2. Mrs. Thankful wife of Joseph Pinckney died Feb. 10, 1850
     ae 23 yrs. 5 ms.
   Also her infant son Joseph Atkins ae 8 days (VR: died
     Feb. 14, 1850)

3. Footstone - T. P. & J. A. P.

LOT #86 -- 1 Stone

1. Joseph Frellick 1826-1882

-237-

HAMILTON CEMETERY

LOT #86 (continued)

    Priscilla F. his wife 1835-1915
    Mary F. 1858-1864
    Charlotte D. 1863-1919
    Jennie W. 1868-1929
    James F. 1854-1941
    Emma J. his wife 1855-1925

LOT #87 -- 4 Stones

1. Capt. Samuel P. Brooks died Mch. 24, 1876 ae 42 ys. 7 ms.

2. Mother - Melissa A. wife of Capt. Samuel P. Brooks Apr. 19, 1836 - Jan. 19, 1896

3. Ella F. Brooks Oct. 17, 1865 - Mar. 19, 1907

4. William C. Brooks 1869-1952
   Ida M. his wife 1879-1955

LOT #88 -- 3 Stones - 2 Footstones

1. Capt. Jonathan Dyer died Jan. 24, 1864 aged 33 yrs.
   His wife Maria West Aug. 5, 1839 - July 23, 1929

2. Ada Maria daughter of Jonathan & Maria W. Dyer died Mar. 11, 1873 aged 10 yrs. 8 ms.

3. Footstone - Mother

4. Footstone - Father

5. Benjamin Sparks 1850-1916 Lost at sea
   Mary C. his wife 1858-1934
   Robert Richardson 1829-1857 Lost at sea
   Ann his wife 1831-1918

LOT #89 -- 1 Monument - 5 Footstones

1. Monument Front: Manuel Rogers died Nov. 2, 1888 aged 65 yrs. 16 ds.
                    Helen P. his wife died Apr. 29, 1916 aged 87 ys. 8 ms. 15 ds.

   Monument Right: Capt. Joseph C. Smith born March 24, 1841 died July 31, 1904
                    Georgia L. (Rogers) (wife of Joseph Smith) Oct. 28, 1844 - (not cut)

   Monument Rear: Abbie D. Rogers died July 24, 1863 aged 3 ms. 24 ds.
                  Salome L. Lloyd (died) Dec. 17, 1944

2. Footstone - Father

3. Footstone - Mother

4. Footstone - Abbie D.

5. Footstone - Georgia

HAMILTON CEMETERY

LOT #89 (continued)

    6. Footstone - Salome

LOT #90 -- 1 Monument - 2 Stones

    1. Monument Rear: James S. Atkins 1829-1914
                       Mary E. Atkins 1831-1851
                       Mary J. Atkins 1836-1894
                       James E. Atkins 1857-1940
                       Francenia R. Atkins 1856-1922
                       Robert S. Atkins 1865-1958
                       Mary E. 1851-1863
                       Harriet W. 1856-1863
                       Susan P. 1859-1859
                       Elisha S. 1862-1863

    2. Elisha West Lost at sea Oct. 1858 ae 52 ys. 9 ms.
       Harriet A. West died Oct. 22, 1853 ae 16 ys. 2 ms. 25 ds.

    3. Mrs. Barbee Ann wife of Elisha West born Feb. 25, 1815
         died Aug. 10, 1851
       James S. their son born Aug. 4 died Sept. 27, 1851

LOT #91 -- 1 Stone

    1. Front: John Garland 1828-1905
             Mary J. his wife 1838-1924
             John L. Garland 1861-1905
             Minnie F. Garland 1865-1876

       Rear: Leonard N. Swift 1868-1944
       Edith C. his wife 1870-1939

LOT #92 -- 1 Stone - 3 Footstones

    1. Joseph Hatch 1841-1909
       Josephine S. Hatch 1845-1891
       Willie R. 1876-1879

    2. Footstone - Father

    3. Footstone - Mother

    4. Footstone - Willie

INDEX TO PART THREE

PERSONS, PLACES & SHIPS BY LOT NUMBER

HAMILTON CEMETERY

ADAMS Carrie E (Mayo) 82
  Clarina Ardelle 66 Lizzie E
  66 Marshall L 66 Mary A 66
ARMSTRONG Gladys (Baker) 33
ATKINS Abigail N 48 E Wilfred 63
  Eddie 48 Elisha S 90 Eugenia
  A (McKennon) 63 Francenia R
  90 Harriet W 90 Helena G 48
  Helena P 48 James E 90 James
  S 90 Jane F 48 John W 63
  Joseph 48 Lizzie B 67 Mary E
  90 Mary J 90 Olive 67
  Rebecca A 48 Robert S 90
  Ruth 48 Susan P 90 Wm
  (William) A 48 William N F 48

BAKER Amaziah 17/18 Clara A 33
  Gladys 33 Lewis H 33
BANGS Ann E 31 Annie M 32 John
  B 32 Lena M 32 Paul L 31
  Peggy 31 Rebecca 32
BAXTER Hannah D 84 Henry 84
  Henry F 84 John D 84
BOARDMAN Evelyn W (Fisher) 70
BROOKS Ella F 87 Ida M 87
  Melissa A 87 Samuel P 87
  William C 87
BROWN Rebecca 24
BUSH Annie 35 Hellen F 35
  Infant son 35 Justine E 30
  Rebecca C 30 William 30

CAMERON Donald 64
CHANDLER Betsey F 1 Franklin D
  1 Freddie 1 Infants 1 Lucin-
  da 1 Susan L 1
CHAPMAN Stephen 14 Thankful
  (Rich) 14
CHASE Hattie N 69
CHILDS Apphia C 78
CHURCHILL Jennie E 37/38
COBB Betsey 71 79 Daniel C 79
  Daniel C Jr 79 James 71 James
  E 71 Susie J 79 Willie F 71
COCKETT John 55
COLLINS Joseph 78 Sarah K 78
COOK Alfred 49 Betsey Kibby
  37/38 Calista 63 Caroline E
  49 Caroline W 15 Carrie Reba
  49 Cassie C 49 Charles A 67
  Charles H 37/38 Clarence A 49

Clarinda 41 Clarinda Tilton
  41 David Jr 47 Delia 37/38
  Eben A 43 Ebenezer 43 Edward
  42 Edwin E 49 Eleanor 26
  Elizabeth K 16 Elizabeth S
  16 Emeline 23 Emma B 16
  Ephraim S 23 Fred W 16 George
  P 67 Hannah C 27 Harriet 23
  Heman S 27 Infant son 47
  Isaac 15 Jennie E (Churchill)
  37/38 Jesse 23 John J 16
  Jonathan 42 44 Jonathan 3rd
  42 Jona (Jonathan) Y 67
  Joseph W 83 Julia F (Higgins)
  37/38 Laura 45 Leonard 37/38
  Louisa 45 47 50 Louise R 47
  Lucy Ann 37/38 Lucy Ann (Wiley)
  37/38 Martha 15 16 Mary A
  (Higgins) 37/38 Nabby 6 Nathan
  44 Nathaniel N 50 Nattie 50
  Olive (Atkins) 67 Rebecca M
  49 Richard W 16 Rosetta (Loth-
  rop) 17/18 Sabra 42 Sally
  37/38 Salome A 47 Samuel 44
  Sarah H (Dunham) 67 Sarah R
  43 Sarah S 23 Sarah W 83
  Stephen 37/38 Sylvanus 45
  Tamsin 44 Thankful H 23 Til-
  ton 41 Winthrop D 83
COVELL Chandler S 4 Edith V 4
  Elijah D 4 Joshua D 4
  Nathaniel 4 Ruth 4
CRANE Abbie Dora (Leach) 2
  George Bond 2
CRAWFORD Edith (Small) 62

DAGGETT Fred W 81 Mabel F 81
  Nettie B 81
DAYS Mamie E C 56
DEAN Susie M 70
DEARBORN Clara W 83 Elizabeth 83
  Emily T 83 J Harvey 83
DITSON Augustus L 34 Sarah D P
  34 Tamsin Ann 34
DOLAN Anna M 75 Charles W 75
  John 75 Olive 75
DOWNER Almena E 77 Elizabeth 77
  Hanna(h) 77 James 77
DUNHAM Sarah H 67
DYER Ada Maria 88 Annie M
  (Bangs) 32 Artie C 45 Ben-
  jamin A 32 David H 54 Eddie

HAMILTON CEMETERY

C 45 Elisha 54 Elisha L 54
Huldah 54 Infant 45 Jonathan
88 Lizzie B 54 Lydia J 54
Maria (West) 88 Thomas W 54

EDWARDS Sarah E 56
EWELL Hattie L 5 Jane N 5
Seneca G 5

FIELDING Grace L 17/18 Rebecca
(Lothrop) 17/18 Warren 17/18
FISHER Evelyn W 70 Helena A 70
Helena F 70 Isaac G 70
Julia D 70
FLUKER Adeline P 51/52 Francis
51/52 Howard E 51/52 Josiah
C 51/52 Temperance 51/52
William T 51/52
FRALECK (see also FRELLICK)
Infant son 57 John 57 Joseph
Arthur 57 Mary E 57
FRANCIS Lucy N 4 Pamelia S 4
FREEMAN A Irving 39 Annie M 66
Arthur C 39 Calvin N 66
Chester C 53 Clarence N 53
Dorinda C 39 Eldredge C 53
Faustina 39 Francis M 53
Grace 55 Hannah N 84 Jennie
Y 39 Jesse 84 John 55 Josiah
C 84 Laura A 81 Lizzie J 66
Mabel F 53 Marion L 53 Mary
55 Mary F 53 Mary J 53 Mary
L 53 Nathaniel 81 Philip
55 Prince I 39 William 55
Willie 66
FRELLICK (see also FRALECK)
Charlotte D 86 Emma J 86
James F 86 Jennie W 86
Joseph 86 Mary F 86 Priscilla F 86
FULLER Angie Y 67 James Wallace 67

GARLAND John 91 John L 91 Mary
J 91 Minnie F 91
GAYLAND Alexander 76 Henry B
76 Rebecca 76
GOTT Charles 33 Gladys (Baker) 33
GRAHAM John M 36 Rebecca A 36

GROZIER Rebecca (Atkins) 48

HALL Grace L (Fielding) 17/18
HANNUM Josiah A 26 Lucy Maria 26
HARTFORD Hattie M 40 Seth N 40
HATCH Joseph 92 Josephine S 92
Willie R 92
HIGGINS Julia F 37/38 Mary A 37/38
HILL Dora A 83
HILLIARD Alice S 28 Almeda Ann
28 Emily 28 Emily Cook 28
Infant son 28 Jairus H 28
Jairus Howard 28 John D 28
Lizzie H P 28 Nellie B 28
Rebecca Helen 28
HOLBROOK Charles H 16
HOLMES Blanche A 41 Caroline B
41 Clara T 41 Clarissa 46
Ellis H 46 George H 41
H Maria 74 Lottie E 41 Mary
A 74 Nathaniel 74 Nathaniel
Porter 74 Rebecca E 41 Sarah
G 74
HOPKINS Joseph S 60
HOWE Lucinda (Chandler) 1
HUNT Adeline P (Fluker) 51/52
Warren F 51/52
HUTCHINGS Hannah W 75 Joshua 75
Thomas W 75

JORDAN Joseph W 70
JUDKINS Mary J (Morrison) 11

KILBURN Hannah (Soule) 40
Harriet P 40 Jonathan 40
Samuel T 40
KILEY John 13 Mary M 13 Sally K
(Rich) 13 Thankful J 13
KNOWLES Albertina F 50

LANCY Benjamin 6 7 Benjamin Jr 6
Ellen M 7 Jane 7 Maria 6
Nabby (Cook) 6 Phebe 8 Seth N 8
LEACH Abbie Dora 2 Mary D 2
Whipple A 2
LLANOS Sebrena S 78
LLOYD Salome L 89

LOCKWOOD George 34
LONG Benjamin 58 Betsey C 58
    Charles H 58 Elsie F 58 May
    58 Melissa V 58 Samuel T 58
    Sylvia C 58 Thomas A 58
LORING Abbie H 42
LOTHROP Adeline 17/18 Eben 17/18
    Marcus M 17/18 Rebecca 17/18
    Rosetta 17/18 Salome C 17/18
    Sarah F 17/18 Thomas 17/18
LUCAS Antone Joseph 56 Charlie
    56 Infant 56 J Arthur 56
    John P 55 Margaret Jane 56
    Mary M 56 Sarah Alletha 56
    Sarah E (Edwards) 56
LYFORD Byley 45 Hannah 45

McDONALD Donald 64
MACK Effie 78 Nellie C 78
McKAY Angus S 12 Annie 12 Frank
    D 12 Frank S 12 Frank W 12
    William F 12
McKENNON Alexander 63 Annie W
    63 Eugenia A 63 Louise A 63
    Ruth (Nickerson) 63
MacPHEE - McPHIE Alexander 64
    Kenneth 64 Mary (Matheson)
    64
MARTIN Bessie M 68 John L 68
    Louisa A 68 Matty 68 Sarah M
    68 William 68 William G 68
    William Jr 68
MATHESON Elizabeth 12 John A 12
    Mary 64 Thankie C 12 William
    64 William B 12
MAYO Alexandrina M 82 Carrie E
    82 Edwin Curtis 82 Elizabeth
    81 Ella 82 Elmira C 82
    Lysander D 81 S Frank 81
MILLS Delia A 24 Elizabeth
    Fernald 24 Joanna C 24
    Rebecca 24 Stephen 24
MORRISON Allen P 11 Annabella
    11 Duncan M 11 Henry J 11
    John F 11 Mary J 11 Nathan
    H 11
MYRICK J Josephine 24 Joanna C
    (Mills) 24 Joseph 24 Osborne
    24

NEWCOMB Lydia F 80 Moses P 80
NICKERSON Alice L 3 Bethia M 3
    Bethiah 43 Charles 26 Charles
    Elliot 3 Clara D 3 Eldridge
    22 Eleanor (Cook) 26 Eliza P
    25 Elizabeth 21 Ellen C 26
    Emeline C 26 Enoch 25 Enos 46
    Eunice 22 Eunice S 22 Freddie
    J 3 Infant dau 3 John 21
    Louisa A (Nickerson) 63 Lucy
    46 Marinda J 22 Rebekah 46
    Richard E 3 Richard F 25 Ruth
    46 63 Seth 2nd 63 Simeon L 10

PAINE Catherine M W 19 Charles
    G 19 Clara Holmes 27 Henry 20
    46 James A 19 James C N 27
    Louise C 27 Louise (McKennon)
    63 Lucy 46 Lucy A 27 Lucy L
    27 Phebe A 27 Rebecca Francis
    20 Sarah H 20 Stephen A 19
PALMER Margarett 40 William 40
PERRY Edwin T 82 Ella (Mayo) 82
    Louise A 82
PIDGEON John 79 Louise M 79
PINCKNEY Elizabeth 85 Joseph 85
    Joseph Atkins 85 Thankful 85
PLACES California Glendale 39;
    Cape Verde Isle de Sal 40;
    England Blackburn 55; Florida
    St Joseph's 65; India Kurrac-
    hee 20; Maine Portland 79;
    Maryland Baltimore 64; Massa-
    chusetts Boston 47 63 66
    Jamaica Plain 78 Malden 82
    North Truro 24 Orleans 24
    Provincetown Cong'l Church 24
    Truro 24; New York Troy 34;
    North Carolina Newburn 34;
    Vermont Middlebury College 24
    Middletown Springs Cong'l
    Church 24 Rutland 24; Virginia
    Danville Prison 2; West Indies
    Cuba, Matanzas 24 Haiti,
    Jacmel 63 Haiti, Port au
    Prince 29 47 Martinique 79
    St Thomas 28
PRATT Ezra T 80 Hannah B 80
    James B 80 James F 80 Lydia
    R 80

HAMILTON CEMETERY

RICH Augustus E 36 Benajmin F 14 Eleazer H 60 Eleazer Osborn 60 Elizabeth H 60 George W 73 Infant 13 James 14 James A 14 Maria C 60 Melissa N 36 Mercy 60 Peggy S 14 Rosilla B 73 Rosilla R 13 Sadie W 73 Sally K 13 Samuel J 13 Samuel R 13 Thankful 14 Thankful J 13 Thankful J (Kiley) 13
RICHARDSON Ann 88 Robert 88
ROGERS Abbie D 89 Georgia L 89 Helen P 89 Manuel 89
RYDER A Maria 43 Angie 43 Benjamin 2nd 43 Clara C 33 Ella K 43 Frank B 33 Stephen A 33 Susie C 43

SHIPS Argo Naves 63 Rienza 51/52 Sunbeam 28 U. S. S. Cumberland 84
SILVA Elizabeth (Matheson) 12 Leon J 12 Raymond P 12
SMALL Abby 2 Abigail C 2 Adelaide F 62 Adelaide L 62 Aylmer F 62 Benjamin 2 Benjamin L 2 Charles G 5 Drusilla 2 Edith 62 Ellen M 5 Emma A 62 Everett 5 Frederick W 62 Hattie E 5 James L 61 Jane 5 Jane L 5 Jesse 61 Jonah G 2 Josiah F 62 Katherine A 62 Nathan 5 Pamelia C 5 Ruth E 61 Seviah H 61 Simeon C 2 Stanley S 62 Taylor 2 Taylor Jr 2
SMITH Georgia L (Rogers) 89 John L 68 Joseph C 89 Nathan 9 Sarah L 68 Winifred 9
SOPER Abby W 72 Samuel T 72
SOULE Hannah 40
SPARKS Anna 59 Benjamin 88 David H 59 Hannah 59 Hannah Y 59 Lurana 59 Lydia K 59 Mary C 88 Mary W 59 Thomas 59
STULL Lydia 65 Moses P 65 Thomas 65 William C 65
SWIFT Edith C 91 Leonard N 91

TALBORT Abbie E 1
TAYLOR Abby C S 69 Charles N 69 E Thomas 69 Elisha N 78 Jerusha S 78 Josephine E 69 Thomas S 69
TUCK Charles Upham 25 Enoch F 25 Francis B 25 Lydia S 25 Mary Louise 25
TURNER Deborah P 73 Ebenezer 73 Hannah 73 Isaiah 73 James R 73 Jennie B 73 Mary 73

WELLS Bertha J 83 Helen C 83 Herman W 83
WEST Barbee Ann 90 Elisha 90 Harriet A 90 James S 90 Maria 88
WHORF Amos 1 Edgar J 29 Henry 29 Henry S 29 Infant 29 Isaiah A 29 Sally 29 Sarah M 29 Susan L 1 Susan M 1 Thannie A 29
WILEY Lucy Ann 37/38
WILLIAMS Margaret 56
WYER Lydia (Stull) 65 Obed 65 William W 65

YOUNG A Waldo 39 Eleazer 39 Ellen M (Lancy) 7 George B 16 Jonathan H 42 Mercy H 39 Nehemiah H 20 Phebe N 39

PART FOUR

SMALLPOX BURIALS

SMALLPOX BURIALS

The people of nineteenth century Provincetown followed the New England custom of burying the victims of extremely communicable diseases, such as Smallpox, in isolated gravesites rather than in the town or church cemeteries. These lonely places are a fascinating footnote to the study of Cape Cod cemeteries. In our search for smallpox cemeteries in Provincetown two slate stones of the 1801 smallpox epidemic and fourteen numbered but unnamed graves of those who died between 1855 and 1873 were located.

It is not difficult to imagine the fear that accompanied these outbreaks of smallpox. The disease is known to have caused many deaths among the native Indians as well as among European settlers during the seventeenth and eighteenth centuries. Thus, smallpox victims were buried almost immediately, and apart from their friends and families, to lessen the danger of contamination. Usually no funeral was held and any articles believed to have been contaminated were burned.

Provincetown could respond at first with only the most rudimentary treatment for smallpox, relying predominately upon isolation to prevent the spread of the disease. Vaccination, as known today, had not been long introduced into this country, especially in areas far from cities. The following excerpts from the records of the town meeting of 1801 give quite a vivid picture of the conditions in the town at that time.

> "At a meeting being warned and holden on the 28th day of December, 1801 on accompt of the Small pocks the following articles wer Voted for... Viz;...
>
> Voted, that a physician be appointed to Attend the house occupied a hospittle & the house of George Whorf & that the Sd. phisician Should not be permitted to go about the town.
>
> Voted, that any person who is the head of any family who Shall permit to the number of Six persons to meet together at his house for frolicking or any unnecessary purpose Shall pay to the use of the town a Sum not Exceeding 50 Dolors.

SMALLPOX BURIALS

>Voted, that all Schools; & meetings on the lords Day & all other meeting Shall be Discontinued until permission is Given by the Selectmen of the town.
>
>Voted, that any person Employed as a nurse Shall not Go Out of the yard around the house on the penalty of 50 Dolors.
>
>Voted, that the house of George Whorf & the house occupied as a hospittle be fenced in; & that the houses to-gether with the hinkses have a watch Set; also that a Smoke house be built.
>
>Voted, that all Dogs and Cats be Ciled also that all hogs & Sheep Runing at large if Out of the Owners inclosure Shall be ciled & the Owner Shall pay 50 Dolors."

We located only two graves of the victims of this early epidemic. The two stones were originally located on a farm and are now part of the new section of St. Peter's Catholic Cemetery. The graves were mentioned in a 1908 deed when the farmland was conveyed from Phebe Ryder to Joseph R. Holmes..."excepting a small lot where two unknown persons are buried". These stones are today located about 75 feet inside the northwest corner of St. Peter's Cemetery and the inscriptions read as follows:

>In memory of Mr. Edward Cook who died of the Small Pox Nov. 11, 1801 aged 55 yrs.
>
>In memory of Mrs. Experience Cook wife of Mr. Edward Cook who died of the Small Pox Dec. 19, 1801 aged 54 yrs.

By 1848, smallpox was again a matter of concern in the town and we found that the selectmen set aside "a certain tract of land commonly known as Eastern plain" on which was built a one-story dwelling to be used as a smallpox house. The land surrounding this hospital was later used for burial of smallpox victims.

There were no smallpox deaths recorded in the town records between the years 1848 and 1855, four deaths between 1855 and 1864, but in 1872 there was what was once again considered an epidemic as described in the Report of the Board of Health in the 1872 Provincetown Town Report:

>"The principal work of the Board however, has been in the management and eradication of the frightful epidemic that has, for over two years past, been raging with increasing severity and prevalence in this country and other portions of the civilized world - the Small Pox."

The report of the Board of Health indicated that, in many ways, the techniques of prevention and treatment had improved since 1801. By December of 1872, however, "Small Pox had been found to be on

a steady increase, in spite of the best efforts of the Board".
On December 4, 1872, Horatio G. Newton, M.D., was appointed by the
Board as consulting physician. He seems to have been a knowledgeable and enlightened physician, experienced in dealing with cases
of smallpox. The success of his efforts is apparent since the
Board's Report for the year 1873 pronounced the town entirely free
of smallpox.

Dr. Newton's report of the epidemic is too lengthy to quote
here in its entirety, but it does give us an accurate picture of
conditions in the town at the time, and the degree to which the
citizens were unprepared to deal with the epidemic. "The community
generally were filled at that time with similar gloomy forbodings,
and painful apprehensions such as I have known to precede a panic."
The continuing spread of the disease could be traced in part to the
reluctance of citizens to report smallpox when it occurred and to
the inexperience of both the citizens and physicians.

Dr. Newton encouraged the Board of Health to continue their
support of compulsory vaccination, a practice which was still believed by many to be almost as bad as the disease itself. He also
stressed the need for good nursing care, complete isolation and
proper ventilation of the hospital area. Upon describing the
existing hospital conditions, he wrote - "The poorest and most
disgraceful one was that owned by the town, known as the Pest
House, a place to which, no patient will hereafter be sent with my
consent, for I should never be willing to go there if I was sick."
Indeed, after reading about the conditions in this Pest House, it
is surprising that there are not more smallpox graves. In 1872,
there were twenty-two patients placed in the Pest House, only six
of whom did not recover.

The members of the Board of Health expressed disappointment in
the conduct of some of their fellow citizens. They had experienced
difficulty in procuring teams to carry patients to the hospital
and to carry the bodies of those who died to the burial place.

During the year 1873 there were only two new cases of smallpox, one of which resulted in the death of the victim. All that
remains of this incredible experience are fourteen numbered grave
markers, which for some unknown reason are placed in a semi-circle
facing northwest. Undoubtedly, the markers were already numbered
and ready for hasty burials and names were never inscribed on them.

It is logical to assume that the numbers on these markers
would correspond with the chronological order of the deaths. In
our attempt to determine the names of these victims, we located in
the Vital Records of the town and in the Pest House records of the
Board of Health exactly fourteen deaths from smallpox, therefore
we feel that our identification of the fourteen persons buried in
this Smallpox Cemetery is an accurate record and one never before
published. Of particular interest is that four of the fourteen
deaths are not recorded in the Vital Records of the town of
Provincetown, but are listed in the Pest House deaths in the annual
report of the Board of Health. The wife of one of the members of
the Board of Health, Tamsin Manuel, is listed as having died of
"heart disease, fright few hours" when in actual fact she had con-

SMALLPOX BURIALS

tracted smallpox and had been admitted to the hospital. Memorial stones for two of the fourteen were found in Cemetery #2...one for Tamsin Manuel and the other for William H. Butler.

The following is a list of the fourteen smallpox deaths in chronological order, citing Volume and Page of the Book of Deaths, or in the case of those not recorded the reference to the year of the annual report of the town of Provincetown:

1. V-1 p18: Adam Dyer died May 9, 1855 age 22 born Truro, Mass., laborer; married; buried Provincetown; son of Adam Dyer

2. V-1 p18: John Roberts died May 15, 1855 age and parents not listed; birthplace unknown; buried Provincetown

3. V-1 p18: Monson W. Barnard died May 19, 1855 age, parents and birthplace unknown; buried Provincetown

4. V-1 p24: Elizabeth Hill died May 20, 1860 age 51 born Truro, Mass., married, wife of Ambrose Hill and daughter of John and Salome Hill; buried Provincetown

5. V-2 p6: Kennis Fergerson died May 20, 1864; male; age 22; single; mariner; parents and birthplace unknown; buried Provincetown

6. V-2 p22: Antone Domingo died Nov. 1, 1872 age 22; widower; mariner; born Western Islands; parents not listed, buried Provincetown

7. V-2 p22: Mary Rogers died Nov. 8, 1872 age 25; widow; born Western Islands; daughter of Frank and Ann; buried Provincetown. (According to the 1872 town report of the Board of Health she arrived from Boston by steamer on Nov. 2 and was removed to the smallpox house.)

8. V-2 p22: George G. Hallett died Nov. 26, 1872 age 31 yrs. 9 mos, born Barnstable, Mass.; married; carpenter; son of Nathaniel and Mary D. Hallett; buried Provincetown

9. V-2 p22: Tamsin Manuel died Nov. 27, 1872 age 73 yrs. 29 days, born Orleans, Mass.; married; daughter of Aquilla and Tamsin Higgins; wife of Alexander Manuel

10. V-2 p23: Frank Sofrine (alias Small) died Dec. 24, 1872 age, birthplace and parents not given

11. -1872- Manuel Terceira died Dec. 24, 1872 at the smallpox house

12. -1872- William H. Butler died Jan. 7, 1873 at the smallpox house

13. -1872- John A. McDonald died Jan. 8, 1873 at the smallpox house; a Scotsman

SMALLPOX BURIALS

14. -1873- Thomas Bussell died May 28, 1873 at the smallpox house; was of Portsmouth, New Hampshire; arrived in Provincetown on board the Schooner Louisa A. of Boston on May 17, 1873. "Buried in the burial ground in the rear of the hospital."

As early as 1872, the Board of Health expressed concern about the condition of this smallpox cemetery:

> "There are, not remote from the Pest House, several graves of those who have died of Small-pox. Some of them were our own fellow citizens who, under former rules, were excluded from a Christian burial within our Cemeteries, and some were strangers, who, though faithfully and even tenderly cared for in their last monents, died where no loving hands of relatives and friends, could lay their corrupting mortal remains beneath the willow or the cypress, nor strew flowers on their graves. Can we, as a Christian and humane community afford to do less, then to have this little consecrated spot properly cleared up, and neatly fenced, that we may thus manifest a fraternal sympathy for that stricken band of our common humanity."

Again in 1873, the Board recommended that "said grounds be taken possession of by the town, properly cleared up, and put in a condition in keeping with our other public grounds, that the graves be marked in some way with the names of their respective occupants."

Today, this burial lot is located within the bounds of the Cape Cod National Seashore Park. It is overgrown with brush, there are no fences, and many of the markers are broken. Nearby, the cellar hole of the Pest House is still visible. We can only echo the words of the concerned citizens of Provincetown when over a century ago they asked that these gravesites be cleared and fenced, and that the identities of the fourteen victims buried there should in some way be preserved.

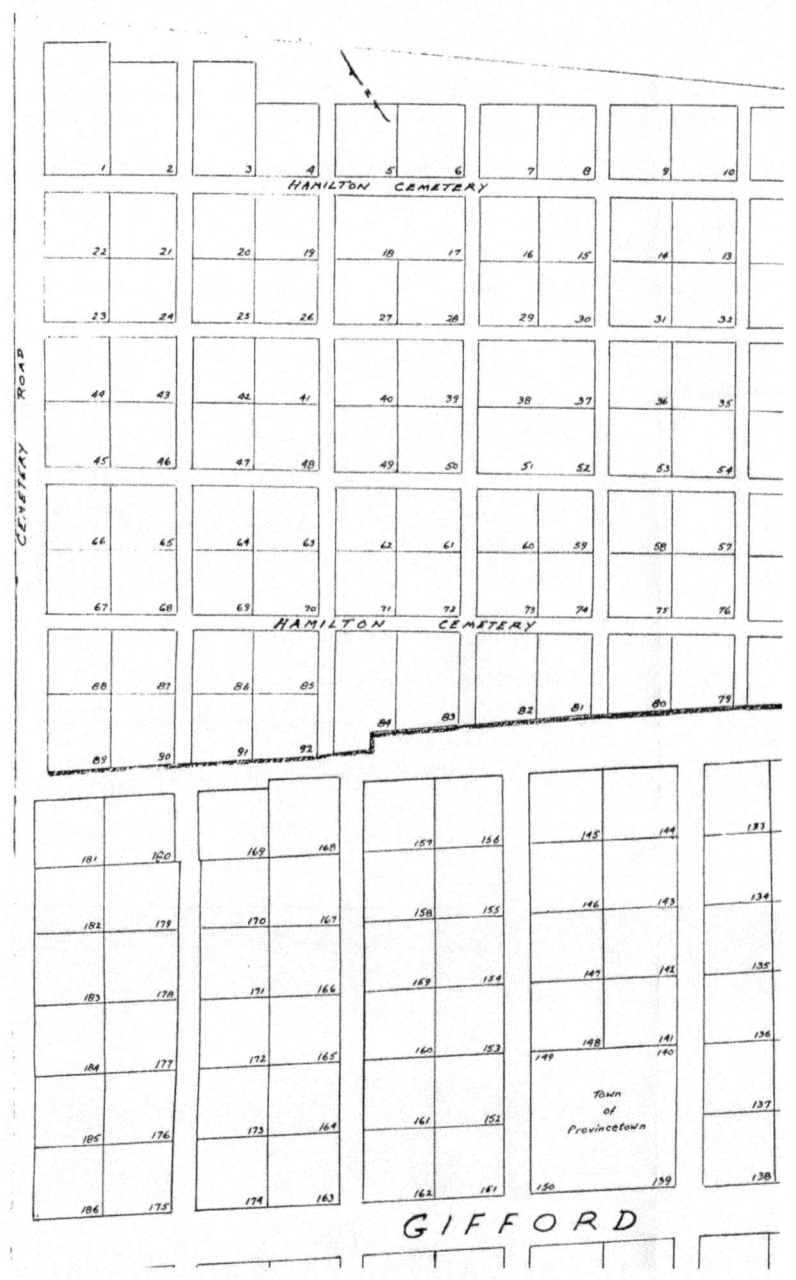

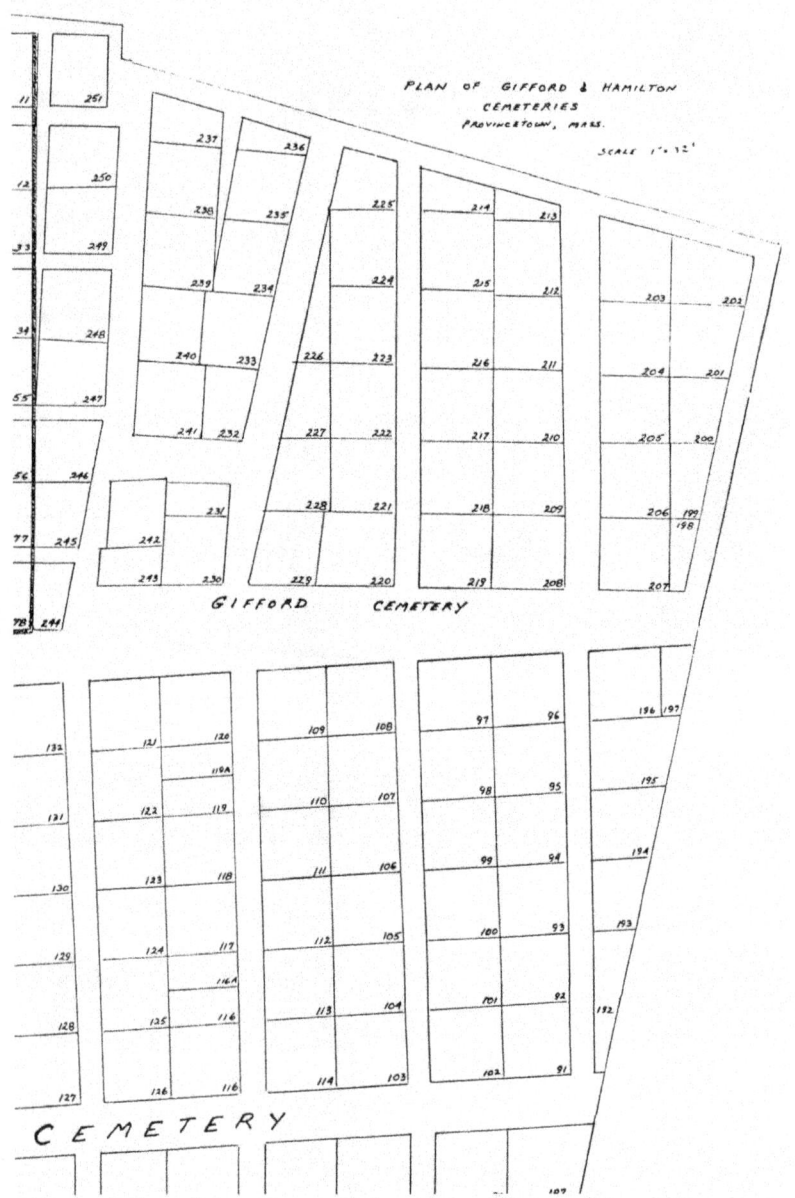

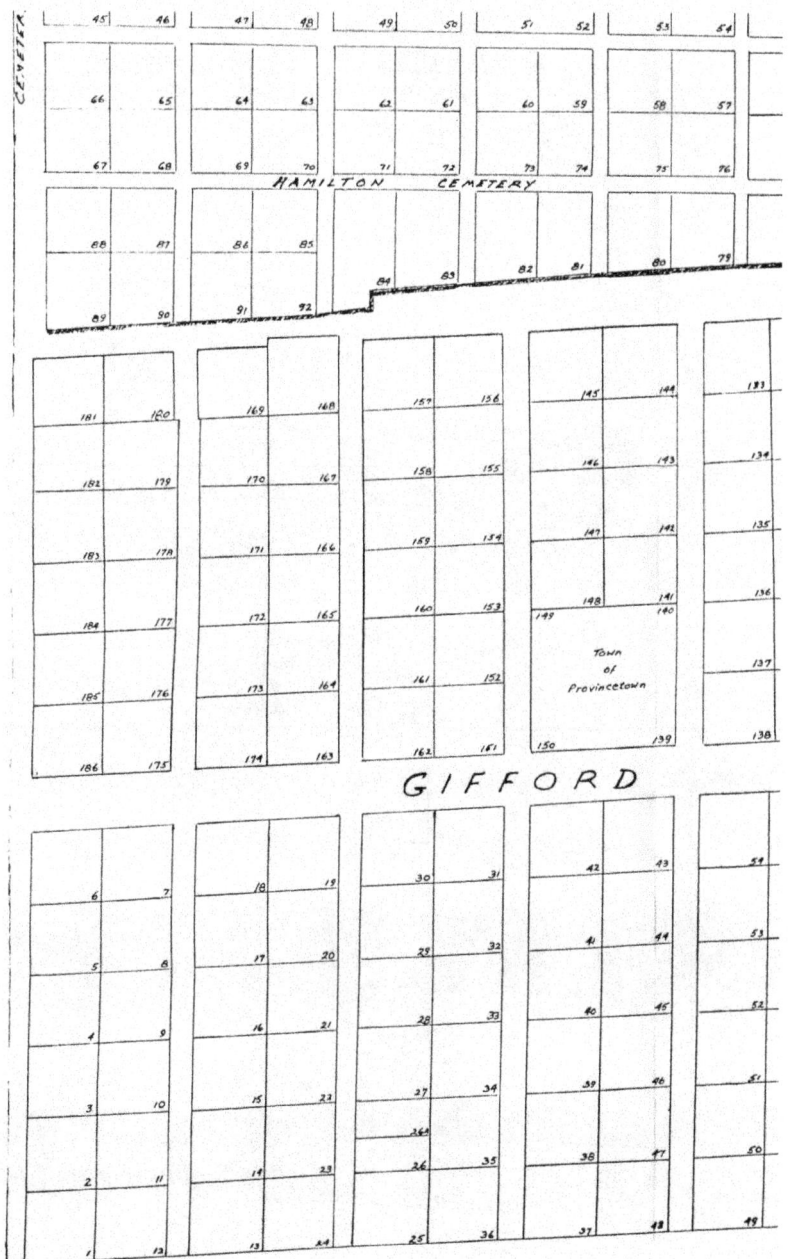

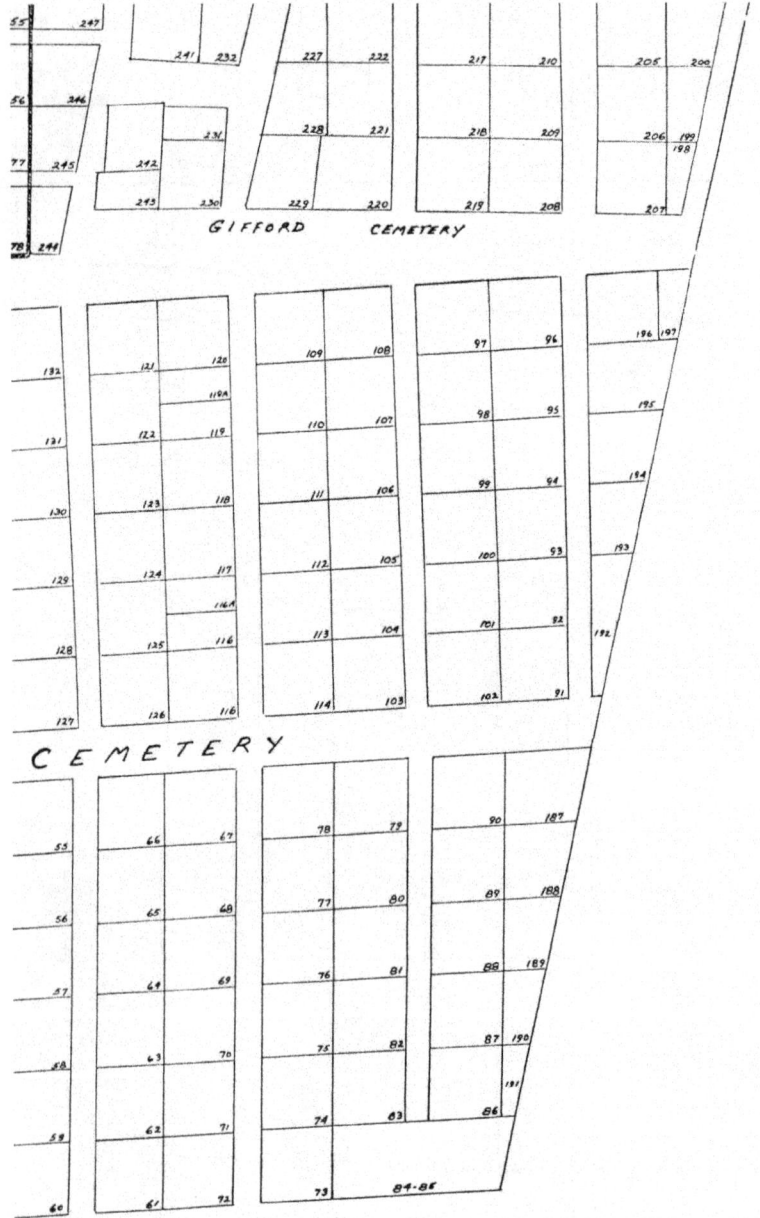

www.ingramcontent.com/pod-product-compliance
Lightning Source LLC
Chambersburg PA
CBHW020806100426
42814CB00012B/346